THE
TREATY

Gretchen Friemann is an award-winning journalist whose work has featured in *The Irish Times, Irish Independent, Business Post, The Sunday Times, The Australian* and the *Australian Financial Review*. She lives in Dublin and recently obtained a first-class Masters in International History from Trinity College Dublin. *The Treaty* is her first book.

—— THE ——
TREATY

Gretchen Friemann

MERRION
PRESS

First published in 2021 by
Merrion Press
10 George's Street
Newbridge
Co. Kildare
Ireland
www.merrionpress.ie

© Gretchen Friemann, 2021

978 1 78537 420 3 (Paper)
978 1 78537 421 0 (Ebook)
978 1 78537 422 7 (PDF)

A CIP catalogue record for this book is
available from the British Library.

Typeset in Sabon LT Std 12/17 pt

Merrion Press is a member of Publishing Ireland.

CONTENTS

In memory of Ron Maher ('the Ref')
and Annette Foley.

1 ▪ CLOSE ENCOUNTERS

In the spring of 1921, David Lloyd George became the first British prime minister to fall in love with Chequers.[1] His secretary and lifelong mistress, Frances Stevenson, described the Buckinghamshire estate, set in 1,000 acres of rolling English countryside, as 'heavenly' and 'indescribably' peaceful. 'There is healing in the atmosphere,' she wrote.[2]

The sense of tranquillity and seclusion would be short-lived. In May, not long after weekend retreats at the Elizabethan mansion had become a regular affair, the crisis that Lloyd George once claimed had 'worried' him 'more than any matter since the war troubles in the spring of 1918', acquired, in the grounds of Chequers, a new and terrifying proximity.[3]

For months the Prime Minister had been warned about threats to his life from Irish republicans. Fears for his safety had intensified in the autumn of 1920, after the deaths of Terence MacSwiney, the Lord Mayor of Cork, and Kevin Barry, an eighteen-year-old medical student turned separatist warrior. The former had died on hunger strike in Brixton Prison, while the latter was hanged for his part in a lethal IRA attack on the Crown forces in Dublin. By the end of November 1920, Irish republican wrath appeared, to the British, to have been whipped into a newly destructive force. First came the IRA shootings on the morning of Bloody Sunday 21 November, when fourteen officers were killed on suspicion of their involvement in intelligence work. Then, a week later, came the Kilmichael ambush in County Cork, which almost obliterated an eighteen-man Auxiliary patrol. IRA attacks had graduated into seemingly well-orchestrated massacres, and privately the British government admitted that the Irish insurgency had undergone an unwelcome transformation. This was no murderous rabble, it was a 'military operation'.[4]

After almost two years of mayhem, the British campaign to crush the rebels looked more complicated than ever. As republican attacks spread to the British mainland, security chiefs warned that Sinn Féin intended to carry its 'war of outrage into England'.[5] (The British authorities frequently failed to distinguish between the separatist movement's armed wing – the IRA – and Sinn Féin, an essentially political body.) Overnight, fortifications sprang up outside Downing Street, while the Prime Minister, now shadowed by armed detectives, was advised by Scotland Yard to decamp to less familiar lodgings.

To those who observed him closely, Lloyd George treated these murder plots with an almost blithe equanimity; on one occasion in the autumn of 1920 he joked to his close friend Lord Riddell that Edward Carson, the fiery Ulster Unionist, was 'first on the list for assassination', whereas he was 'second'. With an insouciant flourish, he added, '"if Fate intends you shall be killed, you will; and if it doesn't, you won't." Not a bad doctrine', Riddell noted approvingly, 'for a threatened man!'[6]

Half a year later, all bravado had evaporated. The Prime Minister appeared a changed man. By then, his government had endured a torrent of abuse for its hard-line policy in Ireland. Antipathy towards the actions of ill-disciplined Crown forces seemed to flow from every direction. One journalist declared that, at last, the country 'has awakened to the hideousness of this hellish policy'.[7] At a Cabinet meeting, Winston Churchill observed that 'we are getting an odious reputation',[8] while in the House of Commons, an increasingly isolated Sir Hamar Greenwood, Chief Secretary for Ireland, continued to lay the blame for this 'orgy of murder' on 'Sinn Fein conspirators'.[9] Perhaps the heavy opprobrium began to unsettle a prime minister who imagined he alone understood the wishes of a mass electorate, and whose 1918–22 premiership has since been characterised as 'one long press conference'.[10]

Or perhaps what Riddell hailed as Lloyd George's 'invincible optimism' simply buckled, momentarily, under the pressure of office. As the Liberal Prime Minister of a Conservative-dominated coalition, his position was always precarious, and survival depended on his ability to ward off the discontents of right and left by turns.

Whatever the reason, the events of Sunday, 22 May 1921 profoundly unnerved Lloyd George. He had spent much of the weekend preoccupied by a protracted coal miners' strike and the nation's ballooning unemployment levels – crises that boosted the Labour Party's appeal, while strengthening Tory hostility to the coalition's welfare programme. As the domestic turbulence intensified, his political foes appeared to be multiplying, and he began, not without reason, to suspect once close allies of treachery. The trouble had been brewing for some time. Churchill, anguished by the failure of the 1918–20 Allied military intervention in Russia – a campaign he spearheaded – and horrified by Lloyd George's decision to open trade talks with the Bolsheviks, became a 'brooding force of discontent' in the Cabinet after the Prime Minister passed him over for the chancellorship in April 1921.[11] The

Treasury's top job – long coveted by Churchill – went to a comparative political lightweight, the Conservative MP Robert Horne. Lloyd George braced for a show of strength from his unruly Colonial Secretary. By mid-May, rumours reached him that Churchill and Lord Birkenhead, the Lord Chancellor, were in league against him.[12]

At the beginning of that gloriously sunny weekend at Chequers, there appeared to be little outward sign that these troubles were weighing on Lloyd George. Frances Stevenson, ever vigilant to the Prime Minister's mood, wrote only of the weather in her diary, and noted that Saturday 21 May 'passed uneventfully' until 'various' guests descended in the evening. On Sunday, Horne arrived 'from Ascot', and for the rest of the day Lloyd George's attention was consumed by the labour and economic challenges roiling his government. That evening, the Prime Minister, still preoccupied with the day's work, ventured out with his guests for a stroll across the estate. He set out deep in conversation with Seebohm Rowntree, a cocoa magnate and prominent social reformer, whom he had known for many years. The pair drifted ahead of the rest of the group and, before long, disappeared from view.[13]

It was then that Stevenson and the other guests spotted 'some people' in the distance. They mistook them at first for Lloyd George and Rowntree, but, drawing closer, realised they were 'strangers'. There was 'a right of way there', she recalled, and so 'we thought no more about it'. Making their way back to the house, they discovered that Lloyd George had not returned. For a full quarter of an hour, no one in his inner circle, least of all his three armed detectives, had the slightest idea of the Prime Minister's whereabouts.

Stevenson's record of this incident is tantalisingly brief, but in her diary she recounts how Lloyd George turned up rattled and convinced that dangerous republicans were roaming the estate. He and Rowntree, he told her, had run up 'against 4 strangers hanging about', 'men' whom they had first seen coming from the 'direction' of the 'little summerhouse on the hill'. So they had hurried into the pavilion and on its walls found scrawled: 'Up the Rebels: Up Sinn Fein; IRA'.[14]

An imperialist to his core, Lloyd George never fully understood the Irish fight for independence. In his view, what was good enough for Wales was good enough for Ireland. Separatists were traitors, and prone, as recent events in Ireland had confirmed, to unfettered violence. To encounter such people in the grounds of Chequers was deeply unsettling.

And yet all around him appeared bemused by the incident. One of his detectives ridiculed the hullabaloo, 'saying they were only visitors making their way across the estate'. Nevertheless, Lloyd George had the men hauled back, locked in a shed, interrogated and then deposited for the night in nearby Aylesbury Gaol, where Countess Markievicz had been incarcerated some five years earlier. Days later, it transpired that one of the four was 'the editor of The Statist', an economics magazine, and a survivor of the Easter Rising.[15]

What is so remarkable about this episode is Lloyd George's reaction to it. All but the Prime Minister remained unfazed. His rebellious daughter Megan 'took a contemptuous view of the affair', dismissing it as nothing more than a prank. Even the local police superintendent, 'a Catholic', Stevenson noted diligently, 'censured ... the P.M.'s detective, for allowing the men to be arrested. "If they had been Englishmen you would not have arrested them", was his comment!'[16]

But Lloyd George refused to let the matter rest. Within days, the Home Secretary, the Commissioner of the Metropolitan Police and Sir Basil Thomson, Assistant Commissioner of the

Metropolitan Police and the government's watchdog on political crime, were summoned to Downing Street to 'discuss' what, by today's standards, would be regarded as an almost inconceivable security breach. Appalled to learn that the men had been let go after only scant questioning, and without any inquiries being made of them in Ireland, the Prime Minister vented his fury upon the flamboyant Thomson, whose career met an ignominious end six months later.[17]

The display of nerves was uncharacteristic. Lloyd George had shown far more sangfroid – according to the IRA man Frank Thornton – after a near collision with the Irishman and his colleague at Westminster station some time towards the end of 1920. At the time of this unexpected encounter, Ireland's guerrilla war had spiralled into a darker, more brutal phase. Increasingly adventurous tactics were being employed to terrorise the enemy. One innovation, adopted by the Auxiliaries – a paramilitary force made up, like the Black and Tans, of ex-servicemen – was to handcuff prominent Sinn Féiners to wooden poles fixed onto the back of British military vehicles, in order to ward off IRA grenade attacks. In response, the republican leader Michael Collins launched an elaborate kidnapping operation. Up to twelve British politicians were to be taken hostage. The wild scheme was abandoned after the paramilitaries stopped employing Sinn Féiners as human shields, but by then Thornton's group had identified twenty-five MPs 'who did a regular thing on the same night every week'.[18]

It was while on a 'routine check-up' for this forthcoming spectacular that Thornton, one of the Bloody Sunday assassins, and Seán Flood, another IRA operative, came face to face with the Prime Minister. They had wandered into Westminster station to catch the Underground to Acton but had just missed the lift to the platform. On the spur of the moment, Flood challenged Thornton to a race, then sprinted 'off in front and disappeared around the second last bend about a few feet in front of me. I heard a terrific crash, and on coming around the corner, I fell over two men on the ground, one of whom was Seán Flood.' The other, they realised to their 'amazement', was Lloyd George. Instantly, his two detectives pulled out guns and demanded that Thornton and Flood raise their hands. The Prime Minister ordered that the weapons be put away, and when the detectives hesitated, pointing out that the men were obviously Irish from their accents, Lloyd George replied: 'Well Irishmen or no Irishmen, if they were out to shoot me I was shot long ago.'[19]

Thornton's story may be apocryphal – we only have his account to go on – but the contrast between this self-assured Prime Minister and the agitated figure sketched out by Frances Stevenson some six months later could not be starker.

In the 1960s, the politician and writer Harold Nicolson reflected that while Lloyd George possessed moral courage, he was most likely 'so far as physical courage goes ... a coward'.[20] The Chequers episode exposed this weakness at a time of severe strain in Lloyd George's premiership. Relations with two of his most influential Cabinet members, Churchill and Birkenhead (known as F.E. Smith up until 1919) were at breaking point, while the government's policy of coercion in Ireland had so far proved a dismal failure and, to the rest of the world, the island now presented a frightening spectacle of lawlessness.

To many within Whitehall and the military, the Sinn Féin-led uprising seemed indistinguishable from the class warfare unleashed by the Bolshevik revolution, and it was seen in some quarters as part of a Moscow-inspired conspiracy to destroy the British Empire from within. Such nightmarish visions rarely disturbed Lloyd George. He had little time for those who pressed a counsel of despair. Yet he nursed a near obsession for social order, believing the first cracks here might presage a slide towards the anarchy that had engulfed large swathes of Eastern and Central Europe.

Since these sentiments were shared to varying degrees by his Cabinet colleagues, the coalition largely avoided heavy-handed reactions to the post-war waves of industrial unrest. Labour militancy was met, in the main, by a policy of consensus and conciliation.[21] To a limited extent, the same can be said of the government's approach to foreign affairs, where the focus was on averting another bloodbath on the Continent. The British strove to compel a lasting harmony in Europe and undermine the appeal of Bolshevism. Above all, the aim was to preserve Britain's global authority and imperial power with a minimum of financial and military commitments. The spectacular exception to this pursuit of stability – leaving aside the Russian intervention, which was abandoned relatively swiftly, and the Amritsar massacre, which repulsed the Cabinet – was Ireland. Despite embracing parliamentary democracy as the model for government everywhere in Europe outside Bolshevik Russia, Britain seemed incapable of offering the Irish population anything other than coercion.

The glaring inconsistencies in this approach alienated many allies. For a brief period, C.P. Scott, the Liberal editor of *The Manchester Guardian*, cut off all contact with Lloyd George, his friend of two decades, so appalled was he at the policy of reprisals in Ireland.[22] But the Prime Minister showed little interest in releasing the pressure. In October 1920, he remarked to Churchill that while he 'had hated being up near the front [during the First World War], and was frightened of shells ... he supposed this was because it was not his duty and business to get killed ... whereas he had no fear of denouncing [Sinn

Féiners] as assassins ... although he knew it sensibly increased his chance of being murdered ... In this case he conceived it to be his duty.'[23] As late as 12 May 1921, Lloyd George told H.A.L. Fisher, President of the Board of Education, that if Britain sought a truce with Ireland 'then we lose the day'.[24] At a Cabinet meeting held on the same date, and after giving the question 'tremendous thought', the Prime Minister was among those who voted 9–5 against a truce with Sinn Féin.[25] Weeks later, he had abruptly discarded this approach.

In private, Lloyd George spoke of the need to beat the 'Sinn Fein militants' and reverse the 'reign of terror' so that he could bargain from a position of strength. The Prime Minister wanted his solution defined as the only feasible alternative to murder and mayhem. There could be no slide towards a republic. 'I see no alternative other than to fight it out,' he told Riddell in April 1921. 'A republic at our doors is unthinkable.'[26]

Yet at the same time, and in typically contradictory fashion, the Prime Minister continued to forge back-channel connections with the revolutionaries, mostly via a handpicked coterie of civil servants who were installed in Dublin Castle in early 1920. Although the change in personnel precipitated a string of peace initiatives, the much hoped-for breakthrough had failed to materialise, and by the time of the Chequers incident in May 1921, the Prime Minister found himself harassed on all sides and confronting a stark choice: negotiate with the gunmen or pursue a policy of unmitigated repression.

He had been boxed into a corner by his own legislation: The Better Government of Ireland Act 1920, which provided for separate Home Rule parliaments in Ulster and the South. Under the terms of the Act, elections for the new assemblies were to be held in tandem, but when nominations opened for the southern House of Commons on 13 May, nationalist parties stuck to an electoral pact and refused to stand against Sinn Féin, so the republicans laid claim to every constituency in the South other than the Unionist stronghold of Trinity College Dublin. The sweeping victory enabled the separatist movement to concentrate its formidable propaganda powers on the elections in the North.

On 24 May – two days after the Chequers incident – polls opened in the newly created six-county territory of Northern Ireland. Almost nine-tenths of the population cast its vote and the lopsided outcome, with one party achieving overwhelming dominance (Ulster's Unionists won forty of the Belfast assembly's fifty-two seats), mirrored the result south of the border, where Sinn Féin controlled 124 of the Southern Parliament's 128 seats.

Although the results in the North were a disappointment (Sinn Féin and the constitutional nationalists won six seats apiece), the republicans saw both contests as an opportunity to undermine and exploit Britain's electoral machinery for their own ends – just as they had in December 1918, when Sinn Féin swept in as Ireland's newly dominant political force in the general election which returned Lloyd George to power. Instead of taking their seats at Westminster, the republicans convened the first Dáil Éireann, a national – and necessarily underground – Irish assembly which purported to represent all thirty-two counties.

In February 1921, Sinn Féin's leader, Éamon de Valera, declared that the movement would follow a similar strategy at the May elections. They would campaign in both territories and treat the contests for the 'partition parliaments' as an election for a second Dáil Éireann. In the North, the move proved a disaster (they split the nationalist vote and intensified Ulster Unionist hostility towards Irish nationalism), but it was a triumph in the South. And so the first elections under the

Government of Ireland Act 1920 entrenched hardliners on both sides of the border: Ulster Unionists strengthened their hegemony in Northern Ireland, while in the South, Sinn Féin was established (whatever the real feelings of the Irish people) as the territory's sole legitimate authority.[27]

For Lloyd George, the Irish crisis now entered a new phase. The elections had copper-fastened partition, sidelining the seemingly intractable Ulster issue; but they had also demolished Britain's constitutional claim to the South, and had exposed the Government of Ireland Act as nothing more than a sham. To make matters worse, backdoor peace negotiations with the illegal Sinn Féin government had confirmed that the revolutionaries were in no mood to entertain a truce on terms dictated by the British. They refused to surrender arms, and Lloyd George's haphazard overtures towards the republicans had infuriated sections of the military and the Conservative Party. Meanwhile the violence raged on unabated. For the Crown forces, the months of May and June proved particularly bloody; one-quarter of all their fatalities were sustained in the last twelve weeks of the conflict as both sides intensified the military struggle by escalating the number of attacks, raids and searches.[28]

The renewed pressure forced the IRA onto the defensive, but for the British, the prospects of a long-term victory had never looked more elusive. With no end in sight to the guerrilla war, ill-discipline among the Crown forces grew, intensifying the psychological and political pressure on the military and the government. In one widely publicised incident on 17 April, the Auxiliaries killed a police sergeant, along with one of their own men, during a chaotic raid on a hotel in County Limerick, prompting the army to accuse them of behaving as if they were 'in the trenches of France'.[29]

In the words of one historian, the 'bankruptcy of British policy was becoming impossible to ignore'.[30] Lloyd George held fast to the belief that the 'Irish job' was a 'policeman's job', maintaining earlier on in the struggle that 'you do not declare war against rebels'.[31] But as the country became increasingly ungovernable, the British had no choice, as Charles Townshend has argued, other than to militarise the Royal Irish Constabulary (RIC).[32] By spring 1921, it was clear that a decisive military victory required a drastic change in strategy, not least because of the failure by the British to establish any unity of command between their security forces. The army and the paramilitaries reinforcing the RIC (the Black and Tans and the Auxiliaries) operated under different command structures, creating tensions and divisions that contributed to disorder and indiscipline. The nature of the combat exacerbated these problems. Although the Crown forces were bearing down on the IRA, they were fighting without a defined front, and as one officer admitted, it had become 'very difficult to "get at" the extremists except by hunting them down'.[33]

Grisly accounts of reprisals filled the pages of British newspapers and, while many of the stories were inaccurate or partisan, the hostile reporting crippled the government's efforts to shore up public confidence in its policy. A particularly effective weapon for the republicans was the *Irish Bulletin*, an underground publication produced five times a week in several languages. British and international newspapers frequently relied upon this organ of Dáil Éireann for details of the military struggle and the misconduct of Crown forces.[34]

Official efforts to counter the negative publicity were sluggish and, at times, heavy-handed. When, in December 1920, Dublin Castle decided to prosecute *The Freeman's Journal* – a nationalist daily the authorities held responsible, together with the *Irish Independent*, for Sinn Féin's popular standing in the country – Fleet Street erupted in protest, forcing the government into a hasty climbdown and the release of the newspaper's convicted proprietors and editor.[35]

The press agitation reflected the British public's intense interest in Ireland's plight. Comparatively little attention had been shown from this quarter during the early stages of the guerrilla war, but by May 1921, Ireland had become a cause of mass grievance. No other issue possessed the power to trigger such anger, solidarity, indignation and revulsion. At Chequers, Lloyd George had received a forceful reminder of the price he was paying for his aggressive Irish policy – both personally and politically. The lack of sympathy shown towards the Prime Minister by the local superintendent underlined how this issue, above all others, fed public antipathy towards the government, empowering and emboldening his political adversaries.

Indeed, public discontent over Ireland contributed to the inexorable rise of the Labour Party. Its staunch opposition to the conflict helped consolidate its power base in Britain's industrial heartlands. By contrast, the Liberals were fixed on a path of irreversible decline. Divided by the overthrow of Herbert Asquith in 1916, one bloc remained in government with Lloyd George, while the other was cast into opposition. Between 1918 and 1922, the Coalition Liberals endured a run of atrocious by-election results, leading Sir George Younger, the influential chairman of the Conservative Party, to question as early as 1920 the wisdom of remaining in such a one-sided alliance. Why should the Tories go on 'propping up the mouldering corpse'?[36]

The Prime Minister's personal appeal was not what it once was, either. By the time of the Chequers incident, the super-human image of him as the man who won the war was on the wane. Conservative distaste for his policies and style of leadership continued to fester, while pulverising economic conditions, which left close to two million unemployed by the summer of that year, threatened to stoke social discontent and undermine Cabinet unity.

In April 1921, when a nationwide strike loomed from a 'Triple Alliance' of miners, dockers and railwaymen, a protest that would have brought the country to its knees, Lloyd George's government threw together an improvised defence force of over 60,000, and against this uncompromising backdrop, the Prime Minister bullied and beguiled trade union leaders into submission. Falling wages triggered that dispute, but Lloyd George never dismissed the possibility that ill-feeling over Ireland had fuelled resentment among the working classes. In 1919, he contended that 'the policemen on strike, [and] the many agitators actively engaged in various parts of the country were generally of Irish extraction and they were creating a vicious atmosphere'.[37]

Yet not till the spring of 1921 did Lloyd George – the 'most pragmatic of statesman' in the words of the historian A.J.P. Taylor[38] – turn his full attention to Ireland, and by that stage the violence had become an international scandal. The search for a solution was not helped by the Ulster hardliners in Cabinet. As early as October 1919, Andrew Bonar Law, leader of the Conservative Party, worried that a revised version of the Third Home Rule Bill, offering limited self-rule for the Irish, might result in the 'break up of the present government'.[39] He had built his career around the fanatical defence of Ulster's interests, and in the pre-1914 years, had preferred to countenance civil war rather than accept a devolved Dublin parliament.

In March 1921, his resignation and retreat from Westminster on the grounds of ill-health cleared the path for a settlement, yet still Lloyd George clung to a policy of repression. For a long time, he had miscalculated the depth of support for Sinn Féin and the strength of nationalist feeling in Ireland. Unlike Bonar Law, whose father was an Ulsterman of Scottish descent, Lloyd George had no strong connections to the Protestant heartlands of the north-east of the island, and so his search for a way out of the Irish imbroglio was not about wrestling with deeply held beliefs. It was more a question, as one historian highlights, 'of how to keep his government together and himself in office'.[40] Tory support for Ulster's Protestants, although of a different character to the pre-war years, still had the potential to destroy his premiership. The formation of Northern Ireland had appeased his Conservative Cabinet colleagues, but until partition was virtually set in stone, Lloyd George continued to hedge his bets with Sinn Féin.

On 24 May, the same day he hauled his security triumvirate over the coals for the Chequers incident, the army in Ireland began preparations for the extension of martial law to all twenty-six counties. On 2 June, the Cabinet signed off on the measure, and days later, the first of the additional battalions rolled into Ireland. Having encouraged tentative peace initiatives in the past, including a secret line of communication with the Sinn Féin businessman Patrick Moylett in the autumn of 1920, Lloyd George now appeared set on an all-out military victory.[41]

The decision flew in the face of his own government's military advice. General Sir Nevil Macready, head of the British army in Ireland, told the Cabinet in no uncertain terms that the troops could not endure 'another winter campaign'. In other words, the British forces had three months to 'break the back of the rebellion' – an unlikely prospect given that for the past two years both sides had been locked in a virtual stalemate.[42]

Appalled at the government's hard-line stance, Macready even wrote to Frances Stevenson in the hope that she would persuade the Prime Minister to abandon all hope of a military solution. 'There are, of course, one or two wild people who still hold the absurd idea that if you go on killing long enough peace will ensue. I do not believe it for one moment, but I do believe that the more people that are killed, the more difficult will be the final solution.'[43]

But Lloyd George, true to form, kept his options open. Under the terms of the Government of Ireland Act, the twenty-six counties would revert to Crown Colony status if the Southern Parliament was not established by mid-July. Constitutionally, it was impossible to impose martial law prior to this deadline, meaning that behind the more aggressive front, Lloyd George could keep his peace moves in play – at least for another six weeks.

Coercion and conciliation were two sides of the same coin when it came to cajoling the republicans to the negotiating table – a strategy not dissimilar to Lloyd George's approach to industrial disputes. When the Cabinet signed off on martial law on 2 June, it was decided that 'no announcement of this policy should be made at present'.[44] The decision would not have helped the government's standing with the public, but it provided a helpful display of bloody-mindedness for the republicans. Shortly afterwards, details of the planned troop surge and martial law arrangements were discreetly leaked to Michael Collins, the charismatic head of the IRA, in an operation overseen by Alfred 'Andy' Cope, one of Lloyd George's trusted civil servants in Dublin Castle. And it was made clear that the British would enforce martial law with the utmost vigour.

At this point, the back-channel negotiating avenues were showing serious signs of congestion. Unofficially, all manner of intermediaries were attempting to forge a truce. But still Lloyd George hedged his bets. British peace efforts in Ireland had failed in the past, he argued at the 12 May Cabinet meeting, 'and they [had] laughed at us', so he saw no point in grasping at just any opportunity – it had to be the 'best opportunity'.[45] Politically the stakes could not be higher. If he was unable to dictate the timing and negotiate from a position of strength, Conservative backbenchers would accuse him of abject surrender, while a slide towards martial law threatened to destroy his reputation on the left and deepen disapproval abroad.

At about this time, Lloyd George experienced some sort of physical breakdown.[46] For weeks, he had been preoccupied by rumours of a 'plot' against him by Churchill and Birkenhead. Frances Stevenson believed the intrigue, which had welled up over a different issue, now centred on Ireland. But while Birkenhead denied charges of a conspiracy, Churchill did not, prompting Lloyd George to remark: 'Winston does not tell actual lies, [and] that is why he will not deny it.'[47]

Drained of all vitality, the Prime Minister suddenly appeared a hapless figure, befuddled and overwhelmed by the great rush of events. Recuperating at Chequers, he wrote to Bonar Law on 7 June and complained of 'one perplexity after another. Crises', he said, 'chase each other like the shadows of clouds across the landscape. Miners, Unemployment, Reparation, Silesia, and as always Ireland.'[48]

Not long after receiving this letter, Bonar Law – his spirits and strength restored by a sojourn in the South of France – journeyed back to England, straight into the drama and intrigue swirling around Westminster. Lloyd George construed the return of the former Conservative leader as further evidence of the plot against him. His anxiety had flared up after Lord Salisbury published a letter in *The Times* urging the Conservatives to abandon the coalition. The Tory dissident – scion of the aristocratic Cecil family – numbered among Lloyd

George's staunchest critics and was on close terms with Bonar Law.

In the fevered atmosphere potential foes multiplied. Frances Stevenson concluded that Churchill and Birkenhead were conspiring with the press baron Lord Beaverbrook, who was thought to be 'engineering for a coup'. The Canadian owner of the *Daily Express*, known before his ennoblement as Max Aitken, had managed Bonar Law's unexpectedly successful campaign for the Tory Party leadership in 1911. They had remained close ever since, and he now beseeched his old friend to return to the fray and lead the Conservatives out of the coalition. At Chequers, Lloyd George also attempted to win over Bonar Law, pleading with him to assume office again and shore up the government. But the ex-Tory leader, who remained hugely popular with his party, rejected their entreaties and within five days was back on the boat to France.[49]

The putative plot never amounted to anything, and by 24 June, two days after the King made his appeal for peace in Belfast, a reinvigorated Prime Minister felt able to slap Birkenhead on the back for the blood-curdling speech he had delivered against the Irish in the House of Lords.

This extraordinary tirade, in which Birkenhead committed Britain to the continuation of the war in Ireland 'at whatever sacrifice', appeared in the newspapers on the same day the monarch opened Northern Ireland's parliament with expressions of hope about a 'new era of peace, contentment and good will'.[50] When the Lord Chancellor fretted about the 'harsh disparity' between the two speeches, Lloyd George insisted that the contrast was 'helpful'. With a fraternal spirit that he might have struggled to muster a few weeks earlier, he reassured Birkenhead that 'in dealing with the Irish you must show that you mean to go on'.[51]

2 · IMPROVISING A NATION

On 28 June 1921, on an afternoon when the summer heat had turned unusually oppressive, a small crowd gathered outside a handsome neo-classical building on Dublin's Upper Merrion Street to witness the opening of the Parliament of Southern Ireland. Since this was a legislature without legislators, the ceremony promised to be notable for its sheer absurdity. The press descended in their droves, determined to milk the occasion for all it was worth. 'Crown forces were to left and right and all points of the compass. So were photographers – platoons of photographers. There were more snapshotters than people and more Crown forces than snapshotters', the *Irish Independent*'s sketch writer recorded. Meanwhile, *The Freeman's Journal* described the antics of a 'barefooted ... unkempt urchin', who amused onlookers by marching up and down whistling 'The Soldier's Song', a rallying tune favoured by the Irish Volunteers.[1]

Some of these observations may have been invented, but it scarcely mattered. They reflected the new reality: outside of a sustained military effort, British rule in Ireland was finished. The old social and political hierarchies had been overturned, and for the first time in a long tradition of rebellion, the concerns of radical republicans had fused with those of the democratic mass of the population. Nationalists of all hues now viewed the British regime in Ireland as degenerate and autocratic.

These shifts occurred with astonishing speed. In the summer of 1914, the vast majority of nationalists supported the Irish Parliamentary Party's demands for Home Rule, or devolved self-government from Westminster. Yet within the space of a few years, those moderate voices and allegiances had vanished, obliterated by a succession of crises that rippled centrifugally over the entire nationalist community. These experiences, from the martyrdom of republican leaders to the conscription ordeal, mass internments, years of violent disorder, the militarisation of the police, and now the imposition of partition and the division of the island into two jurisdictions, each with its own parliament, provoked a unifying hatred of British rule and galvanised popular support for the revolutionaries. Most Irish nationalists were no longer content with the promise of Home Rule; they wanted independence. The revolution had delegitimised the British government in Ireland, but what measure of self-government was worth fighting for was never acknowledged or defined. At this stage, few cared about how to bridge the gap between rhetoric and reality.

In this context, the ceremonies for the new parliaments expressed two divergent visions of sovereignty: while the Northern Parliament opened to lavish fanfare, the southern version was dismissed as nothing more than a 'screaming farce'.[2]

Westminster and Dublin Castle were under no illusion as to the depth of the public's anger. One civil servant faced what he called the 'Ceremony of Bare Benches' with gritted teeth, while Lord FitzAlan, the Lord Lieutenant, cried off sick, as did his second in command, the Lord Chancellor.[3] Although the nationalist papers stressed the presence of Crown forces, it is likely that they tried to keep a low profile on that muggy afternoon outside what are today the Government Buildings of the Republic of Ireland. The unionist *Irish Times* reported that there was no 'elaborate armed display in the vicinity' and the only soldiers visible from the street 'were a few stationed on the roof ... who gazed down with languid interest on the people gathered below'.[4]

Inside, in a room that had been serving as the council chamber for the Department of Agriculture, a large mahogany table separated the Senate from the House of Commons. Towards the centre of the room a raised dais, or speaker's platform, held three wooden chairs, gilt-edged and upholstered in a plush red fabric. A vast crimson curtain, draped along the back wall, gestured towards grandeur, but there was no masking the strangeness or futility of it all. As the newspapers sneered the following day, the pantomime was over in less than twenty minutes. It began just after 3 p.m., when two ushers bearing long, white, gilt-tipped sticks processed towards the dais, trailed by two officials, the Lord Chief Justice and the Master of the Rolls. The dignitaries skipped rapidly through the script. An address from the King was read out, and then Lord Chief Justice Molony, as if 'he were delivering a judgment in the Four Courts', informed the four representatives of Trinity College Dublin, the only members present in the 128-seat House of Commons, that unless at least one half of the chamber took the oath of allegiance to the monarch 'within 14 days from today', the parliament's future was in doubt.[5]

The boycott was not without political risk. Unless the Southern Parliament was properly inaugurated within two weeks – Lloyd George revised the date to 14 July so as to avoid an unfortunate clash with the Battle of the Boyne anniversary on 12 July – the twenty-six counties of Southern Ireland would revert to Crown Colony status and fall under martial law. Some weeks earlier, Andy Cope, Joint Assistant Undersecretary to Ireland, had made sure that the daunting details of the martial law arrangements were passed to Michael Collins, a move clearly designed to jolt the republicans towards the negotiating table and prevent them from stringing out negotiations and extracting further concessions. As a tactic, it foreshadowed the brutal methods of persuasion Lloyd George would apply later that year in London, resulting in the Irish delegates signing the Treaty under the threat of 'immediate and terrible war'. For now, though, the nationalist community, in all its diverse complexity, stood in solidarity against the British.

On 24 June, Lloyd George thrust out the olive branch. He invited Éamon de Valera, as 'the chosen leader of the great majority in Southern Ireland', along with Sir James Craig, Premier of the freshly constituted Northern Ireland, to a conference in London to 'explore to the utmost the possibility of a settlement'.[6]

De Valera received the letter shortly after his release from jail. He had been pitched into a filthy cell in the Bridewell on 22 June.[7] Crown forces were under general orders not to touch him, but the tall man apprehended on the grounds of a large house in suburban Dublin by a detachment of troops from the Worcestershire Regiment initially refused to reveal his true identity. Once in detention, he abandoned the pretence that his name was 'Mr Sankey' and declared himself to be the 'President of the Irish Republic'.[8]

De Valera had become accustomed to this title. It was a constant refrain during his eighteen-month trip to the United States, which transformed him into an international celebrity, although it removed him 'from a crucial stage in the War of Independence', as the historian Diarmaid Ferriter highlights.[9]

Cast as 'the Lincoln of Ireland', de Valera, with his long frame and 'scholarly stoop', captivated the American public, who greeted him, as his official biographers put it, 'in a manner fitting to his position as head of state'.[10] Officially, no such role existed, because there was no Irish state; but de Valera was the head of an Irish republican counter-state that carried out a number of civil functions while prosecuting an armed insurgency against British rule.

By the time Sinn Féin's leader returned from the US, Michael Collins had become the chief prosecutor of the guerrilla war. His power base derived not only from his pre-eminent position within the Irish Republican Brotherhood (IRB), a secret oath-bound society at the vanguard of Irish militancy, but also from his roles as the counter-state's Minister for Finance and the IRA's Director of Military Intelligence. This unrivalled level of political and military oversight gave Collins command over the most effective activists within the republican movement. For the first time since de Valera had been elected as the President of Sinn Féin and the Irish Volunteers back in 1917, a rival source of authority had emerged within advanced nationalism.

As soon as the British government learned of de Valera's arrest, Cope, who operated as the Prime Minister's unofficial go-between with Sinn Féin, sprang into action. 'Nervy and highly-strung by temperament', Cope frequently drove himself to the brink of physical collapse in his efforts to manoeuvre Lloyd George's administration onto the path of peace.[11] And he was now terrified that de Valera's arrest would sabotage the latest efforts in that direction, so, despite the late hour, he dashed to the Bridewell, spoke to de Valera and arranged for his immediate transfer to officers' quarters at Portobello Barracks.[12] Much to the chagrin of the military authorities, plans to launch a prosecution for high treason were knocked on the head, and the following morning, the prisoner was released.[13] Reeling at the speed of his ejection, de Valera concluded that the British were waging some ghastly form of psychological warfare upon him. They seemed to want to 'undermine his authority, to make little of him, and even to make him suspect among his own followers'.[14] While this observation by de Valera's official biographers, writing some fifty years after the event, may have been overly dramatic, Ronan Fanning sees it as a reflection of de Valera's 'enduring paranoia'.[15] But the British were not unaware of the potential dent to his pride. In his diary, the Dublin Castle civil servant Mark Sturgis admitted that he did 'not mind the snub to our hero who has boasted of being on the run and who can't look very grand when we pick him up and instantly let him go'.[16]

Amid this hullabaloo, Cope raced off to London, accompanied by his boss, Sir John Anderson, the powerful Joint Under-secretary to Ireland, and the army chief, Sir Nevil Macready, for the 24 June Cabinet meeting – a pivotal gathering at which the government effectively conceded military defeat. The IRA had won the guerrilla war simply by not losing it. Conscious of the propaganda coup they were about to hand the republicans with the request for peace talks, ministers agonised over the wording of Lloyd George's invitation to de Valera. Staunch Conservatives protested against the 'gush of the letter',[17] but Cope pressed the need for conciliation. As Sturgis put it, 'Andy harangued His Majesty's ministers and even on his own showing must have been pretty hysterical – he says the sweat poured off him. He talked failure without an offer and Greenwood [Sir Hamar Greenwood, Chief Secretary for Ireland], told him "to curb his Sinn Fein tendencies".'[18]

It was Cope who personally delivered the letter to de Valera. Ever since his arrival in Dublin in the spring of 1920, this former customs detective had assiduously cultivated key Sinn Féin and IRA contacts and was on familiar terms with Collins, Minister for Foreign Affairs Arthur Griffith and Eamonn Duggan, a Dáil deputy. Inevitably, his regular forays into enemy territory riled the military and discomforted his colleagues at Dublin Castle. After the Truce, when many in the British army believed they had thrown away a winning position, the distaste towards Cope intensified. One officer recalled that he was 'universally detested by everyone in the Castle, it being generally supposed that he was going to sell us all to the rebels'.[19]

If Cope had assumed that de Valera would leap at Lloyd George's invitation to attend a peace conference in London alongside Craig, his harried nerves were in for another jolt. The Sinn Féin President let days slide by before issuing a reply some hours after the aborted opening of the Southern Parliament. The next morning, the newspapers' damning coverage of that event ran alongside de Valera's letter to Lloyd George, with its insistence on a peace based upon Ireland's 'essential unity' – meaning that no part of the country (i.e. the north-east) would remain within the United Kingdom. Or to put it another way, an Irish administration was to have legal sovereignty over the entire island.[20] In the view of one British civil servant, this attitude implied that Ulster's Unionists were a minority party 'in a country of which de Valera is king', and he characterised the refusal to acknowledge Craig as Northern Ireland's prime minister as 'absurd and insulting'.[21] De Valera had declared that as 'leader of the Irish Nation', he would first have to consult with 'certain representatives of the political minority in this country' before agreeing to any conference in London.[22]

Craig and four Southern Unionists were invited to meet de Valera at Dublin's Mansion House to discuss the next steps in the tentative peace process. Predictably, the new Northern

Parliament's leader declined the offer. Just as de Valera objected to an arrangement that treated him and Craig as equals, Craig refused to engage with the Irish nationalists unless they accepted Northern Ireland's existence. A wholly different dynamic applied to the Southern Unionists. Abandoned, as they saw it, by their brethren in the North, they were now an electorally insignificant group in a twenty-six-county Ireland ruled by republicans. There was nothing for it but to throw in their lot with their former political foes and try to extract the best settlement.

As became the norm over the course of de Valera's and Lloyd George's protracted correspondence that summer, most of the letters between the two leaders appeared in the press; but the British eventually tired of this megaphone diplomacy. Sinn Féin had always been more effective at the war of words than their opponents, since they were appealing to a broadly sympathetic international audience, who viewed their claim to national self-determination as entirely in keeping with the spirit of the age. Parliamentary democracy, which in Europe generally meant a state ruled by an ethnic majority, became the standard of government on the Continent, excluding Soviet Russia, in the early post-war period. The winds of change also swept away the last vestiges of the pre-1914 European order, with its hated practices of secret diplomacy and Great Power alliances. Instead, Wilsonian liberalism promised to reorder the international system on moral principles. Global peace and security were entrusted to a community of independent nations, motivated, or so it was hoped, to act together in the common interest.[23]

No one championed this 'unity in diversity' concept more vigorously than General Jan Christiaan Smuts, a principal architect of the League of Nations and a driving force behind a peaceful settlement to the Anglo-Irish crisis. Tall, lean, fearless and as ambitious as he was self-righteous, this Cambridge-educated lawyer and former Boer commando became, by a strange twist of fate, a messianic defender of the British Empire.[24] He saw it as essential to white South Africa's future: not only in the protection it offered to outnumbered white settlers, but as a 'civilising' force that eventually, in his fertile racial imaginings, would sweep across the whole continent to create a vast white dominion 'stretching unbroken throughout Africa'.[25]

In the aftermath of the Armageddon of 1914–18, these yearnings acquired a fresh urgency. Fearful that the imperial bonds between the self-governing settler dominions of Australia, New Zealand, Canada and South Africa might snap under the cumulative strains of the post-war era, Smuts helped engineer the emergent Commonwealth of Nations. As he spelled out in a speech in London in 1917, the racial ties and common imperial heritage of these countries helped unite far-flung democracies behind a common flag and 'a higher ideal'. The immense sacrifices non-white populations made to the Allied war effort were passed over in silence. Instead, Smuts marvelled at how 'the white inhabitants of the British Empire', who had no direct involvement in the 'struggle and feuds of old Europe', had rushed to help the 'Mother Country'.[26]

His idea that the Commonwealth should exist as a group of co-equal nations served as the model for the League of Nations, as the historian Mark Mazower has documented.[27] For Smuts, the difference between the two organisations was that the Commonwealth represented an organic community of nations bound together by a shared allegiance to the Crown. He and other British imperialists espoused the principle that the Dominions could maintain their close imperial ties even as they became fully independent. Commonwealth theorists saw the entity as a 'social organism unified by a common moral purpose and culture'.[28] But the vicious guerrilla conflict between Britain and Ireland made a nonsense of such high-minded sentiments, and Smuts knew it. At the Paris Peace Conference in 1919, he warned that Ireland was a 'chronic wound' capable of destroying the British Empire.[29] By June 1921, when Smuts and the other Dominion leaders were in London for the Imperial Conference, these sentiments were expressed with even greater force. 'The present situation is an unmeasured calamity,' Smuts fulminated in a letter to Lloyd George; 'it is in negation of all the principles of government which we have professed as the basis of Empire ... and it must more and more tend to poison both our Empire relations and our foreign relations.'[30]

It was in this crusading spirit that Smuts stepped off the boat at Dún Laoghaire (then Kingstown) on the morning of 5 July 1921 as an 'unofficial' intermediary to the stalled peace process. His mission was to persuade the Sinn Féin leaders to relinquish their demands for a Republic and embrace the 'free membership of the British Empire'. Lloyd George had assumed negotiations would go ahead in London without a formal truce, but in the atmosphere of mutual suspicion between the two capitals, the Dáil ministry wanted the ceasefire terms in writing.[31] A fear, verging on paranoia, swept through the Irish Cabinet. Perhaps Lloyd George's unexpected u-turn was an elaborate bluff, designed to entice them into a deadly trap – a prospect that tormented Collins. If the 'truce should fail' and 'we come out into the open, it is extermination for us', he reportedly told one comrade.[32] Not everyone was so wary. Art O'Brien, an indefatigable republican activist who gave up a relatively lucrative career in engineering to become the Dáil's representative in London, could barely contain his euphoria. 'England is beaten in regard to us,' he declared in a long missive to Collins, in which he urged his leader to accept Lloyd George's invitation as 'genuine' and a crucial 'first step from … which there can be no going back'. The Prime Minister 'has played into our hands,' he wrote triumphantly, and 'we must use our strength to get what we want.'[33]

De Valera had been weighing the tactical considerations in a far more cynical frame of mind. At the palatial Georgian residence of Dr Robert Farnan, a gynaecologist whose home on Merrion Square provided regular refuge to IRA men on the run, he told Smuts he intended to refuse the invitation. As far as he was concerned, Lloyd George was playing him off against Craig, in order to 'exploit their differences'. The South African Premier was appalled. 'You are making the mistake of your lives,' he warned de Valera, who was flanked by Griffith, Robert Barton and Eamonn Duggan, all of whom had just been released from jail. The blunt-speaking Afrikaaner laid out what was at stake. They would squander their advantage in public opinion if they spurned this 'olive branch'. Smuts reported back to Lloyd George that while Griffith seemed to agree with him, de Valera harped on 'about generations of oppression and seemed to live in a world of dreams, visions and shadows'.[34]

Nevertheless, Smuts departed Dublin in buoyant form. He concluded, correctly, that Sinn Féin's leaders would accept Lloyd George's invitation if Craig was excluded from the talks, but mistakenly assumed he had succeeded in winning over even de Valera to the merits of Dominion status. He had tried to impress on the revolutionaries the perils of a republican system of government that lacked international support and solidarity, warning they would become prey to the twin dangers of external aggression and internal division. These were not empty words; he spoke from experience. The old Transvaal Republic, he assured the Irish, had been marred by internecine strife as well as fractious relations with the British, culminating in a war that reduced 'my country ... to ashes. If I can give you any warning it is to avoid that fate.'[35]

The insurgency appeared to reach a fresh pitch of intensity as a truce approached. In the days after Smuts returned to London, negotiations between Sinn Féin, the Southern Unionist leader, Lord Midleton, and Britain's Commander-in-Chief in Ireland, Sir Nevil Macready, resulted in the agreement of an armistice at 8 p.m. on Friday 8 July. At the end of this 'epoch-making day', as Macready put it, the IRA and the British forces committed to officially ending hostilities by midday Monday, 11 July.[36] Significantly, however, no truce document was signed, a situation that stored up difficulties for the long peace talks ahead, and which provided, in the words of the historian Charles Townshend, a 'fruitful source of dispute' between the two sides.[37] During these last days of war, there was no perceptible let-up in the fighting. On the morning the guns were due to fall silent, the British recorded ten deaths and a total of sixteen casualties. That did not include the four off-duty soldiers kidnapped the night before in Cork city, who were discovered lying in a field on the morning of 11 July, blindfolded and shot in the head.[38]

On 20 July, Lloyd George offered the Irish Dominion status. What precisely he meant by this remained unclear, for at the Imperial Conference that summer, the Australian Prime Minister, the pugilistic Billy Hughes, brusquely repudiated Smuts' efforts to clarify the concept. The South African Premier, supported by Arthur Meighen of Canada, wanted a written Imperial constitution that would formalise the ties of empire and legally institute the settler nations' independence from London. But Hughes, who in 1919 led a Dominion-wide revolt against a proposal to enshrine the principle of racial equality in the preamble of the League of Nations, now rounded on Smuts, snarling at him to 'leave well alone'.[39] And so Dominion status would remain a fluid, ill-defined concept throughout the 1921 Anglo-Irish peace talks. In fact, it was not given a coherent status until the Balfour Report of 1926.

It was within the Commonwealth's 'sisterhood of nations – the greatest in the world' as Lloyd George trumpeted it during one of a handful of post-Truce meetings with de Valera in London that July, that Ireland's future lay. At first, the Prime Minister attempted to cajole the long-limbed revolutionary into acceptance of this fact. He ushered de Valera, who had insisted on meeting alone and whose arrival in the capital drew emotional crowds chanting the rosary, into the Cabinet room at 10 Downing Street. On the wall, as Frances Stevenson wrote in her diary, hung a large map of the British Empire 'with its great blotches of red all over it'. That evening the Prime Minister told her that this was 'to impress upon DeV the greatness of the [British Empire] and to get him to recognise it, & the King'. Yet his Irish adversary, she recounted, 'kept going off at a tangent'. Lloyd George had gestured to the long table in the centre of the room, at which the various representatives of the Dominions had sat earlier in the day, during a session of the seven-week Imperial Conference, and had indicated that one chair could belong to an Irish prime minister. 'All we ask you to do is to take your place in this sisterhood of free nations. It is an invitation ... we invite you here.' That approach fell on stony ground, so the velvet glove came off. 'I shall be sorry if this conference fails,' Lloyd George reflected:

> [T]errible as events have been in Ireland, it is nothing to what they will be if we fail to come to an agreement. The British Empire is getting rid of its difficulties ... [and] we

shall [soon] be able to withdraw our troops from other
parts of the world. I hesitate to think of the horror if the
war breaks out again in Ireland.

An agitated de Valera protested that this was 'a threat of force
– of coercion'. 'No,' responded Lloyd George, 'I am simply
forecasting what will inevitably happen if these conversations
fail, [and] if you refuse our invitation to join us.'[40]

The Prime Minister's words may have brought home the
crude realities of power politics to de Valera, but the evidence
suggests that even before the Irish leader met Lloyd George,
he understood that an all-Ireland separatist republic was
beyond the reach of the revolutionaries. While the IRA had
prevented the British from administering power in the twenty-
six counties, full independence could not be won by force of
arms. And as de Valera conceded in writing that summer, there
could be no forcing the six counties of Northern Ireland to join
an independent republic. Some form of political compromise
was unavoidable.[41]

Earlier in the year, much to the alarm of a number of
leading Sinn Féin activists, de Valera appeared to row back
on the question of the Republic. As he told the gregarious
revolutionary Harry Boland, a close friend of Collins, there was
no point in making 'it easy for Lloyd George by proclaiming
that nothing but so and so will satisfy us. Our position should
be that we are insisting on only one right, and that is the right
of the people to determine for themselves how they should be
governed. That sounds moderate but includes everything.'[42]

In April, when Seán T. O'Kelly, Dáil Éireann's envoy in
Paris, wrote to de Valera urging him to hold firm 'to the stand
we take on an Irish Republic or nothing', his intervention
drew a sharp rebuke. Cabinet policy was not up for debate;

the Dáil's overseas representatives were expected to 'carry out the instructions of the Department, whether they personally agree with policy or not'. The alternative 'way out', de Valera reminded O'Kelly, was resignation.[43] And after the Truce, he repeatedly dampened down excited political expectations, remarking on one occasion that if Sinn Féin only made 'peace on the basis of the recognition of the Republic, they were going to face war'.[44]

During these early days of the fragile peace, de Valera trod carefully through the political minefields and, in the judgement of one historian, 'appeared to show a greater willingness to bend in order that talks could begin'.[45] On 20 July, he angrily rebuffed the Prime Minister's formal peace proposals. But the following morning, when the two leaders reconvened for the last of four one-on-one encounters, he made sure to steer clear of the cliff edge. People on both sides of the Irish Sea were thoroughly war-weary and neither de Valera nor Lloyd George could afford to wear the blame for a return to conflict. The problem was that Britain's proposed political solution, far from advancing the cause of peace, seemed only to have exposed the depth of the divide between the two governments. Tom Jones, the deputy secretary to the Cabinet, and the Prime Minister's principal official on Irish matters, summarised the offer as '"Dominion status" with all sorts of important powers, but no Navy, no hostile tariffs, and no coercion of Ulster'. Effectively what this meant was internal autonomy (the Dominions still lacked full sovereignty over foreign policy at that point) to be curtailed by six conditions relating to defence, trade and Ireland's unspecified debt obligation to the UK. A separate seventh qualification outlined Ulster's 'powers and privileges'. In Jones' judgement, the 20 July proposals represented 'one of the most generous acts in our history'.[46] Smuts wholeheartedly agreed. He told Austen Chamberlain, the monocle-wearing leader of the Conservative Party, that the Irish 'cannot reject this ... unless they are smitten with madness'. But as Chamberlain wrote to his sister, de Valera did 'reject it. Is that his last word? No. But will his next word be any better? Nobody can say.'[47]

De Valera's 'next word' turned out to be every bit as unacceptable to the British as his demand for a republic. His formal reply, dispatched some three weeks later on 10 August, proposed an alternative solution: 'External Association'. The concept, which became the basis of the Irish negotiating position, was designed to bridge the gulf between a separatist republic and British Dominion status. Under this formulation, Ireland would be externally associated with, but not a member of, the British Empire. The idea hardly set republicans' souls on fire: there was no rousing reception when he introduced it in Cabinet, where it was neither liked nor properly understood.[48] Nonetheless, all approved it – even the doctrinaire Cathal Brugha and Austin Stack. Decades later, when Britain re-invented the Commonwealth, relations with the ex-colonies were restructured along the lines laid out by de Valera. In 1921, however, the British were having none of it. 'We have gone to the utmost limits of concession both in substance [and] in form,' Chamberlain told his sister.[49]

De Valera's reply threw the British Cabinet into a fit of despair and confusion. In the Prime Minister's absence, Chamberlain hastily convened a meeting, at which the Conservative leader's 'nervous manner', as Jones later recounted to Lloyd George, 'conveyed a feeling of mild panic to his colleagues who had been drawn hurriedly from their several luncheons'. Without having seen the response, Sir Laming Worthington-Evans, the Minister for War, and Hamar Greenwood, Chief Secretary for Ireland, 'became anxious ... as though Michael Collins was about to break the truce in ten minutes or at most a quarter of an hour'. That made up Chamberlain's mind. Nothing was to be done, he said, 'to give the slightest cause for alarm', until the Prime Minister returned.[50]

Yet de Valera's deliberately vague reply left Lloyd George equally baffled. An aggressive assertion of sovereign independence was qualified by a proposal for an association with the Empire, a promise not to coerce Ulster, and a commitment to give ground on trade, debt liability, arms limitations and communications. It was impossible to determine de Valera's intention: did he mean to walk away or was he signalling his willingness to continue negotiations?[51] Lloyd George inclined to a pessimistic reading, writing glumly to his wife that these 'Irishmen are once again most troublesome. It looks for the moment as if they mean to refuse.'[52]

The British hit back with an unequivocal repudiation of de Valera's demands, ruling out any advance on the 20 July proposals. The Cabinet agreed the response should be 'brief, clear and precise'. There was no talk of turning their backs on Sinn Féin, however, thanks largely to the mediation of Andy Cope, who attributed de Valera's enigmatic letter to posturing and his need to accommodate the 'extremists of Dail Eireann [sic]'.[53] On the other hand, expectations had been raised by the negotiations, both at home and abroad, and it was scarcely conceivable that Lloyd George could allow them to end in failure. Even so, the protracted correspondence that ensued between the two leaders gave little ground for hope. To the British, the endless wrangling looked destined to end in rupture.

On 7 September, Lloyd George declared that 'this correspondence has lasted long enough'. He proposed a conference to 'ascertain how the association of Ireland with the community of nations known as the British Empire can best be reconciled with Irish national aspirations'.[54] Although carefully formulated, his invitation precipitated another bout of arm-wrestling as de Valera pressed for the delegates to be recognised as 'representatives of a sovereign and independent State'.[55] Holed up in the splendour of Flowerdale House in Gairloch, Scotland, where he had retreated on the advice of his doctor, Lloyd George contemplated his options. It was out of the question to compromise on Ireland's 'allegiance to the crown' or 'the integrity of the Empire', he reassured Chamberlain, who had returned to his home in Kent rather than remain in Scotland for a second Cabinet meeting in Inverness – the nearest major town to Gairloch. (Like other ministers, the Conservative leader had been outraged at having to embark on a long journey north at the whim of the Prime Minister. When summoned to the first Cabinet meeting in the Highlands two weeks earlier, which Lloyd George had called in response to de Valera's latest letter, he had told his sister that 'I simply splutter with rage'.)[56] Now, having held up the Crown and the Empire as non-negotiable, Lloyd George impressed upon Chamberlain the importance and inevitability of peace talks with Sinn Féin. For in the absence of a conference, he wrote, the 'country ... will not be quite satisfied that everything has been done to prevent rupture'.[57]

While the Prime Minister wanted a settlement in Ireland to restore his battered political credibility, his eyes were on a potentially more significant prize: a successful outcome at the looming disarmament conference in Washington. The security of the Empire remained Britain's chief concern in the post-war era, but there could be no certainty on that front if it failed to forge close ties with the United States. This realisation was brought home at the Imperial Conference that summer, when the Dominion leaders divided over whether London should renew the Anglo–Japanese alliance due to expire at the end of the year.

To do so would risk hostile relations with Washington, which regarded Japan as its principal foe and the greatest future threat to the Pacific equilibrium. Worse, it might pitch a cash-strapped Britain into a costly naval race. On 23 July, Churchill warned that the US could become 'the strongest naval power in the world'.[58] Ultimately, a decision was deferred until talks could reconvene in Washington later that year – a move that preserved Dominion unity, but which also served to underline America's ascendant status in the post-war international order. As the historian David Stafford has written, 'The Imperial Conference marked a turning point for Britain. No longer could it maintain the balance of power in Europe without the help of American muscle.'[59]

An unravelling peace process in Ireland was the last thing Lloyd George needed as he grappled with the growing problems of empire, economic decline and the rise of rival global powers. He reminded Chamberlain of the 'great importance of carrying the opinion of the Empire, and of this country in particular with us'.[60]

By the end of September, relations between the Prime Minister and de Valera turned a corner. The two governments essentially agreed to disagree. Negotiations in London on a political settlement would go ahead without preconditions. Crucially, there would be no prior recognition of Ireland's sovereign independence. Lloyd George restated his categorical rejection of this idea in their final exchanges. As a parting shot, de Valera replied cryptically that 'we can only recognise ourselves for what we are'.[61] Then, at last, he accepted the invitation to a peace conference.

In three months of negotiations with Lloyd George, de Valera had failed to extract any concessions on the principal issues: Irish sovereignty and partition. Nonetheless, he decided to raise the stakes with the British government that summer by formally changing his title to President of the Irish Republic – a title he had sometimes traded under in the past. Later, uncertainty was expressed over exactly what de Valera's status had been up until that point. Diarmuid O'Hegarty, the Dáil Cabinet Secretary, claimed the correct term was 'President of the Ministry or Príomh-Aire [prime minister]'.[62] But whatever the truth of the matter, de Valera was clearly intent on emphasising his status as the leader of the Irish counter-state, and probably wanted to signify directly to the British that he was the legitimate head of a legitimate state.

The new Dáil Éireann, which met for the first time in mid-August, unanimously backed the move, even though the scope of de Valera's powers remained undefined. The President himself laboured under no such confusion. He told the Dáil, 'I more or less concentrate in myself the whole Executive responsibility.'[63] Not everyone was comfortable with this sudden refurbishment at the top. George Gavan Duffy, a fastidious republican lawyer who had overseen the defence of Roger Casement at his trial for high treason, objected to de Valera holding the dual titles of president and prime minister on the grounds that it was a 'dangerous precedent'.[64] Others, too, expressed disquiet. But these reservations were swept swiftly aside by the far more pressing problem of who should represent the 'Republic' at the forthcoming peace conference.

In a somewhat hectoring speech on 23 August, the day his confirmation as president was put to the Dáil, de Valera instructed the one-party revolutionary assembly not to 'fetter me in any way whatever'. He would accept office only 'on the understanding that no road is barred'. Then he announced perhaps the most controversial decision of his career: he would 'stay at home' rather than lead the Irish delegation in the upcoming talks. He did not want to 'be a member ... of the particular body that would negotiate peace'. He noted that 'We are not in the position that we can dictate terms, we will, therefore, have proposals brought back which cannot satisfy everybody.' In that instance, de Valera explained, 'I will be in a position, having discussed the matter with the Cabinet, to come forward with such proposals as we think wise and right. It will be then for you [i.e. the Dáil] either to accept the recommendations of the Ministry or reject them.' The latter course, he warned, would involve the creation of 'a definite active opposition'.[65]

De Valera had kept External Association under wraps: it was not to be discussed beyond the Cabinet or the bilateral discussions with the British government. Clearly the idea was to hold it in reserve from Dáil Éireann and the Irish public until the negotiations with Lloyd George hit the buffers.

If de Valera was keeping his powder dry, so too was Collins. Fêted as the hero of the guerrilla war, he exercised a fascination over the public that the less photogenic de Valera never possessed. But in the post-Truce Cabinet meetings, Collins cut a very different figure. He contributed little to the discussion on how to secure a peace settlement – unlike Arthur Griffith and Cathal Brugha, revolutionaries who represented the polar extremes of moderate separatism and republican extremism. And in this tendency to play his cards close to his chest and reserve judgement on the path ahead, Collins' approach mirrored that of de Valera's.

There is not much direct evidence of de Valera's internal calculations in declining to lead the negotiating team. In the Dáil that summer he spoke of himself as the 'Head of State' and the 'symbol of the Republic', which should be left 'untouched' by any arrangements made in London.[66] After the Treaty was signed, he would tell Joe McGarrity, a key American supporter, that he had anticipated conciliatory overtures from Griffith and Collins serving as 'bait' for Lloyd George, 'leading him on and on, further in our direction'. He also told McGarrity that he had felt 'we would be able to hold them from this side from crossing the line'.[67]

On 9 September, more than a fortnight after he informed the Dáil of his intention to remain in Dublin during the upcoming peace talks, he encountered the first significant challenge to his authority in the Cabinet, when, at a meeting, Griffith, Collins and W.T. Cosgrave, the Minister for Local Government, demanded he reverse his decision. Pitted against them were Brugha, Stack and Minister for Economic Affairs Robert Barton. It took de Valera's casting vote to settle the debate in his favour, and once that was done, he proposed Griffith as the Irish delegation's chairman. Collins was to accompany him, along with Barton, Eamonn Duggan (a lawyer), Gavan Duffy and Erskine Childers (Sinn Féin's divisive director of publicity and a cousin of Barton's). The last two were intended to represent de Valera's interests and provide a counterweight to Collins and Griffith.

Scarcely a week later, on 14 September, the dissent spilled over into the Dáil. Cosgrave leapt into the fray, arguing that without de Valera's 'extraordinary experience' of negotiations, they were effectively leaving their 'ablest player in reserve'. Collins interjected along the same lines, adding tersely that he himself 'would very much prefer not to be chosen'.[68] One former comrade, Batt O'Connor, recollected the 'deep distress' that de Valera's decision caused Collins: 'He came to see me [and] would not sit down but kept pacing the floor, his face set in lines of pain and anxiety.' Collins felt de Valera was making a terrible mistake and told O'Connor how he had pleaded with the President to change his mind. 'Who ever heard of the soldier who fought the enemy in the field being sent to negotiate the peace,' he cried, according to O'Connor. 'I am being put in an impossible position.'[69] In this telling, the row over who should go to London becomes a set-piece contest between Collins' patriotism and de Valera's treachery. It is the story of the hero soldier choosing the nation over politics, while the Machiavellian de Valera forces him to risk his life for a battle he cannot possibly win.

Little of this stands up to scrutiny, at least with regard to Collins. As Peter Hart, the most scholarly of his biographers, has shown, Collins was, above all, 'a revolutionary politician' with little combat experience,[70] whose role within Cabinet, position on the executive of Sinn Féin, and evident skills as an administrator and strategist all qualified him for the delegation. Collins had been disappointed not to be included in the delegation that accompanied de Valera to London in July, and Hart argues convincingly that, far from wanting to quit the main stage at this momentous hour in Ireland's history, he found the opportunity irresistible. What Collins dreaded was de Valera's absence, for if the negotiations failed, his 'natural power base in the army and among republican militants' risked being fatally compromised.[71] In any event, Collins accepted the responsibility.

It was the ambiguity over the powers conferred on the delegates that created the catalyst for all that was to come. De Valera described the negotiators as plenipotentiaries, which would ordinarily mean that they had full powers of independent action, though that ran contrary to what he had told the Dáil in August. On 14 September, moments after Cosgrave attacked de Valera for excluding himself from the London talks, Gavan Duffy warned that Lloyd George would take advantage of the delegates' plenipotentiary status and he urged the President to think again. De Valera retorted that plenipotentiaries were 'people who had power to deal with a question subject to ratification', then immediately contradicted himself by stating that the Irish representatives would 'go first with a Cabinet policy ... on the understanding that any big question should be referred home before being decided by them'.[72] This was de Valera's have-your-cake-and-eat-it formula. He wanted to remain aloof from the negotiations, but still be involved and in full control.

Nothing exemplified this more than the decision to issue the delegates with private, contradictory instructions, requiring them to refer any draft settlement first to 'the Members of the Cabinet in Dublin'.[73] The negotiators were informed of these fresh orders on 7 October, the eve of the delegation's departure for London and weeks after the Dáil had voted unanimously to approve the delegates' plenipotentiary powers. The last-minute manoeuvre enhanced de Valera's ability to reject any agreement in London, since the new instructions bypassed the Dáil's authority and, in the absence of three ministers who formed part of the delegation (Collins, Griffith and Barton), gave the first right of refusal to a Dublin cabinet dominated by hardliners who had not been prepared to negotiate directly with the British.

The ambiguity of the delegation's powers and responsibilities injected a potent source of conflict into what was already a highly combustible situation. From his perch in Dublin Castle, civil servant Mark Sturgis recorded how the republicans were 'to a certain extent all to pieces' and too suspicious of each other 'to act off their own bat'; or as the historian Tom Garvin put it, the real problem for Sinn Féin was 'not their natural distrust of the British but their intense distrust of each other'.[74]

The Truce presented a new challenge for the revolutionary movement. As the galvanising pressure of warfare subsided, republicans were forced to confront the fundamental uncertainties about what they were fighting for, a process that immediately strained the fragile solidarity that had prevailed over the previous four years. The frictions and personal rivalries that surfaced within the Dáil Cabinet were symptomatic of these long-dormant, unresolved tensions. For while conflicting social, cultural and economic priorities had been subordinated to the nationalist cause, there was no unanimity over how far the struggle should go, or whether it was worth fighting to the death for 'absolute independence', as de Valera termed it in 1917.[75] Nor was there any consensus about what constituted republican loyalty. Radical separatists like Brugha and Stack, both of whom refused to participate in the London peace talks, conceived of it in black-and-white terms. To them, the Dáil's oath of allegiance to the Irish Republic and its government, first sworn in 1919, was sacrosanct. Others displayed a more pragmatic or ambivalent attitude. Among this constituency, as the historian Michael Laffan observed, the counter-state's republican policy was 'an admirable and worthy objective which could nonetheless be sacrificed in a compromise settlement'.[76]

Ambiguity over republican aims fostered unhealthy civil-military relations, a problem that mired in toxic factional disputes the state-building process that began in earnest after the Truce. A long-smouldering feud between Brugha and Collins ignited into a vicious power struggle, as the austere Minister for Defence renewed efforts to wrest the army away from the control of the IRB and subordinate it to his own political authority. It was a move bound to end in division and rancour, for, as an organisation, the IRA was poorly coordinated and loosely controlled. Most within its senior echelons were IRB men who owed their loyalty to Collins in his capacity as president of the Brotherhood's Supreme Council. And since March 1919, the day-to-day running of the army had been in the hands of his close ally, Richard Mulcahy, the IRA's Chief of Staff. By the summer, Brugha's relations with both these men lay in ruins. This dysfunction at the top came as the army was engulfed by a series of crises, including chronic shortages of weapons and ammunition, fracturing hierarchies, ill-discipline, spiralling costs, and mounting unease among seasoned gunmen at the influx of post-Truce recruits.[77]

During the months between the cessation of hostilities and the start of the Treaty talks, the issue of Ireland's sovereign status continued to eclipse all others. In August, when the President was asked in the Dáil to define his Ulster policy, he ruled out any coercion of the province, since they would then 'be making the same mistake ... as England had ... with Ireland'. This met with some dissent, but the debate quickly switched to other matters.[78] In the remaining time before the delegation's departure to London, de Valera supplied no further details of the Ulster strategy, nor did he issue any instructions on the subject until the Treaty talks were well underway. Unlike the British, who remained united around the 20 July proposals, the Irish delegates were packed off to London unsure of what they wanted and without a coherent plan for the battle ahead. They would have to hope that luck, that incalculable component which exists in any diplomatic situation, would be on their side.

For his part, Lloyd George refused to relinquish the menace of war. From the Truce to the commencement of the Treaty talks, and right up until the dénouement on 6 December 1921, the negotiations were overshadowed by the threat of renewed violence. As this book will show, there was no inevitability about the eventual outcome. On the contrary, the perceptions and behaviour of the decision-makers were structured by a constant sense of imminent crisis. Conflict hovered at every turn, and after two years of war, these anxieties held a nightmarish plausibility.

3 ▪ LONDON

6 October–11 October

At a Cabinet meeting on 6 October, the British government selected its delegates for the upcoming peace talks with Sinn Féin. By any measure it was a formidable line-up, with the Prime Minister enlisting Chamberlain, Churchill and Birkenhead to join him as principal negotiators. The 'Big Four' as they were later called, entirely overshadowed the rest of the delegation: Hamar Greenwood was too loathed by the Irish to wield much influence, while Worthington-Evans, the low-key Secretary of State for War, possessed few attributes other than a reputation for loyalty. He was regarded as more of a civil servant than a politician. The seventh member of the team was the Attorney General, Gordon Hewart, who would be involved only in relation to constitutional matters. But any one of the 'leading quartet', the historian Frank Pakenham declared in the mid-1930s, 'could have played Prime Minister with distinction'.[1]

Not that the names were a surprise, much less controversial. All had been drafted onto the Ireland Cabinet Committee established at the start of September, when de Valera nearly derailed plans for the conference by insisting that Britain first recognise Irish sovereignty. His demand split the Cabinet between those willing to engage with Sinn Féin unconditionally, and those implacably opposed to an open invitation. To head off a potentially ruinous schism, the Prime Minister created a committee with 'full powers to deal with the Irish situation ... [arising] out of the reply ... sent to de Valera' on that day.[2] A month later, as the dire economic conditions in Britain intensified, triggering public unrest in cities across England and Scotland, including Churchill's constituency of Dundee, the logic of circumstances took hold: committee members Robert Munro, the Secretary for Scotland, and Edward Shortt, the Liberal Home Secretary who had been a moderate Chief Secretary for Ireland for some months in 1918, were both ruled out. So too was Lord Curzon, the Foreign Secretary. He faced similarly all-consuming challenges, and his imperious character would likely have proved a liability. In any case, he disliked conferences, regarding them as tedious and too conducive to endless exhibitionist speech-making. He hated how Lloyd George monopolised these events and once described them as nothing more than 'a stage on which he is to perform'.[3]

Few Cabinet members would have deviated substantially from this view; most found the endless post-war conferences onerous and exhausting. On this occasion, Lloyd George made no bones about the arduous nature of the task ahead: the talks were likely to be 'difficult' and 'prolonged', and in order to tackle every issue on the agenda they 'would probably have to form many sub-committees'.[4] The prospect filled Chamberlain with dread. The following day he wrote to his sister that he expected 'the meetings will drag on for a long time and I look forward to them with anything but pleasure'. Unlike Joseph, or 'Joe' as his famous statesman father was known, Chamberlain lacked the stomach for political battle, and had no taste, in the words of one biographer, for 'prolonged hard work'.[5] Now in his late fifties, it often left him physically and mentally drained. He was prone to debilitating attacks of sciatica and lumbago that struck out of the blue, rendering him incapacitated for days. But it was the perceived absence of ambition, drive and resolve – all qualities his father possessed in abundance – that crippled him in the eyes of his contemporaries. Harold Macmillan described him as 'respected, but never feared',[6] while Leo Amery judged him 'wooden in face and manner, pompously correct, impeccably virtuous, but frigidly uninteresting'.[7]

As the leader of the Conservatives, Lloyd George could scarcely have excluded Chamberlain; on the contrary, his presence was vital if any settlement was to be sold to the Tories. The diehards, infuriated by the Truce – or as they saw it, the capitulation to Southern Ireland's 'murder junta' – were already marshalling their forces in protest at the government's decision to enter into a conference with Sinn Féin. On the same day that the Cabinet approved the choice of delegates, the Duke of Northumberland, a Tory peer whose personal animus against Lloyd George went beyond the standard hostility most aristocrats felt towards the 'dirty little rogue'[8] who had eviscerated their class privileges, fired the opening salvo in what was to become a sustained campaign against the peace talks. In a letter published in the diehard daily, *The Morning Post*, he attacked the government for its lack of 'moral courage' in suppressing the 'rebellion by force of arms', and accused Lloyd George's administration of 'betraying the Conservative cause'. Calling on the party's grass roots to rise up against any settlement that left the 'Irish Republican Brotherhood in control of Southern and Western Ireland', he urged Conservatives to sever ties with the coalition until 'this condition is fulfilled'.[9]

The diehards were always a fringe group within the party, and yet they proved a constant thorn in the government's side. No other faction within the Conservatives or Coalition Liberals came close to offsetting their influence. Mostly this was because they were noisy and persistent, but also because they were organised and acted collectively. Chamberlain had few ways of disciplining them; diehard MPs occupied traditionally safe Conservative seats and were not dependent on political patronage, and peers were untouchable. Aware of their unassailable position, they behaved with impunity, launching anti-coalition campaigns in the press, and voting against the government time after time.[10] Although many, like the Duke of Northumberland, were mere parliamentary curiosities, visual embodiments of obscurantist snobbery and inherited privilege peddling theories about the Jewish–Bolshevik conspiracy threatening the Western world and the British Empire – Northumberland believed Sinn Féin was an integral part of this 'great combined attack' – they were, on the whole, politically experienced. And after the Truce, their numbers appeared to be growing. Two Conservative MPs, including the diehard leader in the Commons, Colonel John Gretton, had already seceded from the coalition in protest at the concessions to Sinn Féin.

The emotions roused by the Irish question, and its potential to fuel divisions among the Tories, made Birkenhead as strategically important to Lloyd George as Chamberlain. Pakenham described him as the greatest of the 'Big Four',[11] a conclusion that few historians would concur with these days, but in his time he was a dazzling and intimidating figure. Known as Carson's 'galloper', a soubriquet earned for his part in Ulster's anti-Home Rule rallies, he still wielded influence in unionist circles, and for the Prime Minister, it was this that mattered most. Chamberlain was regarded as too much of a moderate to cut much ice with the right wing of the party and, despite his father's reputation as an aggressive unionist, he lacked the personal connections to Ulster. Lloyd George clearly did not rate him either as a negotiator. He was kept at arm's length from the preliminary London talks with de Valera over the summer, due to what Tom Jones described as 'his disconcerting way of butting in with speeches'.[12] Birkenhead, on the other hand, was an entirely different creature.

Whereas Chamberlain was schooled for political greatness – an ambition he ultimately failed to fulfil – Birkenhead, who took the title of his native town when he was raised to the peerage, had vaulted into the top legal and political echelons by dint of ambition, drive and sheer intellectual brilliance. He was, as David Cannadine wrote, 'endowed with a gigantic ego and towering self-confidence' together with 'mesmeric oratorical gifts of lightning wit, stinging retort and poisonous vituperation'.[13] Importantly, he was associated with the extremists in his party, although unlike Arthur Balfour, a former prime minister and elder statesmen within the Cabinet, whom Lloyd George cannily packed off to the disarmament conference in Washington, he could not be categorised as an 'irreconcilable'. What counted was Birkenhead's fearsome re-putation, which provided the Prime Minister with the requisite level of menace that he deemed essential to any successful negotiation. As Pakenham put it, the Lord Chancellor exerted a 'sinister, even satanic power' over the imagination of the Irish nationalists, who remembered him chiefly as the prosecutor of Sir Roger Casement, the charismatic revolutionary hanged in London three months after the Easter Rising.[14]

Between them, Chamberlain and Birkenhead held the key to the conference's success, for without their advocacy and agreement, a settlement with Sinn Féin was unlikely to win Tory support. But there was another motivating factor for Lloyd George: the need to fortify his premiership against any further challenges from within. By drawing Birkenhead and Churchill into every twist and turn of the Irish saga, the 'plotters' who had caused him anxiety earlier in the year were absorbed into a process that promised to make or break their political careers. Churchill, as Colonial Secretary, could expect to play a major role in the negotiations, and yet without Lloyd George's careful manoeuvring at this juncture, there was no guarantee the government would present a united front on the fraught issue of Ireland. His diplomatic efforts erased the frictions of the summer and bound the most powerful personalities in the Cabinet into a mutually dependent enterprise that, if successful, promised to prolong the coalition's spell in office. Not that Churchill was the type to harbour a grudge. He likely heeded his wife Clementine's advice when she wrote in July 'that as long as [Lloyd George] is P.M., it would be better to hunt with him than to lie in the bushes & watch him careering along with a jaundiced eye'.[15]

Chamberlain resolved to pursue the same course. In August, he calculated that the backbench rebellion on Ireland could rise to above forty Conservative MPs, with the resistance, as ever, centred on the party's right wing, where discontent on so many other aspects of government was already widespread. The Irish question threatened to transform these simmering tensions into outright revolt, potentially triggering the return of Andrew Bonar Law, whose credibility among the Conservatives remained as strong as ever. Having returned permanently to London at the end of September, he was now hovering on the political sidelines, and his presence served as an uncomfortable reminder of the obstacles ahead. Yet Chamberlain was prepared to risk all for a settlement. When it came to Ireland, he had never been an orthodox unionist, and was the only member of the British delegation, with its three Liberals and three Conservative politicians, to have pushed for a conference free of conditions – other than no separation and no republic.

Later, he argued that Birkenhead was converted to his view long before the conference began. In a memoir published shortly before his death, he recalled how, one morning in July, Birkenhead strode into his room in 11 Downing Street:

> [J]ust as I was telephoning to say that I must see him. 'You and I,' he said, 'bear a great load of responsibility. Unless we are agreed, we shall smash the party and destroy any chance of settlement. It is time we knew exactly where the other stands.' And then he proceeded to explain his views with that clarity and brevity which always distinguished him in council. I found that he had come to say to me what I had come to say to him, and thenceforth we cooperated without a shade of difference.[16]

According to Birkenhead's most recent biographer, John Campbell, his acceptance of Dominion status for Southern Ireland marked the 'turning point' of his career.[17] It also opened him up to accusations of betrayal. In the House of Lords, just before parliament broke for the autumn recess, the Lord Chancellor energetically defended himself against charges of disloyalty to the old alliance between the Tories and Ulster's Protestants. Under attack from Salisbury, the influential diehard leader of the peers, Birkenhead vowed never to 'abandon' Ulster and insisted that he still held fast to the belief that a 'complete and unbridgeable gulf separated the North of Ireland from the South'. Repudiating the accusation that talks with Sinn Féin were a source of 'shame', he argued that the weight of public opinion, throughout the Empire and the country, rested with the government. But if all else failed, there would be a renewal of hostilities on a 'scale never heretofore ... undertaken by this country against Ireland'.[18]

Birkenhead's public rebuke to the diehards underlined the relative isolation of the British landed elite from the majority of the Conservative Party. Although their numbers were comparatively strong in the House of Lords, most pro-coalition Conservative MPs were businessmen. The diehards, on the other hand, were typically landowners or military men with family connections in Ireland. In this context, Birkenhead's repeated assurance that Britain would wage war with ruthless efficiency if the republicans failed to compromise was intended to calm Tory nerves at the prospect of Sinn Féiners traipsing in and out of 10 Downing Street. The Truce and the move towards peace had disabled the attacks on the coalition from the left but risked provoking a far deadlier onslaught from the right.

A similar problem confronted Michael Collins. The IRA was in no mood for compromise. The men at the heart of the movement felt the Truce had been a vindication of all their sacrifices and struggles over the previous two years. They grew increasingly confrontational with policemen and soldiers, as all around them the machinery of the British state appeared to be in inexorable retreat. Many assumed that not only were the people united behind the Volunteers (as the IRA was known up until 1920), but that the ultimate prize, the Republic, was imminent. Collins did little to disabuse IRB officers in the south of this impression when he met them in Cork days before his departure for London. However, there was a gentle warning that the revolutionary ideal they had been fighting for in the hillsides of Munster might not survive the rigours of a settlement; there might have to be, he suggested, some modification of the full republican demand.[19] But even this tentative admission of the need to compromise provoked anger from Liam Lynch, the influential IRA leader of Munster's 1st Southern Division.

By 6 October, Collins was back in Dublin, where the preparations for London were in full swing. Unwilling to share digs with the rest of the delegation, he arranged for separate lodgings that would house an inner circle of trusted comrades, some of whom were from the 'Squad', his band of young and devoted gunmen. Characteristically, Collins kept a tight lid on his plans and demanded oversight over every detail of his household. This tendency to monopolise information and ensure that all lines of communication ran through him had proved effective during the guerrilla war when he was running the IRA's intelligence operations. But Erskine Childers, who was in charge of the delegation's secretariat and logistical arrangements, found such behaviour suspicious and irritating. He also disliked Collins' quick temper, which flared up that day with inexplicable intensity. As Childers noted in his diary, there was an odd altercation over the domestic staff. It seemed Collins did not approve of one of the housekeepers, or he objected to her travelling ahead with the rest of the hired help. On 6 October, Childers wrote, 'Sent off Staff and Housekeeper Miss O'D. M.C. furious & countermanded her!' The following day's entry read: 'Ordered Housekeeper to go. M.C. explained but did not apologise.'[20] Whatever the source of this dispute, Miss O'Donoghue remained in her post and presided over the living arrangements at both houses.

These were, of course, turbulent times for Collins, both on the political and the personal front. Barely a week earlier, his close friend and fellow carouser, Harry Boland, had blurted out that he and the glamorous Kitty Kiernan, who was also the object of Collins' affections, were engaged to be married. While this was wishful thinking – the Tiggerish Boland had proposed but received no firm answer – Collins appeared anguished at the news. Immediately, Boland wrote to Kitty and confided to her that Collins 'was most upset'. Summarising the conversation, he revealed that 'I told him as well as I could that you and I are engaged, and further that if he (M.) had not entered into yr life that I w'd. now have you as my very own Wife ... He assured me that "it did not follow if you did not marry me that you would marry him."' Despite this devastating twist in the long-running tussle for Kitty's hand, Collins showed up early the next morning at Cobh harbour to see his friend off to New York. In another letter to Kitty, Boland marvelled at this display of loyalty. 'I know he has a warm spot in his heart for me and I feel sure in no matter what manner our Triangle may work out, he and I shall be always friends.'[21] Boland sailed to America on 2 October. On 8 October, a day before he left under the cover of darkness for London, Collins proposed to Kitty in the Grand Hotel, a rambling Victorian structure that overlooked the sea in Greystones, County Wicklow.

By this stage, the rest of the delegation were on their way to England. Early that morning crowds had thronged Dublin's Westland Row station as the delegates embarked on the first leg of a nine-hour train and sea journey to London's Euston station. A large press pack monitored their every move.

The *Irish Independent* noted that Robert Barton was the first to arrive at the station that morning, while George Gavan Duffy was the last, and among the friends and 'distinguished personages' who chatted to them, before the train 'steamed' away at 8.25 a.m., was the historian and veteran nationalist Alice Stopford Green.[22] Fine weather ensured the crossing from Dún Laoghaire to Holyhead was 'pleasant', although one reporter recorded that as they approached the British coast, 'conditions changed and a thick fog lay on the sea'. Eventually it lifted and 'the sun shone out in splendour', surely 'an omen', the writer ventured, for the conference ahead.[23] Later that night, however, a passenger steamer, SS *Rowan*, crossing the Irish Sea from Glasgow to Dublin suffered two catastrophic collisions in the fog and at least twenty people died.

The delegation travelled in style; on the boat, two staterooms and three deck cabins were reserved for their exclusive use, while at Holyhead they boarded a special saloon on the express train to London. It was a large party, with the four plenipotentiaries accompanied by three of the four secretaries to the delegation: John Chartres, an English barrister who worked for the British government during the First World War, investigating and reporting on subversive labour groups; Fionán Lynch, a close friend of Collins; and Childers. In addition, there were typists, personal secretaries, spouses – Duggan travelled with his wife – and the Dáil's debonair head of publicity, Desmond FitzGerald, another close ally of Collins. At times, the journey appeared more like a procession.[24] When they arrived in Chester, the whole cavalcade disembarked to meet representatives of the Irish Self-Determination League (ISDL), the main republican organisation in the country, whose branches served as recruiting grounds for the British IRA. Founded in 1919, its chief purpose was to publicise the Irish cause, although, even at its peak, its membership never crept above a disappointingly small 27,000.[25]

After another two stops and more meetings with ISDL members, the train finally pulled into a seething Euston station. Thousands crammed onto the platforms, and the London Irish pipers' band belted out 'The Soldier's Song'. People cheered and waved republican flags, and when the delegates stepped off the train, the press photographers surged forward, flash bulbs blazing. A reporter from *The Freeman's Journal* declared that 'such a scene of unbounded enthusiasm has never been witnessed at Euston or at any other railway station in England', while *The Manchester Guardian* noted that 'Women as much as men shouted their hardest, real hearty shouts ... with a note of joyous exuberance.' Through it all Griffith remained unmoved and was 'at all times', the Press Association observed, 'as emotionless as the sphinx'.[26]

By coincidence, the Royal train bearing the King and Queen back to the capital from an official visit to Manchester arrived at Euston station half an hour before the Irish delegation. While the Sinn Féin supporters 'good-naturedly' cheered the monarchy, one British paper pointed out that 'two sets of people ... got mixed up without knowing it'. There were the 'loyal, peace-loving Londoners who wished to greet the Royal Family ... and perfervid Irish who went to hail their heroes'.[27]

Yet the one man who all had come to see was nowhere to be found. As one reporter recorded, the cry that went up 'on all sides' was: 'Where is Collins?'[28] It was his face the international press were desperate to print; the 'man of mystery', the 'MOST "WANTED" MAN IN THE WORLD' even, as the *Dundee Evening Telegraph* described him back in March of that year.[29] His glamour, his reputation as a ruthless man of action, specious as it was, transformed an otherwise nondescript political delegation into a global sensation. But where was he? The delegates were bombarded by this question, until finally Barton quipped, 'It's a state secret.'[30]

After yet more greetings and formalities, the Irish escaped into a waiting motorcade and made their way to Knightsbridge. And it was here that all the joy, excitement and exuberance of the past few hours suddenly evaporated. At least it did for

Childers, who was appalled at the house Art O'Brien had selected for the delegation, regarding it as 'grand' but entirely inappropriate. Number 22 Hans Place is a tall, narrow, late-Victorian red-brick townhouse discreetly tucked away behind Harrods department store. Childers thought it 'hopeless' for its 'purpose' and wrote in his diary that he had a 'scene with Art' soon after they arrived. Meanwhile, crowds flocked to nearby 15 Cadogan Gardens, the address that most newspapers gave as the delegates' residence. It was, in fact, the property reserved for Collins and his entourage, and while the police were called in to direct traffic outside this rather gloomy-looking Chelsea townhouse, the delegation sat down to their first dinner at the far more upmarket Hans Place.[31]

The next day, as southern England sweltered in an unseasonable heatwave, Griffith and the other delegates took off to the Thames Valley, where they stopped at Reading Gaol, the infamous institution immortalised by Oscar Wilde. Griffith, it seems, could not resist another glimpse at the colossal Victorian penitentiary where he had spent six months locked up without trial in the aftermath of the 1916 Rising. Terence MacSwiney, Ernest Blythe and Darrell Figgis numbered among his fellow inmates, but of the twenty-eight nationalist writers and intellectuals held at Reading, the short, stocky, bespectacled founder of Sinn Féin was, at the time, by far the most prominent.[32] And yet Griffith, a prolific printer, writer and journalist, had played no part in the insurgency. For reasons that remain obscure, the man whose teachings and ideas had done so much to inspire the revolutionary generation found himself on the sidelines when Dublin erupted into armed rebellion.[33]

In the lead-up to the Rising, Griffith, unperturbed by the nationalists' increased militarisation, had continued to advocate a dual monarchy as a viable step on the path to freedom. In a theory first elaborated in a series of newspaper articles in 1904, and then republished in 1905 as *The Resurrection of Hungary*, he argued that Ireland would recover the prosperity and population declines suffered under the hated Union if the only bond to Britain was a shared monarchy, similar to Hungary and Austria, which recognised each other as two equal, independent nations. In his view, only then would Ireland amass sufficient strength to finally sever all ties with her neighbour. Unsurprisingly, these theories jarred with active young zealots championing more drastic measures, and Griffith cut a poor figure among his old separatist colleagues.[34] Even Sinn Féin, the political organisation he continued to dominate, fell from view, eclipsed by the rapid ascent of the Volunteer movement. But the Easter Rising abruptly reversed Griffith's fortunes and propelled him back to the centre of the nationalist stage. The events of 24–29 April were instantly labelled a 'Sinn Féin Rebellion', transforming the once moribund party into a mass movement. And it was this concentration of various nationalist elements into one body that gave Sinn Féin, or 'Ourselves Alone' as it translates into English, the party's devastatingly effective, but short-lived power.[35]

Thrust onto an entirely different trajectory by the repressive aftermath of the Rising – a staggering 3,400 people were interned, in addition to the execution of the principal insurgents – Griffith made no attempt to retain his previous position in the organisation. In October 1917, he cleared the way for a new Sinn Féin president, the previously unknown revolutionary Éamon de Valera. And yet, despite Griffith's unimpressive record of 'militancy', he remained at the party's core, skilfully tiptoeing around the hardliners who turned the organisation inside out. He was there to oversee its hour of triumph: the 1918 elections. And it was his long-conceived battle-plan of local opposition, effectively a mass withdrawal from the entire British edifice in Ireland – the courts, the police, local authorities – that underpinned the movement's post-electoral strategy. The 'indignant little chap', as James Joyce once characterised him, had proved an unexpectedly agile survivor.[36] Perhaps Griffith reflected on these strange twists of fate when, five years later, gazing up at Reading Gaol's red-brick battlements and towers, he 'expressed pity', as one member of that day's excursion recalled, 'for the unfortunates confined there'.[37]

But there was more to this Sunday outing than just a trip down memory lane, or a 'sentimental journey' as Griffith's famous biographer, the playwright and poet Padraic Colum, described it.[38] By the time the delegates motored out to Reading, public outrage in Ireland at the plight of thousands of political prisoners still incarcerated without trial was reaching fresh peaks of intensity. Three months after the Truce, internment camps in Ireland were overflowing, and while the cessation of hostilities resulted in the release of a small number of inmates, including all those elected to Dáil Éireann, the vast majority remained in indefinite detention. In September, a memoir published by one former internee from the Ballykinlar camp, County Down, afforded a glimpse into the misery and camaraderie of life in captivity. There, as in Frongoch, the celebrated internment camp in north Wales that helped produce a revitalised Volunteer movement after the 1916 Rising, committed republicans seized the opportunity to instruct and inspire their fellow inmates. Yet intermixed with tales of defiance and grandiose schemes to escape – a failed attempt to tunnel out led to the British constructing a spiked trench across the camp – were details of the 'terrible mental suffering' many experienced, and the physical depredations endured by the elderly; prisoners ranged in age from seventeen to seventy and, according to one official, at least one-fifth had no involvement with Sinn Féin or the IRA.[39] Newspapers highlighted the economic and emotional devastation of the families left behind, with publicised accusations of arbitrary arrest, abuse and maltreatment from former internees adding to what the Irish saw as yet more British brutality. Two men at Ballykinlar were shot dead for straying too near the miles of barbed-wire fencing that surrounded the camp, while stories abounded of the incarceration of invalids and the mentally ill.

At the time of the Truce, almost 400 women also remained behind bars, though female political prisoners were kept clear of the internment camps.[40] In this context, the delegates' visit to Reading Gaol was no whimsical reminder of Griffith's stint in captivity, it was an affirmation of what was at stake in the forthcoming negotiations.

Expectations were riding high of a swift resolution to the problem of those still in prison. When the Irish delegation left Dublin for London, it was thought the release of all untried prisoners would soon follow. In that Sunday's edition of *The Observer*, Stephen Gwynn, a journalist and former Irish Party MP (1906–18), argued that 'very convincing reasons of State need to prevail when in time of peace persons are detained without charge or trial'.[41] From the British perspective, however, mass releases risked strengthening the ranks of the IRA and they categorically rejected the idea. When the British delegation held its first meeting on Monday 10 October, the unanimous decision was to downplay the issue. As Tom Jones recorded, the general 'view was in favour of ... creating a friendly atmosphere and avoiding an early reference to the truce and internees.' He then added, 'What was to be feared was some unexpected explosion which would plunge the conference into the wrong atmosphere.'[42]

Of all the hair-trigger sensitivities accumulated on both sides, it was the persistent breaches of the Truce that threatened to upend the talks first. Furious at what they saw as 'flagrant' violations of the armistice, the British resolved to pressure the Irish delegation into a revised agreement. They wanted to eliminate the ambiguity of the Truce's terms and decided that unless the IRA stopped the 'ostentatious' drilling, training, parade and arms-bearing, along with the 'commandeering of houses and property' and the 'importation of weapons', they would be 'compelled to take steps ... calculated to prejudice the results of the conference'.[43]

The next step was to familiarise themselves with their negotiating opponents, the Sinn Féiners, whom the British once dismissed as nothing more than a 'murderous rabble'. Thumbnail sketches of each of the Irish delegates, possibly prepared by Cope, were circulated for background reading. Aside from Gavan Duffy, who was considered 'vain and self-sufficient', the British were told the rest were likely to be 'nervous and ill at ease'. They had 'never been in conference with men of experience before', and there was a high likelihood they would be 'rude and extravagant in speech'. Although Griffith was an exponent of the 'dual monarchy idea', he tended to approach the current crisis from a 'historic' perspective, 'even more so than de Valera'. In this case, he would probably 'start somewhere about AD 1100 and argue up to the sovereign independent right of every nation'. They should expect him to be 'silent' for the most part – he 'was not a good speaker' – and remember that while not as 'attractive as de Valera', he was 'the real power in Sinn Fein'. Barton, a 'Protestant', privately educated and 'a substantial farmer', possessed 'no outstanding qualities', while Duggan was 'completely under the influence' of Collins. As for Collins himself, he was 'a Cork man' and 'therefore impetuous and rather excitable'. Evidently the 'strongest personality of the party', he was a 'quick thinker' and 'full of physical energy'. But the precise scope of his power in the republican movement remained obscure. He 'claims influence', the writer noted, 'which at this juncture would be exercised on the side of moderation'.[44]

By this point, Collins had slipped into London unnoticed, a feat that sent a thrill through the British press. It was an inspired act of theatre, one that exploited his celebrity status to the full and guaranteed that when the conference opened the following morning, there would be blanket coverage of 'the Sinn Fein Mystery Man'. The *Daily Express* was first on the scene, crowing that its photographer had 'captured' him on his way to dinner at 22 Hans Place. Lathering it on thick, the paper described him 'as elusive as in the days when a price was set on his head and thousands of detectives and policemen searched for him in vain'.[45] Never mind that in March, the same paper had published a picture of Collins, complete with a relatively accurate profile piece, headlined 'The Bad Man of Ireland'.[46] Treated as a celebrated outlaw turned revolutionary hero, roles for which his looks were ideally suited, his fame had become self-perpetuating. He was a media phenomenon. Throughout much of the guerrilla war, the British public were kept on tenterhooks by sensationalised stories of his murderous exploits and endless hair's-breadth escapes. Whether he was cycling insouciantly away from onrushing troops 'with an umbrella under his arm', shimmying out of a window in a night shirt, or donning 'feminine attire' during a police raid, it all read like something out of an adventure novel. He was the Irish Scarlet Pimpernel, a 'master of disguise', operating independently of law or convention.[47] To a press and public often confused by the ferocity of the Irish conflict, the Collins legend both simplified and sanitised the narrative; and to many in Labour and Liberal circles, his image appealed precisely because it threw into unflattering relief the chaotic brutality of the Crown forces' behaviour as they inflicted reprisals of their own devising.

But there were always two sides to the legend. Collins was both the symbol of Ireland's patriotic fortitude and a murdering mastermind, whose flair for outwitting the authorities and evading capture seemed to border on the superhuman. It was a reputation that thrived in the half-light, and there was no certainty his mythic status would survive under the full glare of publicity. So, when the *Daily Express* reporter asked him how he managed to arrive in London incognito, Collins played up to the role of the dangerous rebel. 'I always watch the other fellow instead of letting him watch me,' he replied. 'I make a point of keeping the other fellow on the run, instead of being on the run myself. That is the secret of success that I have learned during the past year or two.'[48]

Youth added to his appeal, whether he was being denounced as a criminal or lionised as a national icon. Born on 16 October 1890, Collins was still just thirty when he leapt out of a car full of armed men and bounded through the open door of 10 Downing Street. As he crossed the threshold, barely a stride behind Griffith – trilby hat slightly askew – the crowds massed behind police barricades erupted into cheers. Inside, Lloyd George stood waiting for them, one hand outstretched in greeting. But for the rest of the British team, such formalities were a bridge too far; they could not bring themselves to shake hands with the Irish republicans and left that duty to the Prime Minister. In Tom Jones' account, the two delegations 'stood opposite' each other while Lloyd George 'named our people'.[49] Shortly afterwards, at just before 11.10 a.m. on that Tuesday,

11 October 1921, the 'P.M. began ... proceedings', initiating the greatest historic shift in Anglo-Irish relations since 1801, when the Act of Union transformed the separate nation of Ireland into a province within the United Kingdom.

Seated at the colossal, rectangular Cabinet table, a relic of the Gladstone era, the two negotiating teams listened first to a ten-minute address from Lloyd George, long fêted as one of the greatest orators of his age. But there were to be no fireworks just yet. Instead, as Jones noted in his diary, the Prime Minister spoke 'very slowly and rather gravely' of the opportunity 'for putting an end to the tragic story of misunderstanding and war between the two countries'. Previous efforts, he thought, had been doomed by the fatal misfortune of bad timing. 'When England was in the mood for peace Ireland was not, and when Ireland had been in the mood for peace, England was not.' Then he injected the usual hint of menace. 'He did not wish to hurry the proceedings in any way, but he could not conceal the fact that there were forces at work in this country which thought the Government had gone too far already and certain details were being fastened upon which if pressed would make peace increasingly difficult.'[50]

Griffith then took the floor, and it struck the British as if a lion had given way to a mouse. Tom Jones recorded that his voice was so soft, it was barely 'audible' and, unlike the Prime Minister, he spoke 'only for a very few minutes, five at the outside, and when he stopped the P.M. was taken rather by surprise'. But contrary to expectations, he steered clear of AD 1100, and seized upon 'the days of Pitt' as his embarkation point. For ever since that precociously young prime minister had yoked Ireland into an unwanted union with Britain, 'it has been the policy of this country to keep [the Irish] in a subordinate position'. He conceded that it is 'possible that there is a new England: a new attitude in the people over here towards Ireland', before wrapping up with the suggestion that, as to procedure, 'we are in your house and will follow your suggestions'.[51]

It seems that no one had much interest in maintaining a detailed chronicle of events. Documents in Britain's National Archives state that both sets of secretariats agreed that the 'records of the discussions' should be 'purposely made very short'.[52] They were united on the need to avoid any 'surprising' of the press.[53] After the difficulties of the summer, when de Valera and Lloyd George communicated in a blaze of publicity, the Prime Minister was determined to keep a tight lid on the negotiations.

But there could be no hiding the Irish delegation's woefully inadequate preparations. Right from the outset, the British dictated the flow of the talks, an advantage they secured not only as a result of their greater negotiating experience, but because the Irish arrived without any comprehensive plan of action. De Valera had packed them off with a set of proposals – known as draft Treaty A – which ran to a meagre six articles and which he had derived from a memorandum written in the wake of his own talks with Lloyd George. A second document, draft Treaty B, was essentially a face-saving exercise, a 'propaganda document' as Barton referred to it, to be relied upon in the event the conference collapsed.[54] Incredibly, no position on Ulster, the issue the Dáil Cabinet regarded as its strongest source of leverage, was formulated until almost a week into the discussions, leaving the Irish on the back foot from the very start, forced to parry a succession of demands from the British.

With the opening speeches out of the way, Lloyd George leapt straight to the proposals first put to the Irish on 20 July. As Jones handed out copies of the letter sent to de Valera, the Prime Minister casually raised the subject of the Truce. There were question marks over its 'observation', and these should be dealt with in a sub-committee, he suggested. Immediately, Collins chimed in, claiming he too had concerns about this issue, and so, without further discussion, the Truce was ring-fenced from the plenary sessions, and with this small but fateful decision, the scales tilted further towards the British.

None of this would be apparent for some time. To the Irish, that first meeting seemed to go entirely to plan. Like their counterparts, the Sinn Féin delegates wanted to appear amenable, and so Griffith avoided attacking the substance of the 20 July proposals. When invited to comment on them, he confined his objections to that document's six attached conditions, which, he argued, undercut Britain's offer of Dominion status. They would strip Ireland of her vital freedoms, he contended, particularly as Britain demanded exclusive access to Irish waters. Effectively, it meant continued British 'domination'. An aggrieved Lloyd George replied: 'This is a most amazing statement ... We wish no military domination over Ireland any more than we wish it over Canada', before pointing out that 'the coast of Ireland is essential to us'. It was imperative, he explained, that Britain secured itself against invasion by air or sea, and they must be able to achieve this 'without parley or negotiation'. Everyone in the Cabinet room would have been familiar with this depiction of Ireland as Britain's back door. English concerns about its vulnerable western flank had dominated Anglo-Irish relations for centuries – the Act of Union was essentially a defensive move – and it was inconceivable to the British negotiators that they should relinquish these strategic outposts.

Anticipating this line of attack, Griffith dangled an olive branch: a resolution would be possible on these matters, he said, 'if we reach an agreement on the general question'.

Attention then shifted to the thorny issue of free trade. In their 20 July proposals, the British had stressed the need to avoid 'ruinous trade wars' between the two islands, and Lloyd George now repeated this line, dwelling on the importance of Britain and Ireland's entrenched economic ties. Trade barriers, he warned, would lead to 'exasperation' and 'retaliation', and would damage 'peaceful relations'. In a debate shot through with contemporary resonances, Griffith countered that they 'had no objection to the Free Trade in English goods, [but they] must protect themselves against foreign goods sold by English merchants'. Churchill, who had stood consistently for free trade since 1903, was flabbergasted by this attitude. 'We are offering you the most terrific guarantee that Ireland can have. The market secure to you quite independently of all the fluctuations of our political parties.' With an air of strained tolerance, Lloyd George reiterated that 'tariff wars' would 'only antagonise [both countries'] populations', and when Collins reminded him that de Valera had given the British an assurance on this front during the summer, the Prime Minister snapped back: 'I don't want a general assurance; I want it in the Treaty.'[55]

After about an hour and a half of this back and forth, both sides took a break. At four in the afternoon, the delegates resumed their seats at the Cabinet table, although once again Chamberlain was absent, laid low by one of his sporadic attacks of lumbago. He had missed the morning session for the same reason. The gap in the ranks left Collins facing the imposing figure of Birkenhead, while next to him were Griffith and Duggan on one side and Barton and Gavan Duffy on the other. Lloyd George took up his usual position at the centre. To his right were the Lord Chancellor, Churchill and Hewart, with Worthington-Evans and Greenwood to his left. The secretaries were spaced slightly behind the delegates – Tom Jones, as ever, at the Prime Minister's elbow.[56]

By now, according to Pakenham, 'some of the tension was gone from the atmosphere'.[57] But if anything, the second round offered a sharper reminder of the challenges ahead, as the delegates turned to Ireland's demand for neutral status, a question destined to bedevil Anglo-Irish relations for decades. Griffith advanced the case first, arguing that Irish neutrality would benefit Britain because it would eliminate the fear of a hostile state on her doorstep. Unimpressed, Lloyd George reminded him that 'Britain's offer was that Ireland should be in the same position as the Dominions'. Sending troops would remain 'a voluntary act', but there could be no question of neutrality. To illustrate the point, he explained that while Canada could withhold 'her resources', that was as far as she could go constitutionally, 'for to allow her to be neutral would be to repudiate the King's sovereignty'. Neutrality, in other words, put Ireland outside the Empire. The discussion began to veer into dangerous territory. Dominion status appeared to imply that Ireland's right to self-government was nothing more than an imperial concession. At this point, Gavan Duffy interjected. 'Ireland's neutrality could be guaranteed by the League of Nations,' he suggested, 'and by the United States and Germany.' Lloyd George changed tack. Were the Irish, he asked, 'coming into the community of Free Nations with the same rights as Canada, Australia and the other Dominions?' Griffith replied: 'We cannot enter freely if it is not a free choice.'[58]

Towards the end of the session, Collins finally brought up the question of the 'prisoners and the camps'. He wanted a 'joint visiting committee' with both British and Irish officials allowed access to the internees. Lloyd George thought this was jumping the gun: 'We are most anxious to do our best in the matter of treatment,' he replied but the 'truce is not a treaty'. And then he cut off any further discussion by suggesting it was a matter for the Truce sub-committee.[59] The Irish agreed, and with that, the opening day of the conference was brought to an abrupt close.

Later that evening, Griffith rounded on Barton and Gavan Duffy for 'being too emphatic and creating the wrong atmosphere' in their exchanges with the British on trade and neutrality.[60] Overall, though, he was pleased, and felt there were grounds for optimism. As soon as he returned to Hans Place, he dashed off a report to de Valera. The British are 'anxious for peace', he wrote, in an upbeat but cautious assessment. Admittedly, no headway had been made against their demands for naval bases, and the 'question of the Crown and Ulster' had yet to be broached. Nevertheless, the discussion was 'amiable and both sides were polite to each other'. Lloyd George was a 'remarkably suave and astute man', but Griffith, brimming with misplaced confidence after that first encounter, thought the Irish had proved a match for him. '[O]n the whole,' he concluded, 'we have scored today.'[61]

4 · WAR OR PEACE?

12 October–21 October

Churchill described the first meeting with the Irish delegates as 'not without its shock'.[1] Enforced intimacy with the enemy had evoked something akin to horror in Collins too. Writing to de Valera the following morning, he claimed he had 'never felt so relieved at the end of any day, and I need hardly say I am not looking forward with any pleasure to resumptions – such a crowd I never met'. He signed off with the declaration that 'this place [is the] bloody limit. I wish to God I were home.'[2]

It was not a promising start. Biographers have laid the blame for this outburst on the 'strained and formal atmosphere of the talks' and the British delegates' 'diplomatic and political etiquette', which jarred with Collins' 'blunt', 'pragmatic' and, according to one account, 'shy and rather self-conscious' personality.[3] Those intent on de-mythologising Collins argue that he was simply out of his depth.[4] In his letters home to Kitty at this time, he complains of wakeful nights and of feeling in 'a queer mood', even of being a 'bit unstrung'; all recognisable symptoms, these days, of intense psychological stress.[5]

Half a year later, when the Treaty had changed everything

and civil war loomed, Collins glossed over these initial pangs of frustration and hostility, telling his first biographer, Hayden Talbot, that from 'beginning to end the English plenipotentiaries dealt candidly, fairly [and] sympathetically' with the Irish. The real 'menace', he fumed, was Erskine Childers, a former British civil servant and de Valera's trusted constitutional expert. 'I considered him ... altogether too radical and impractical and, at worst, an enemy of Ireland', Collins stated, with undisguised venom.[6] Yet there is no evidence that animosities on this scale predated the Treaty talks, even allowing for tensions that flared up over the summer; Robert Barton later insisted that up until these fault lines emerged, all relations within the delegation 'were quite formal, if not cordial'.[7]

It was the British who reviled Childers from the start, seeing in him not only a traitor but an implacable obstacle to any compromise. At the eleventh hour, they drafted in his old schoolfellow Lionel Curtis as co-secretary to the delegation, and ensured that the two sat opposite each other in the Cabinet room on that first day. This was an experience Childers apparently found uncomfortable, although his diary entries, copiously long in previous years but now reduced to a series of short, staccato-like observations, make no mention of his reaction.[8] Ostensibly, Curtis' task was to advise the British on 'historical and similar matters';[9] in reality, he was there to bring precision to the offer of Dominion status to Southern Ireland, and ensure that it did not, as Smuts maintained, equate to independence. His presence on the secretariat filled some unionists with glee: it stoked their expectations of an early collapse in the talks. Pitting a crusading imperialist against a doctrinaire republican, it was thought, could only end in deadlock and failure. In a letter to the Prime Minister's secretary, one staunch unionist predicted that 'the collision of the Prophet', as Curtis was known, and 'the ghazi', the label he whimsically applied to Childers, would 'finally disrupt the proceedings'. And he scoffed, 'I offered a prize the other night at dinner to that person who should render best the glances which the two yogis are interchanging across your council table ... For obvious reasons I did not invite a competition in dialectic or we might have got to bed the next morning.'[10]

Ironically, for much of their early lives Curtis and Childers appeared as if cast in the same mould. The two attended Haileybury College together, an English public school of the 'imperialist hue' and a former recruiting ground for the East India Company.[11] After degrees at Oxbridge – Curtis, the younger by two years, went to Oxford, and Childers Cambridge – the patriotic fervour unleashed by the South African war swept them both into the socially elite City Imperial Volunteers, an amateur corps drummed up by London's Lord Mayor, as a 'much-publicised gift to the nation'.[12] Childers, a short, lean man in his youth, whose limp rarely thwarted his love of sailing or his lust for adventure, was still an ardent Tory then, and regarded Lloyd George's open sympathy for the Boers as 'perverse and treacherous'.[13] Although he paid little heed at the time, the hard-fought effort by Britain and her imperial armies to obliterate the republics of the Transvaal reinvigorated Irish nationalism and left a lasting impact on the movement. Weeks before the Treaty talks opened in London, Collins wrote an adulatory letter to the old Boer General, Christiaan de Wet, telling him that his 'great fight against the same foe was the earliest inspiration of the men who have been fighting here for the past two years against foreign aggression'.[14] Childers, too, had admired the Boers' military skill, but for a long time he maintained that the conflict was just and necessary.[15]

By 1906, the year Collins left the family farm in west Cork to embark on a four-year stint as a lowly clerk at the Post

Office Savings Bank in West Kensington – then a prized route of advancement for many of Ireland's youth, since Dublin Castle remained a Protestant, Anglo-Irish bastion[16] – Childers seemed destined for a life at the heart of Britain's political and social elite. He had become a celebrated author whose connections, particularly his friendship with Edward Marsh, Churchill's long-serving private secretary, could open doors to the halls of power. More importantly, Childers was now married to Mary Alden 'Molly' Osgood, a strong-willed, intelligent, affluent Bostonian, whose captivating personality and 'luminous brown eyes' never failed to enrapture her admirers. As a wedding present, her father, a distinguished physician and friend of Sigmund Freud, gifted the happy couple a sturdy gaff-rigged ketch called *Asgard*.[17]

Childers had lost his father at the age of six and, after his mother was removed to a sanatorium, he and his siblings were shipped off to relatives in County Wicklow (the Bartons of Glendalough), for an upbringing that, in his own words, was 'steeped in the most irreconcilable sort of Unionism'.[18] His mother's relations occupied the minor gentry rung of the Anglo-Irish ascendancy, so, despite the immediate success of his 1903 spy thriller, *The Riddle of the Sands*, which tells the story of a German plot to invade Britain, there could be no question of giving up the day job. Employed as a parliamentary official, a role that confined him to the back rooms of Westminster, Childers continued to write prodigiously, although he never returned to fiction. Instead, he churned out analytical military histories, and it was as he entered the final throes of volume five of *The Times History of the War in South Africa*, published in 1907, that his transition away from Toryism manifested itself in a withering attack on Alfred Milner, former High Commissioner for South Africa and Lieutenant Governor of Cape Colony. Childers had always sympathised with the Boers' determination to preserve their 'white prestige', maintaining that 'unlike coloured barbarians ... they were accustomed to free institutions'. In his view, the Boer and the Briton, 'two white races' as he put it, were 'destined to live side by side in the midst of a vast coloured population'.[19] The reflexive racism of this logic, the link between whiteness and the right to self-government and the advocacy of a 'fusion' of Boer and Briton all overlapped with Smuts' views. But now Childers began to agonise over the Afrikaners' humiliation and what he saw as their lost sense of national identity.[20]

It would be another year or two before he underwent something of a spiritual conversion and embraced the cause of Irish nationalism. The tangled loyalties of his childhood were not so easily displaced. At first Childers endorsed Home Rule as the 'salvation of Ireland'. But almost a decade later, not long after George V pinned a medal on him for his service in naval intelligence in the First World War, he turned his back on the political principles inculcated in him from his youth and flung himself into the pursuit of an Irish republic.[21] From that point on, the fight for Ireland's independence became the single theme that shaped his fate, leading him ineluctably on, until one cold, bright morning in November 1922, at Beggar's Bush military barracks in Dublin, he was cut down by an Irish firing squad, condemned on the trumped-up charge of illegally possessing a firearm. Childers became, as Frank O'Connor recalled, the one man whom Ireland's post-Treaty Provisional Government 'was bent on killing'.[22] Loathed for his perceived influence over de Valera, he was derided until the end as that 'damned Englishman'.

Curtis, by contrast, never lost his faith in British imperialism: for him, it grew into an all-consuming passion. He spent his entire life devoted to a concept that was 'already out of date by the end of the First World War': imperial federation.[23] To him, the ideal state was an imperial one; he saw it as the best means to secure mankind's peace and prosperity, and believed that if the British Empire's ramshackle possessions were reorganised into a single political framework, a kind of 'Britannic' superstructure, nationalism and ethnic conflict would subside. And ultimately this global Britain would provide a model for world-government. Dismissed as an 'imperial crank' by the time of his death in the mid-1950s, he clung to the vision of an 'organic Commonwealth', enlightened by Anglo-Saxon leadership and united by the common bond of imperial citizenship. While Britain and the white Dominions were to be equal participants in this federal structure, Curtis assumed that non-white communities would attain the same status once they had undergone a period of British political tutelage of unspecified duration.[24]

Curtis, who was raised in an evangelical Anglican environment, emerged from under the coat-tails of Milner, the great proconsul in South Africa whom Childers loathed, but who, as the historian Paul Addison wrote, had 'the flair of the dangerous don for gathering around him a group of young men and converting them into disciples'.[25] His circle of acolytes, mostly young male graduates from Oxford, had been drafted in to rebuild South Africa along British lines after the Second Boer War and were known forever after as the 'Kindergarten'. Each Milner devotee believed implicitly in their idol's vision of a reformed, centralised Empire, an imperial union, and it was this cause that Curtis would remain faithful to for the rest of his life. An obsessive attention to detail distinguished him from the outset. Set to work on the constitutional rewiring necessitated by the union of South Africa, he ensured that pre-existing discriminatory legislation, which opened the road to apartheid, was enforced with water-tight legality.[26] Years later, the nucleus of the 'Kindergarten' reassembled into an imperial pressure group called the 'Round Table', and over the years, its members began to populate Britain's business and political elite. Some ended up in Lloyd George's famously expansive secretariat, and it was through this extensive Milnerite network that Curtis found himself playing a starring role in the drafting and implementation of the Anglo-Irish Treaty.

On that first day of the conference, and doubtless with a degree of irony, the Prime Minister suggested that Curtis and Childers collaborate together and produce a paper mapping out 'how Dominion status actually works'. Griffith objected, driven partly perhaps by his animus against Childers. He had always been uncomfortable that an 'Englishman' stood as a central spokesman for Irish freedom. On the other hand, as Pakenham pointed out, it made little sense for them 'to commit themselves at this stage to an estimate of their opponents' scheme' and so 'the piquant idea was dropped ... and a museum piece was lost to posterity'.[27]

For the next week or so, Curtis grappled with how to present Dominion status in a light sufficiently alluring to the Irish, but without weakening or undermining in any way the constitutional powers of the Crown. He thought it essential that Ireland's sovereignty should be derived from this authority only – as opposed to the Irish legislature or the Dáil. To yield on this vital constitutional procedure would, he feared, endanger the Commonwealth's very existence. In a memo to the British delegates, he stressed that a slippage here would result in disastrous consequences; it would precipitate another 'desperate struggle between these two islands' and would inspire India's nationalists to agitate for exactly the same deal. They, too, would claim 'an exclusive right to legislate for India, and to formulate an Indian constitution'.[28]

Curtis had spent the last years of the Great War lobbying for constitutional reforms in that country in an effort to conciliate the moderates and marginalise the extremists. But, characteristically, he misjudged the 'sophistication and deep roots of Indian nationalism'. Rather than alter or re-evaluate his views, he simply moved 'his campaign', as one historian observed, 'to a different imperial front – Ireland'.[29]

In Dublin, meanwhile, de Valera was casting a jaundiced eye over Griffith's jaunty appraisal of the situation so far. Owing to the Irish delegates' justifiable fear of British surveillance, they had resolved to avoid, as far as possible, the use of telephone calls, telegrams or the postal service for sensitive material, and to rely instead on couriers shuttling between the two capitals. As a result, de Valera received his first report from London some time on the morning of 12 October. It was this concern about British eavesdropping that prompted Art O'Brien to install a private phone line linking 22 Hans Place with 15 Cadogan Gardens, although historians have long speculated about the success of these defensive measures. As Robert Barton later explained, the delegation's cooks, waiters and domestic staff were brought over from Ireland 'as a safeguard against espionage'.[30] All this, of course, meant consultations with Dublin were limited and time-delayed; disputes within the delegation would have to fester or be resolved without adjudication from colleagues at home. So, by the time Griffith digested de Valera's disgruntled reply, his attention had already turned to the preparations for day three and the conference's third plenary session, to be held at noon that day, Thursday 13 October. (The second day was given over to the Truce sub-committee.) Under instructions from the President not to continue traipsing over ground already covered with Lloyd George that summer, Griffith was to 'pick [the Prime Minister] up soon on his "further than this we can't go stunt". De Valera, irritated by what he saw as the Prime Minister's intransigence, insisted, "Two can play at that."[31]

Griffith's high spirits were not shared either by the British, who were despondent, increasingly suspicious of the motivations of their opponents and frustrated at the conference's slow start. After recovering from his lumbago attack, Chamberlain informed his sister Hilda that after two meetings there had been 'no progress forwards or backwards ... Opposition to the Conference & to our action is growing among our own people,' he wrote fretfully.[32] The newspapers were full of reports of IRA breaches of the Truce and the headlines centred on the activities of the revolutionary Dáil courts. The republican movement had rolled out its alternative – unauthorised – legal system in summer 1919, as part of a wider strategy to undermine and supplant the authority of the British administration. It proved an instant propaganda triumph. But the revolutionary justice system was not an unmitigated success. During the guerrilla war, many separatists took the law into their own hands, seizing the opportunity to settle old scores with rivals or neighbours, or simply to better themselves, which could mean escaping a long-standing debt. And despite agrarian unrest and mounting rural poverty, problems that stemmed from a combination of factors – including emigration curbs, rising land and agricultural prices, and the weakened coercive powers of the RIC – the Dáil courts continued to protect the status quo and uphold existing laws relating to private property ownership. As a result, some separatists had tired of what they saw as the social conservatism of Sinn Féin and the Dáil. For the revolutionary leadership, sovereignty trumped all other priorities. But with lawlessness on the rise after the Truce, the counter-state government's efforts to quell unrest, even with the public's widespread acceptance of this alternative justice system, often provoked dissent, leaving the Dáil courts unable to restore order or dispense justice.[33]

Towards the end of the guerrilla war, repressive British measures had brought these shadowy civil structures to a standstill, and so, over the summer, the Dáil Cabinet encouraged the revival of the republican courts. There were fears, too, that the gains of the past few years would be lost unless Sinn Féin consolidated its control over local government and administration. But Austin Stack, the bumbling, dogmatic Home Affairs Minister, made it his mission, during this delicate time, to expand the republican justice system. The scant terms of the Truce made no reference to the Dáil courts, although the RIC regarded their revival as a provocation and a breach of the peace, and on occasion the constabulary broke up sittings. In response, Stack exhorted justices to take a strong stand on the matter, stipulating that courts should adjourn only if forced to by 'enemy interference', adding that their work should continue as unostentatiously as possible.[34] In the meantime, the Dáil's publicity department fell to admonishing unruly citizens. In August 1921, the *Irish Bulletin* expressed revulsion at the 'lawless invasion of private rights ... gross intimidation, cattle-driving, fence-levelling and an "ugly rush" for land'.[35]

To the British, however, the courts – which attracted much outraged coverage in the British press – were like a red rag to a bull; they inflamed sentiment among Tory hardliners and appeared to justify fears that Sinn Féin was using the Truce to consolidate its position. One police report noted that control of the country was swiftly 'slipping into the hands of those who were the hunted a couple of months ago'.[36] At a strategy meeting of the British delegates, convened an hour before the conference's third session, Lloyd George attempted to calm the jangled nerves of his Conservative colleagues. Brandishing a copy of the previous evening's *Star*, which referred to the opening of a republican court in Dublin with the words 'I now declare this Court open in the name of the Irish Republic', the Prime Minister raged that this was 'not the status quo'. It would have been unthinkable, he argued, if after the 1902 Treaty of Vereeniging, which ended the South African war, the Boers had set up courts in the 'area [of] our military occupation ... I shall have to tell them that we shall have to scatter these courts'. Birkenhead shot back, 'I am glad to hear you say so. Otherwise it would have been impossible to carry on.'[37]

This was typical Lloyd Georgian bluster, designed to smooth relations within his own delegation and force the Irish on the defensive by implying a grave offence. It was not so much the courts themselves but the publicity surrounding them that rattled the government, and, after an avalanche of intelligence reports about increased IRA activities throughout the country, which did little to lessen the justifiable suspicion that the Irish were preparing for renewed conflict, Lloyd George resolved to wield the stick. The press coverage provided him with easy leverage.

It was not just the tabloids that were up in arms about the courts. *The Times*, once a trenchant critic of Britain's policy of reprisals, described the proceedings in Dublin that week as 'utterly and defiantly illegal'.[38] Fired up, the Prime Minister stormed into the third conference meeting discharging a volley of accusations about serious breaches of the Truce. He pointed to press photographs of armed men drilling, and warned that a 'repetition of incidents which had recently taken place would make it very difficult for the British to continue the Conference'. Griffith counter-attacked. British forces had recently occupied the County Council buildings in Sligo. This was no 'maintenance of the status quo', he argued but 'the occupation of a strategic point'. Suddenly, the Prime Minister, having orchestrated the row, appeared to back down. The matter should be referred to that afternoon's meeting of the Truce sub-committee, he suggested, before steering the conversation onto trade.[39]

As with the opening sessions on 11 October, this was a debate overshadowed by the Belfast Boycott, an economic blockade against the North's unionist strongholds. Officially implemented by the Dáil government in January 1921, the boycott was a local initiative that arose in the west of Ireland in the summer of 1920, before spreading to Dublin, and was intended as a retaliatory measure to the expulsion of Catholic workers from Belfast's shipyards. The republican leadership mistakenly assumed the campaign would awaken loyalists to the perils of partition, by reminding them of the South's economic strength. Instead – as some in the Dáil had feared, including Griffith and Collins – it achieved precisely the opposite effect, inflaming sectarian tensions and entrenching political and economic divisions. In other words, it accelerated the process of partition, and the ill-feeling it created among the North's Protestant communities partly explained Lloyd George's firm stance on the debate over the two nations' future trade relations.[40]

He now repeated his demand that tariff-free access between Ireland and the UK should be preserved and inked into the Treaty. Barton led the attack on this position. 'The fact that nine-tenths of our exports go to you is due to an artificial situation,' he asserted. Favoured 'nation status' was a better policy, he argued, before tactlessly pledging not to penalise Britain 'as regards other nations'. In a swift reminder of where the economic power lay, Lloyd George snapped back, 'No, we need not wait for a tariff to be put on against us by you. We can hit first.'[41]

Immediately, Collins interjected with a more conciliatory line. 'Is it not reasonable,' he asked, 'to give us safeguards for

our development?' After all, if Ireland were to prosper outside
Britain, he reasoned, there would need to be some protection
for her growing industries. Chamberlain, whose 'frosty eyes'
were later to make an impression on the Conservative MP
Henry 'Chips' Channon, observed that 'the question ... of the
crushing of an infant industry in its cradle' was 'rather in the
nature of a police measure'.[42] That brought the third session to
an end, and once again, after an hour and a half's discussion,
neither side had conceded a thing.

But the psychological dynamics were shifting. That evening,
Griffith wrote to de Valera, claiming victory on the dispute
over the courts. 'We were able to turn the tables on account
of the Sligo incident,' he recounted, but warned the problem
would flare up again since the 'whole die-hard element is at
work publicly and privately to smash the Conference over
the ostentatious publicity of the Courts'.[43] His words scarcely
reflected the cold sweat that Collins and Childers had worked
themselves into. The former was so worried that he immediately
dispatched instructions to GHQ in Dublin to restrict IRA
activities, while Childers notified de Valera, in an unusually
long epistle, that the publicity over the courts was 'so serious
that we cannot exaggerate its importance'. He thought it best
to compromise and keep court sittings private because 'to break
off negotiations ... on a matter of this kind would be absurd'.[44]

The following day, Friday 14 October, the Irish delegation
agreed to a joint declaration 'that no courts shall be held in
Ireland otherwise than as before the Truce'.[45] Childers felt
precious time had been wasted on this issue when they should
have been making up their 'case on the serious questions'.[46] The
British, too, were anxious to cover more substantial ground,
and after the courts issue was settled, Lloyd George opened
a conversation on Ulster, for which the Irish were entirely

unprepared. As Griffith explained hours later to de Valera, 'We could not defer it any further as only it and the question of the Crown remain for the moment outstanding.'[47] The lack of preparation, and the failure to produce an alternative position paper to the British delegation's 20 July proposals at the opening sessions, lost the Irish vital leverage.[48] It was in their interest to make the running on Irish unity and deal early on with the question of allegiance to the Crown.

Instead, with de Valera still to formulate his Ulster proposals, the Irish delegates were forced to play for time. And so Griffith launched the traditional Sinn Féin attack on partition, characterising it as 'unnatural' and an alien English solution to an Irish problem. He went on to portray the 1920 riots in the North as the work of Belfast politicians and accused the city's industrial heavyweights, the linen manufacturers and shipbuilders, of fomenting religious strife to prevent 'concerted action' by their employees. Gavan Duffy chipped in with, 'If England would stand aside there would be no difficulty.'[49]

The incompatibility of these Irish arguments – first holding Ulster Unionists accountable for sectarianism, then blaming the whole problem on 'England' – reflected the incoherence of Sinn Féin thinking on the North, as well as the delegates' poor preparation. But if the analysis was weak, the grievance was genuine. Northern Ireland's creation was fundamentally unjust, its borders established without consultation with a substantial Catholic minority. Protestants in Monaghan, Cavan and Donegal were also shoved out into the cold, despite having made their feelings on the matter clear with the signing of the 1912 Ulster Covenant, a popular protest by the Protestants of the north-east against an all-Ireland parliament.

During a long and laborious debate, the Irish delegates repeated de Valera's earlier promise not to coerce Ulster, which led Lloyd George to concede that there was a 'majority in Tyrone and Fermanagh against partition', but that, in 1914, nationalist politicians 'had accepted a crude division of the six counties as being preferable to setting up a boundary commission'. This appears to be the first reference in the Treaty talks to what proved to be one of the most controversial aspects of the 1921 settlement. Intriguingly, and almost as if he was musing out loud, Collins retorted that the Ulster question would be settled by 'a plan for a boundary commission, or for local option, or whatever you may call it'. He then immediately added, with characteristic swagger, that the Irish decision not to use force against Ulster had little to do with military considerations; rather it was because a victory over the north-east 'would not settle the matter'.[50]

As the fourth session drew to a close, there was general agreement that 'all parties', as Collins put it, were after a settlement. But Chamberlain implored the Irish delegation not to push their demands 'too far'. 'You are not aware', he said, 'of the risks we are taking with our whole political future.'[51] After an exhausting week, Lloyd George retreated to Chequers in a fug of disappointment, where he predicted that the conference would collapse within a fortnight. Over the weekend, he told Riddell that the Irish delegates were 'impossible people. They came to the point but could not make decisions.' Worse, their leader, Griffith, had 'no power of expression'; he was 'clever but incoherent'. Collins, on the other hand, was 'undoubtedly a considerable person'.[52]

After a week in the company of 'Shinners', the acerbic head of the British military forces in Ireland, Sir Nevil Macready, who sat on the Truce sub-committee, returned to Dublin with a completely different perspective. For him, Collins was a 'great disappointment, flippantly trying to get out of corners by poor jokes in bad taste', while Griffith seemed 'a strong, silent man'. Art O'Brien looked as if 'he was dying of drink, and Erskine Childers of consumption' and he didn't care 'which of 'em goes off first!'[53]

In his reference to Collins' 'poor jokes', Macready may have been thinking of the one made by the IRA leader on his way out of Downing Street at the end of that historic week. Noticing a rifle in the hallway – an antique from the American Civil War – Collins asked, 'What is the meaning of this provocative display?' Then he called on the Prime Minister to send for a photographer so he could pose with the gun in his hand. As the *Belfast News-Letter* recounted with bitter sarcasm the following day, this joke 'between His Majesty's Ministers and the rebel junta' was much enjoyed by the Prime Minister, who 'has a highly cultivated sense of humour'.[54] The episode rebounded well on Collins in the press, where he remained a romanticised figure, although the focus had become less about his adventurous exploits and more about his apparent heart-throb looks: his fine figure, 'raven's wing' black hair and 'typically Irish blue eyes'.[55]

Lloyd George's difficulty, on the other hand, was that increasing numbers of Tory MPs now believed that the coalition government spent its time entertaining murderers. A year earlier, the Prime Minister had welcomed Lenin's Bolsheviks to 10 Downing Street, infuriating the diehards and his Liberal ally, Churchill, and igniting a firestorm of protest in the press, with *The Times* describing Leonid Krasin, the head of the Soviet Trade Delegation, as the representative of 'a blood-stained despot'.[56] During that first week of the Treaty talks, as rampant unemployment triggered another mass demonstration in London, the political atmosphere grew ever more toxic. Reports circulated that while Lloyd George was enjoying

Collins' jokes, Churchill was listening 'with interest' to his 'adventures', prompting one unionist newspaper to assert that 'Ulster is more fastidious in her friendships, and is as immovable by threats as by temptations.'[57] Predictably, the diehard bible, *The Morning Post*, was the source of the Churchill story and caused enough consternation for his secretary to fire off a letter to the paper's editor categorically denying that Churchill had spent any time being regaled by Collins.[58]

When the fifth plenary session began at 3.30 p.m. on Monday 17 October, the Irish launched a blistering assault on the British, accusing them of negotiating in bad faith and of plotting to restart the war. The source of this angst was an alarmist intelligence report from a senior member of the Crown forces, which dated back to the start of the month and which the IRA had recently laid its hands on, testifying to the continued effectiveness of the republicans' own intelligence operations. In the Cabinet room, Griffith read out excerpts from the secret British military document, concentrating on the instructions to hunt down rebels 'at the first sign of the termination of the Truce' so that the Crown forces could ensure that 'all important leaders [were] arrested or satisfactorily accounted for'.[59] Lloyd George passed the report to Worthington-Evans, who questioned whether the directions had even been issued; he judged it to be nothing more than a contingency plan in the event that the negotiations collapsed and hostilities recommenced. At this, Collins sneered, 'We know. You can't issue these documents without my knowledge.' The bravado thinly masked Collins' genuine terror at what was in store if the talks failed, and, in the swiftly souring atmosphere, all trace of the first week's bonhomie vanished. From the outset, Collins and his intelligence network within the IRA had worried that the conference was doomed and that its collapse would provide the catalyst to an unwinnable war. It was why Emmet

Dalton, one of his loyal gunmen, arranged access to a private aeroplane – in case the IRA leader had to be bundled out of London in a hurry.[60] Months later, Collins would tell Hayden Talbot that when he first shook hands with Lloyd George 'there was still in existence the Dublin Castle reward of ten thousand pounds for my capture, dead or alive! Subsequently I reminded the British Prime Minister of this incongruous state of affairs – but that did not happen until I had discovered that he knew how to laugh.'[61]

At the Cabinet table that afternoon, Collins cut a very different figure. The British had engaged in espionage against him, he complained. An 'English agent' had even shadowed him at mass the previous morning, to which Lloyd George curtly replied that 'they had to contemplate a possible break-down of the truce and consider what must be done in that event'. Furious, Collins lashed out again, demanding that the Prime Minister take concerns about his safety seriously. 'I have asked what you thought of a soldier who during the truce circulated a photograph of myself, and the question was treated as a joke.' Keen now to end this confrontation, Lloyd George conceded that 'these matters make me anxious about the prolongation of the negotiations'. The Irish had little to show for such a forceful attack. The British simply shrugged off the accusations, while Collins' emotional outburst provoked another reminder from Chamberlain about the risks he, too, was taking. 'My position is becoming more difficult every day,' he said, prompting Griffith to conclude limply that 'No doubt an early decision would be the best thing.'[62]

It was the British who were more effective at exploiting the risk of war that hung over the conference. During the Truce committee sittings, which commenced on 12 October, the Irish were steadily thrust onto the back foot, acceding at

each meeting to a fresh set of British demands aimed at curbing
the activities of the IRA. At this fifth plenary session of the
talks, Griffith confirmed to the British delegates that Dublin
had agreed to the conciliatory formulas submitted the previous
week on IRA drilling and the Dáil courts. Within days, more
concessions were extracted as the Irish agreed to restrict IRA
levies, parades and funerals. By doing so, the Irish delegation
had effectively assumed responsibility for the insurgents' future
actions, which, in view of the army's loose command structure
and weak discipline, risked handing a fresh tactical advantage
to Lloyd George. Sinn Féin's compliance had come cheap, and
from now on, any further infractions of the Truce could be laid
at the feet of the Irish delegates.[63]

The remainder of that session was turned over to the vexed
issue of Ulster. De Valera's long-awaited 'draft clause' on the
subject was now complete, but Griffith chose not to present
it, a decision Ronan Fanning puts down to its 'tortuous and
convoluted provisions'.[64] The President's proposal stipulated
that all constituencies in the six counties could opt out of an
all-Ireland assembly. If they exercised this right they could
'maintain [the Belfast] legislature', but it would be Home
Rule under Dublin rather than Westminster. This meant that
the Northern Ireland MPs who sat in the British parliament
would instead attend an all-Ireland assembly. While this alone
would have infuriated Ulster's unionists, more troublesome still
was the caveat that parliamentary sovereignty would apply
only to 'contiguous' constituencies that formed a 'territorially
continuous group', meaning that if the local vote was based
on the 1918 parliamentary constituencies – and de Valera
intimated that it would be, without actually spelling it out –
Northern Ireland would be reduced to a tiny outcrop on the
island's north-eastern coast.

While this was ultimately an objective that Griffith shared – like most southerners, he detested partition, regarding it as unnatural and illegitimate – he opted to return to his theme of 14 October. If the British government stood aside, he argued, Sinn Féin would make the people of the north-east a 'fair proposal'. That meant allowing those in the six counties to 'choose freely whether they should be in the North or the South'. And what would happen, Lloyd George asked, 'in the case of scattered, non-contiguous areas?' Griffith suggested that isolated minorities could strike a deal, or 'exchange such areas'. The Prime Minister shot back, 'That is not self-determination, [that] is a deal.'

After a lengthy debate, Lloyd George finally demanded that the Irish go away and choose whether they wanted to preserve the status quo or have all of Ulster – meaning the province's nine counties – vote together on partition or unity. The Prime Minister knew that neither Ulster's unionists nor Sinn Féin would accept this second solution. Craig did not want the three additional counties. He had already pledged to 'sit on Ulster like a rock', declaring over the summer that 'we are content with what we have got',[65] while Griffith feared further territory losses for the South on a plebiscite of that scale. He wanted the vote in the six counties based upon 'local units', meaning the 1918 constituencies or Poor Law areas, so as to ensure a more favourable outcome for the Catholic nationalist population.[66]

As a consequence of this stalemate, another plenary session closed without a significant breakthrough. The conference was in danger of turning into a labyrinth without a thread, and Lloyd George struggled to stifle his anxiety. At the end of the Ulster debate, he scrawled a note to Jones: 'This is going to wreck [a] settlement.'[67] But a string of unexpected events soon raised the pressure to far more drastic levels. The first shock was de Valera's public slap down of King George V on 20 October, via a telegram to Pope Benedict XV. The dispute erupted after the King replied to a papal message hoping for a successful outcome to the London peace conference. De Valera complained that 'ambiguities' in the monarch's response meant that the 'uninformed' would assume Ireland's troubles were a domestic difficulty, whereas the fault lay with 'British rulers [who] by brutal force have endeavoured to rob [the Irish] people of the liberty which is their natural right and their ancient heritage.' He claimed 'the independence of Ireland' had been 'proclaimed by ... elected representatives' and 'no consideration' would ever induce the Irish people to abandon 'their natural freedom'.[68] The President published the exchanges in the press to counter what he, with some justification, saw as a 'propaganda' stunt between the Pope and the monarch. But it was an unnecessary and ill-judged intervention.

Predictably, this inflammatory rhetoric triggered a storm of outrage in Britain. In an editorial, The Times solemnly declared that if de Valera spoke for the majority of Irish people, 'the chances of peace are small'.[69] Other newspapers speculated the move was designed to poison Anglo–American relations ahead of the forthcoming naval disarmament conference in Washington – a line that likely came from Riddell. He was scheduled to travel to the American capital within a fortnight as Lloyd George wanted his old friend, and the proprietor of the News of the World, to act as unofficial spokesperson to the British delegation.[70]

De Valera's intervention would not come to light until the following morning, when the delegates reconvened for the sixth plenary session. (A three-day adjournment had allowed both sides to focus on the conference's various sub-committees.) Unaware of the storm that was brewing, Collins skipped off that evening to Wormwood Scrubs, where almost 200 Irish internees were being held.[71] In April 1920, when a number of these mostly untried prisoners embarked on a hunger strike, their treatment triggered questions in the House of Commons.[72] Now Collins arrived to rally their spirits. But unbeknownst to him, fairly detailed reports of his visit filtered back to the Prime Minister. Prison guards claimed he was drunk, handing out cigarettes and loudly 'boasting about all the loyal people he has shot'. They vowed to resign if he was allowed in again.[73]

Under the circumstances, it was a misdemeanour the Irish could ill afford. For, at the same time, reports were pouring into Westminster about a freshly uncovered IRA gun-running plot in Germany. During the War of Independence, Collins and his agents had attempted to establish an arms-trading network on the Continent, even though these routes generally proved expensive and unreliable. After the ceasefire, British security services began to close in on these IRA intrigues, and their efforts culminated on 21 October in the port of Hamburg with the discovery of their largest haul yet – a ship laden with weapons and bound for Ireland. To complicate the situation, another IRA gun-running plot was under investigation in the north of England, after explosives were found stored in a house in Newcastle-upon-Tyne. The munitions had been robbed earlier that month from nearby Bebside Colliery. An intelligence report submitted to the government that week claimed that the republican running this operation, who had been arrested in Cardiff, was also behind 'a wide conspiracy spreading from South Wales to the Tyneside'.[74]

As the clock struck noon on Friday 21 October, the Irish delegation resumed their seats at the Cabinet table at 10 Downing Street, quite unaware of the extent of the charge sheet against them. Lloyd George spoke first, displaying an almost sinister level of politeness. 'I wonder, Mr Griffith, have you any preliminary questions which you would be anxious to raise before we proceed with the business?' Having woken up to the Pope telegram controversy that morning, the Irish were well aware this was not going to be plain sailing. They decided to attack first. Griffith gave the floor to Duggan, who immediately upbraided the British for failing to evacuate all local council buildings in Sligo. 'The Military are still in the possession of the offices of the district council,' he complained, '… and military permits are required from the staff before they can enter the building to perform their ordinary duties.' Worthington-Evans retorted, 'Is there only one entrance?' Duggan plodded on: 'The usual practice in such cases,' he replied, 'is to surround the building with barbed wire.' 'We will look into that,' Lloyd George purred. There was no obvious sign of rage to begin with, but after an initial apology for the 'two or three preliminary questions' he had that were of the 'gravest character', the Prime Minister poured out accusations one after the other, and within minutes he had launched into a full-blown tirade, as the Irish were excoriated for the German ship 'with arms on board for your people' and the 'serious conspiracy in this country for the accumulation … of bombs and other destructive weapons' which were to be shipped to Ireland, 'and it is clearly evident that this action was done in concert with your people'. The 'third matter of which we have to complain,' he exclaimed violently, 'is the publication of Mr de Valera's telegram to his Holiness the Pope'. Not only was this 'document … offensive to the King … it will make our task almost impossible … It looks like a deliberate attempt to break up the Conference.' Now at full tilt, he blasted the Irish for submitting 'a complaint regarding the non-observance of the Truce in Sligo', dismissing it as a 'trivial matter'. It was time the Irish showed their hand. 'We must know without delay our exact position. If we do not,' he warned, '… these sittings cannot be prolonged.'[75]

Under sustained fire, the Irish became defiant and defensive. As Pakenham tells it, Griffith believed de Valera's telegram to be a 'grave mistake' but betrayed no sign of this to the British. Instead, he argued that the President had 'only stated ... facts', since the troubles were not 'between Irishmen ... but between Ireland and Great Britain'.[76] There was no mention, of course, of the ongoing inter-ethnic violence still raging in Ulster, or the fact that the region's majority Protestant population refused to contemplate, let alone accept, citizenship in a united Ireland. Addressing the division within the country had never been a priority for Sinn Féin.

But Griffith was keen to lower the tensions in the room. He held out the possibility of a compromise on trade and defence, saying, 'I do not regard these as insoluble.' Collins was more belligerent. He wrestled with Churchill over the issue of Irish neutrality, arguing that this would be a 'greater safeguard' to Britain than any commitments on ports or naval bases. 'No!' Churchill thundered. 'The position of neutrality would have been a great difficulty to us in the late war ... we must consider that there might ... be ill-will in Ireland.' Chamberlain cut in with the observation that 'neutrality means that you would be outside the Empire'.[77] The British had always seen this issue as another way for the Irish to pursue de Valera's goal of External Association, and both sides traipsed over these arguments numerous times during the defence sub-committee meetings.

Collins refused to back down. He tried a different tack, making the running this time on the ambiguities of Dominion status. Quoting from a recent statement issued by an influential Canadian lobby group, which advocated the British Empire becoming a 'partnership between nations free and equal', he turned to the Prime Minister and said, 'I put it to you, Mr Lloyd George, that the lines on which we are going are very much like those lines.' Griffith went further, arguing that what the British were offering was an 'inferior' version of Dominion status, since, unlike the other Commonwealth nations, the Irish would not even have the 'right' to build a navy.[78]

But at that point, the debate was brought to an abrupt halt by the British delegates' decision to confer privately. They returned after ten minutes with an ultimatum: no later than Monday morning, the Sinn Féin delegation was to spell out its position on the three key British demands of allegiance to the Crown, membership of the Empire and naval defence guarantees. Otherwise, the talks were finished. These were not 'real negotiations', Lloyd George railed; they were being 'spun out' to enable the Irish to equip their forces. 'The British government', he declared, 'could no longer waste time in conferences which would lead to no result.'[79]

By browbeating the Irish over breaches of the Truce, the Prime Minister hoped to undermine their position and soften them up for a compromise on the Crown and the Empire. The strategy had the added bonus of placating Birkenhead and Chamberlain, who had to face down the diehards. But the Irish refused to show contrition, challenging the veracity of the British charges and alleging that the importation of arms was not forbidden under the Truce. Griffith asserted, 'If this conference breaks down we will have to fight' and 'if we have to fight we have to prepare'.[80]

The talks were now on a knife-edge. That afternoon a codeword was issued to the British military in Ireland warning of the imminent resumption of hostilities. The following day, Worthington-Evans confided to a colleague that the conference was headed for collapse. He predicted that 'our army is likely to have work soon' in Ireland.[81]

5 ▪ OPPOSITION AND DIVISION
21 October–30 October

The sharp deterioration in the talks quickly became public knowledge. Evening newspapers afforded the 'crisis' front-page treatment, while unnamed government sources laid the blame for the 'extremely difficult' situation on the 'attitude of the Sinn Fein delegates'. It was their 'utter disregard of the fundamental facts of the situation' that had tipped the negotiations towards disaster, and they were carrying on as 'if they were masters of the position'. Another, described as a 'leader of political opinion', marvelled at Lloyd George's reserves of patience: 'If anyone but the Prime Minister had been presiding,' he told the *Pall Mall Gazette*, 'the whole business would have ended before now.'[1] Yet the briefings against the Irish stopped short of any meaningful disclosures, leaving the newspapers to conclude that the trouble stemmed solely from de Valera's 'bombshell' telegram to the Pope.[2] At the weekend, *The Freeman's Journal* reflected that the 'grave' expressions of the Irish delegates as they filed out of Downing Street on the Friday afternoon had given the game away, since it appeared, 'for the first time', that 'all was not going well in the Conference Chamber'.[3]

In fact, the Irish delegates assumed the end was now in sight. At a crisis meeting at Hans Place shortly after the explosive encounter at Downing Street, they instructed Childers to draw up a memo to de Valera setting out the parlous state of the negotiations and the uncomfortable choices now confronting them. They wanted answers on two questions: firstly, whether arms importations into Ireland should cease while the conference was underway, and, secondly, whether the President advocated an immediate refusal on the question of the Crown – an action that would have severed all further discussion. In the starkly worded memo, the delegation made clear its opposition to the continued importation of munitions, and said that on the Crown, they were prepared to 'neither … refuse … nor accept it at the present stage', but to delay any resolution until it was clear what the British were prepared to offer in return. This had been Griffith's strategy all along. He had hoped to defer discussion of the Crown for as long as possible, but the outcry over de Valera's telegram to the Pope rendered that impossible, and so now he demanded that the President explicitly approve the negotiating plan – either that or suggest an alternative one.[4] They could risk no more mishaps.

Collins then tore off to Euston station for the long, overnight journey back to Dublin. He took with him the minutes of the sixth session and the hastily written memo. De Valera assumed Collins had returned 'about the wire to Rome' and swiftly convened a Cabinet meeting. Yet, as Austin Stack recollected some time later, the telegram to the Pope was not mentioned. Instead, Collins asked de Valera to join the delegation in London; 'the President refused, saying he saw no necessity'.[5] In a letter to Griffith during the week, he explained that he would change his mind only if 'the position imperatively calls for it' but refrained from specifying what those compelling circumstances might be, and a century later it remains impossible to establish what would have altered his strategic calculation that he could achieve more in Dublin than London.[6] In any case, the effect of de Valera's approach was to deepen the existing schism within the Cabinet, sowing confusion and suspicion among one faction, while inspiring a misplaced complacency in the other. As the historian J.J. Lee observed, 'it was never quite clear' what de Valera 'stood for; or with whom he stood, at least from December 1920 until June 1922'.[7]

The letter to Griffith ended with a hope that it would be possible to 'secure unanimity for whatever action is taken', but rarely had unanimity within the Cabinet looked such a distant prospect.[8] The rifts were widening not narrowing, driven in large part by Cathal Brugha's renewed attempts to overhaul the IRA. He wanted the territorial, volunteer guerrilla force turned into a non-territorial professional army under civilian control; a move that would entrench his authority, sideline Collins and weaken the power of the IRB. There was a broad acceptance within GHQ that reform was needed, but Brugha's ham-fisted interventions were widely seen as a malicious power grab, particularly by Collins and the IRA's Chief of Staff, Richard Mulcahy. It didn't help that the truculent Minister for Defence, who was in his mid-forties by the time of the Treaty talks, lacked credibility with the generally far younger gunmen. One Cork commander recalled that he received just one communication from Brugha throughout the War of Independence, while Mulcahy later dismissed his contribution altogether: 'Brugha did no systematic work in connection with carrying on of the military organization.'[9] A special bone of contention to some contemporaries and historians alike was his part-time status: he juggled ministerial duties with the demands of running a candle-manufacturing business on Dublin's quays.[10]

But there can be no dispute about Brugha's devotion to the separatist cause. The reserved, abstemious minister – who embraced teetotalism in 1917 rather than contribute to His Majesty's Treasury by paying the tax on alcohol – was always most energetic when in pursuit of his grand passion: the assassination of the entire British Cabinet, which he meticulously planned in 1918, 1920 and 1921. Brugha's problem was that effective control of the IRA rested with Collins, a fact humiliatingly reinforced when he revived the scheme for the third time. Brugha had instructed the Volunteer charged with leading the operation to relay the details to Collins, who promptly barked at the officer to drop the 'mad plan', then sent him off with the withering reminder that he should stop 'thinking [he was] some vest-pocket Bonaparte going over to conquer England'.[11] (Of course, Collins was susceptible to his own hare-brained schemes. He authorised unjustifiable killings in the War of Independence, and is suspected of ordering the murder of Field Marshal Sir Henry Wilson in 1922.) For his part, Brugha seized every opportunity to undermine Collins' role in the army and degrade his achievements. In fact, there are signs his hatred grew into an obsession, which, at times, quite literally unhinged him, and while the awkward relationship between the Dáil and the IRB fuelled this struggle, at heart, it was the result of a brutal personality clash.[12]

De Valera mostly refrained from taking sides, but his style of leadership meant Machiavellian plots were easily laid at his door. Collins and his allies became convinced that the President, Brugha and Stack were conniving against him while he was in London, and it is likely their fears were fed by petty disputes over the delegation's personnel and the knowledge that Childers was in secret communication with de Valera.[13] Days before his controversial telegram to the Pope, the President waded into battle on behalf of Brugha and Stack, arguing that the defence and constitutional experts drafted in to help with the London negotiations should have been summoned by the ministers for Defence and Home Affairs. Unexpectedly, de Valera also demanded the return of Diarmuid O'Hegarty, the Cabinet Secretary who had been co-opted to the delegation's secretariat, insisting that he was not to be kept in England 'an hour longer than is necessary'.[14] To make matters worse, Brugha launched a broadside at Mulcahy over a key appointment in GHQ. The latter promptly penned a furious letter of protest to de Valera, condemning the 'nagging spirit' of the Minister for Defence and describing the dispute as 'devitalising and degrading'.[15]

Mostly, the British remained in the dark about these difficulties. They understood there were high-level splits within the republican movement but misjudged where the fault-lines lay. Restrictions imposed by the Truce added to the knowledge deficit. Under the terms of the ceasefire, both sides were prevented from running intelligence operations against each other, although neither the British nor the Irish observed this rule to the letter. For the Crown forces, the curbs represented a serious setback. Towards the end of the guerrilla war, they had relied on overt intelligence-gathering methods: large-scale sweeps and searches that allowed them to seize documents and capture and interrogate prisoners. Now, forced to fall back on covert surveillance operations, and with the talks at a tense juncture, Irish-based British intelligence chiefs kept a close watch on Collins. Files in the UK National Archives show that he was followed that weekend in Dublin, although the agent picked up little of value and, judging by his report – which revolved around a conversation overheard at the Gresham Hotel in the city centre – the IRA leader was fully aware that he was under surveillance, just as he had been in London.[16]

At any rate, Collins appeared to be leaving nothing to chance. On Monday 24 October, hours before the two sides were due to face each other again for the seventh plenary session, he ordered Art O'Brien, who controlled the Dáil's purse-strings in Britain, to provide the delegation with more cash. Under instruction, a colleague dashed off a note that read: 'As there may possibly be some emergency calls during this week it would be well to cancel my application for £300 and make an issuance of £500 instead.'[17]

Yet Collins had more than just the unfolding crisis at the conference on his mind. This was the week he hoped Kitty Kiernan would visit. On his way back to London on the Sunday evening, he had confessed, not for the first time, to feelings of loneliness, writing in a short letter to her that he wished she were with him now and that it was 'so sad being far away'.[18] On Monday, Kitty received a telegram from one of the delegation's female staff, urging her to catch the overnight boat the following day. When there was no reply, Collins had Duggan's wife, May, wire her twice on Tuesday 25 October, pointing out that if she still wanted to come to London, she must travel the next day because there was 'not the slightest use after that. Cross Wednesday night or not at all.'[19]

Not much is known about Kitty's visit, not even the dates, although it is thought she responded to this injunction and arrived in England that week. Her sister Helen, who was on her honeymoon, was also in London and, according to Kathleen Napoli McKenna, one of the four secretary-typists to the delegation, 'Mick was very much in love with Kitty' and was a 'proud man' when he walked out of Cadogan Gardens 'with a sister on each arm'.[20]

At that stage, aside from his relations with Kitty, little else appeared to be going Collins' way. The talks were teetering on the brink, while the strains and divisions within the Cabinet and the delegation threatened to erupt into open acrimony. On 24 October, as Collins' train pulled into Euston station at 5.30 a.m., a fresh chill hung in the air. The Indian summer had vanished without warning. Collins would have felt the cold as he made his way first to 15 Cadogan Gardens, and then on to Hans Place, which was a hive of activity that morning. The British were expecting Sinn Féin's written answers to the questions of the Crown, the Empire and defence by early afternoon at the latest. Yet as Childers recorded in his diary, and also scrawled on a copy of the memorandum which Collins took back with him to Dublin, there had been no response from de Valera. This lack of direction, combined with last-minute debates among the delegates about neutrality and defence, along with a fair amount of organisational chaos, meant the documents were not delivered to Downing Street until 3.20 p.m., less than an hour and a half before the seventh session was due to begin.[21]

When the two sides finally confronted each other across the Cabinet table that evening, thirty minutes later than anticipated, Lloyd George was in no mood for cheery salutations. Immediately, he reprimanded the Irish for their tardiness, complaining that not only was their 'memorandum ... received too late for effective examination', but it failed to adequately address the vital questions. Time was running out, he reminded them, 'and we cannot much longer prolong discussion on these questions ... especially having regard to the political position'.[22] Earlier in the day, in the House of Commons, the Prime Minister had fended off a noisy attack from the diehards. The agitator on this occasion was Rupert Gwynne, a hard-line Tory notorious for his inflammatory rhetoric towards Irish and Indian nationalists. He stirred up the House by demanding that Sinn Féin remove the republican flag displayed in the doorway of 22 Hans Place, which another Conservative MP condemned as a 'great provocation to people who live in that neighbourhood'. When Lloyd George insisted they were mistaken, the 'Sinn Fein colours' were not on display, the Conservative benches chorused back at him, 'They are ...!', prompting another MP to chip in: 'Put there by the enemies of this country.' Inevitably, the pantomime-like scenes filled the newspapers' main pages the following day.[23]

The British were perplexed and annoyed by the Irish counter-proposals. They took exception to the strident language, which emphasised that Ireland was not a colony 'but an ancient and spirited nation',[24] and in a meeting held minutes after the memorandum was deposited at Downing Street, they had debated whether to break off the negotiations. The conclusion was that while the Irish had 'by implication refused or evaded' the three key questions, the responses were too 'ambiguous' to justify a rupture.[25] Based on draft Treaty A, which itself was a recapitulation of de Valera's July statements, the counter-proposals advanced the case for External Association. The delegates claimed that Ireland was not interested in becoming a Dominion, but, if it were, the British proposals 'did not confer that status'. This was followed by a hazy summary of what the relationship between the two nations should look like: Ireland's 'freedom and integrity' were to be defined as international concerns, enshrined by guarantees from the British Commonwealth, as well as from the League of Nations and the United States – if they agreed. Irish neutrality would come with a commitment to uphold this sovereignty, thereby providing the 'best security' for Britain; and, in exchange for complete autonomy on taxation and finance, the 'free State' would enter 'into reciprocal obligations' on trade and civic rights. The Ulster clause was not included, but Sinn Féin restated its determination to treat the six counties as a domestic matter, and if an agreement proved impossible, then the decision would be decided in a plebiscite. On the basis of all this, Ireland consented to 'adhere' to the Commonwealth 'for all purposes of agreed common concern'.[26]

What does that mean, Lloyd George demanded: 'are you prepared to come inside the Empire, as New Zealand, Canada?' 'That is not quite our idea of association,' Griffith replied stiffly, forcing the Prime Minister to redouble his efforts. 'Association is not the position of Canada and Australia. What is the distinction between association and coming inside the Empire?' Rather at a loss, Griffith responded: 'We should be associated with you – outside that a free people.'[27]

Like Dominion status, External Association was never clearly defined during the talks. De Valera had yet to finalise his thinking on the idea, which, by definition, acknowledged that there would be no clean break from Britain. But just as the Irish were unwilling to accept the 'still expanding freedom' that came with Dominion status, the British refused to contemplate any solution that compromised the symbolic authority of the Crown and Empire.[28] External Association, unveiled only at this seventh plenary session, struck the British negotiators as a thinly disguised request for a republic. They equated it with separatism and, as the historian Bill Kissane observed, the country's 'political elite did not emerge from the First World War to contemplate humiliation in their own backyard'.[29] Imperial considerations were of paramount importance, not just from a strategic point of view, but because they reflected fundamental assumptions about Britain's identity. As he went into the conference that autumn, the Prime Minister was all too aware that domestic and Dominion opinion favoured Ireland remaining in the Empire.

Pressed to explain exactly what Sinn Féin meant by External Association, Griffith floundered, so Birkenhead moved the discussion on to defence and proceeded to demolish the case for Irish neutrality. Dismissing the policy as a sham, he argued 'no country' would recognise that status if Britain retained access to Ireland's naval bases. It would be 'reduced to a shadow – a meaningless trophy'. Unwilling to contest the logic of this argument any further, Griffith gave way. 'We accept the principle that your security should be looked after.'

At once, the Prime Minister suspended the meeting, declaring: 'I think we must confer amongst ourselves.'[30] Then the British delegation left the room.

In a sitting room next door, Birkenhead claimed to be 'shaken' by the answers of the Sinn Féin delegates, while Chamberlain fixated on their 'evasion of allegiance'. When the Prime Minister pointed out that it would be 'more useful' to dwell on the progress so far, there was general acknowledgement that Griffith's comment 'marked an important advance in the negotiations'.[31] Lloyd George had good reason to strike such an optimistic tone – he was battling to recover lost ground. Earlier in the day, Collins and Griffith had agreed to a private meeting with the Prime Minister and Chamberlain ahead of the afternoon's session. But when the Irish counter-proposals arrived, the British delegation developed cold feet and suspended the plan. Lloyd George learned of the change only when he returned to 10 Downing Street shortly before 5 p.m. He had rushed out of that crucial meeting to keep an appointment with the Prince of Wales (the future Edward VIII) and arrived back to be told by his colleagues that the 'preliminary interview' was off because they wanted clarity on the Irish position. Another hurried meeting ensued, this time in Chamberlain's rooms in 11 Downing Street, and while there are no records of the discussion, it was presumably at this point that they decided to press ahead with the earlier strategy if Sinn Féin adopted a more ameliorative line.[32] So when Griffith ceded ground, Lloyd George pounced. Here was an excuse – the first that presented itself – to close out the seventh plenary session on a positive note.

With the flurry of British nerves over, the Irish delegation was herded into one of Downing Street's drawing rooms, while Collins and Griffith were instructed to remain in the Cabinet room and await the arrival of Lloyd George and Chamberlain. Over the decades there have been conflicting accounts about who initiated this meeting, but its effect was to tighten the circle of people at the table for the Treaty talks.[33] Under the new format, secretaries were banished, and so Childers was excluded from all further meetings, while the minor delegates were left with an obscured view. There would be twenty-four, in total, of these sub-conferences before the Treaty was signed. Griffith attended twenty-two and Collins nineteen. By contrast, Barton went to three, while Gavan Duffy and Duggan attended just two each.[34]

Despite the accusations levelled at Collins, this first request for a private interview was undoubtedly a British initiative. Ostensibly, the Prime Minister wanted to exclude the more troublesome members of his team, Greenwood and Worthington-Evans, but he was far more bothered by Childers, Barton and Gavan Duffy.[35] He knew, too, as his former private secretary Geoffrey Shakespeare recalled, that Collins and Griffith 'were likely to discuss the issues more freely if the other Irish delegates were absent', and probably calculated that his ploys and devices would work more effectively in an informal session. 'Lloyd George always disliked arguing with a committee,' Shakespeare wrote. 'He preferred direct dealing with individuals, man to man.'[36]

The Prime Minister, Chamberlain, Collins and Griffith spoke in private for an hour and fifteen minutes. Afterwards, in what was turning out to be a marathon day, the British delegation gathered again for an update: the Irish were prepared to consider Dominion status, but only if there was an end to partition; they had also agreed not to import any more arms into Ireland out of 'an anxiety for peace'. Finally, Lloyd George reassured his colleagues that he was now confident the Sinn Féin delegation 'would take down' the republican flag outside Hans Place, which had been the cause of such controversy in the Commons earlier in the day.[37]

Then he rushed back to parliament just in time to witness the diehards throw down the gauntlet. The much-threatened right-wing revolt was underway. That evening, thirty-eight backbenchers tabled a motion condemning the government's negotiations with Sinn Féin. Marshalled by Colonel Gretton, a Staffordshire brewer who was married to the daughter of an Anglo-Irish peer, the rebels included Gwynne and a number of parliamentary curiosities, most notably Admiral Sir Reginald 'Blinker' Hall, a member for Liverpool and the former head of Naval Intelligence. (His handling of covert information ahead of the 1916 Rising has fuelled questions about whether he intended the rebellion to occur, knowing as he did that Dublin Castle's reaction would be a policy of repression.)[38] The diehards, in their desire to defend the traditional order and avert what they saw as a humiliating surrender to Sinn Féin, were all in favour of brute force. They believed Southern Ireland could be rid of the 'murder junta' within months, given 'fifty thousand additional men and a free hand'.[39]

Neither de Valera nor Collins showed much sympathy for Lloyd George's political plight. Rightly suspicious of his capacity to exploit the threat from the far right, the President reminded Griffith that while the Prime Minister certainly had 'the die-hard crowd to fight ... he should realise there are people in this country who are just as determined on their side'.[40] Collins proved equally inflexible. Later that week, as the pressure in parliament intensified, C.P. Scott, the editor of *The Manchester Guardian*, intervened to press the Prime Minister's case. He had arranged to meet the IRA leader at 15 Cadogan Gardens and, in a lengthy diary entry, recalled how Collins had turned up in 'immense force' and ejected everybody from the office with a 'sweep of his arms', 'including an unhappy typist'. During their hour and a quarter conversation, the 'telephone rang at intervals when he sprang upon it fiercely as an enemy and yelled a challenge that might have split the instrument'.

But what unnerved Scott the most was Collins' refusal to consider the British perspective. 'Lloyd George was fighting their battle hard,' he stressed, 'and had done wonders in bringing over the Tories', to which the IRA leader replied, 'I know nothing about your politics. I have only to think of Ireland.' In exasperation, Scott shot back, 'You have got to think of our politics if you want to get anything done.' Afterwards he reported the conversation to Lloyd George, as agreed. The Prime Minister had dispatched his old friend and confidant to the Sinn Féin camp to gauge whether the worsening conditions at Westminster were having the desired effect: he wanted to know if the Tory rebellion had persuaded the two main Sinn Féin negotiators to adopt a more conciliatory approach. Yet, in the event, only Collins had been available, whom Scott judged a 'straightforward and quite agreeable savage'. The venture had not been entirely unavailing, for Lloyd George now knew where to concentrate his powers of persuasion.[41]

Encouraged by the fresh momentum that emerged from the meeting with Collins and Griffith, the British resolved to adopt the sub-conference format as their new modus operandi. Although Gavan Duffy, Barton and Childers were unhappy at this development, de Valera kept quiet, confident that any important decisions would be referred back to the Cabinet. Griffith viewed the change as a minor victory: it gave him a freer hand in the negotiations. But the impression of having overcome a crisis proved fleeting, for within days the hard-won advance was offset by a dispute of even more alarming proportions; one that threatened to destroy the Sinn Féin delegation and collapse the talks.

It began, most likely, with a misunderstanding. On Monday evening, soon after he had returned to Hans Place, Griffith dashed off a brief letter to de Valera, providing only a bare-bones account of the discussions with Lloyd George and Chamberlain so the messenger could catch the train and over-night mail boat back to Dublin. He related how he and Collins had driven the British hard on Ireland's 'essential unity', making clear that 'association of any kind with the Crown' would hinge on concessions on Ulster.[42] The following afternoon, Tuesday 25 October, unaware that his missive had caused ructions in Dublin, he and Collins pursued this same line at a second sub-conference, this time in Chamberlain's rooms.

That evening, with de Valera's response still to arrive, Griffith dispatched another letter to Dublin, summarising the afternoon meeting with Chamberlain and Attorney General Gordon Hewart. The British had organised it in the hope that it would point a way out of the Ulster quagmire. But Griffith trumpeted how he and Collins had stood their ground, hammering home that partition needed to be determined by a plebiscite structured on the 1918 constituencies, not, as the British insisted, on the province as a whole. 'Eventually,' Griffith recalled, 'they suggested the six-county area remaining as at present, but coming into the All-Ireland parliament.' Although he and Collins believed this 'might be a possible basis' for an agreement, he reassured de Valera that they had turned down the proposal. 'In the end,' Griffith wrote, 'I told them that no Irishman could even discuss with his countrymen any association with the British Crown unless the essential unity of Ireland was agreed to' by both sides.[43]

But de Valera was less focused on Ulster than the Crown, and it was this promise of 'association' that caused the ensuing uproar. Griffith had used the same phrase in his Monday evening dispatch, and when de Valera digested it the following morning he immediately wrote back:

> We are all here at one that there can be no question of our asking the Irish people to enter an arrangement which would make them subject to the Crown, or demand from them allegiance to the British King. If war is the alternative, we can only face it, and I think that the sooner the other side is made to realise that the better.[44]

His letter arrived in London on Wednesday 26 October, and as soon as Griffith saw it, he exploded in indignation. That evening, at a meeting in Childers' room at Hans Place, he threatened to 'go home unless the Cabinet left their hands free'. As festering resentments boiled over, Collins accused 'those in Dublin' of 'trying to put him in the wrong' so that he could 'do the dirty work for them', and, in a towering fury, vowed to quit the delegation.[45] Gavan Duffy and Barton, who were less troubled by de Valera's unwarranted intrusion, agreed to sign a letter of protest, as did Duggan. In a rare show of unity, the plenipotentiaries censured the President for what they saw as 'the interference with our powers', reminding him that these 'had been given by the Cabinet as a whole, and can only be withdrawn or varied by the Cabinet as a whole'. They declared, 'We strongly resent ... the position in which we have been placed', accusing de Valera not only of 'tying their hands in discussion', but of threatening, by 'this intervention', the 'very slight possibility' of a settlement. And the blame for this failure, they warned, would not rest with the delegates. If all this was not sufficient to ensure his retreat, they made it clear that they would return home 'immediately', if the powers 'given to them on their appointment ... were withdrawn'.[46]

Thrown by the delegation's combative stance, de Valera backed down. 'There is obviously a misunderstanding,' he wrote to Griffith the next day. 'There can be no question of tying the hands of the Plenipotentiaries beyond the extent to which they are tied by their original instructions', he said, adding that his memoranda were 'nothing more than an attempt to keep you in touch with the views of the Cabinet'.[47] But the swiftly patched-up rift left a thick residue of bitterness. In a letter to Joe McGarrity at the end of December, when the signing of the Treaty had uncorked a toxic mix of furies, de Valera claimed that it had struck him then that some in London 'were looking for an excuse to return and throw the blame of the breakdown of the negotiations on us who were at home'.[48]

Once the letter of protest to de Valera had been typed and signed, there was a mad dash to the Royal Albert Hall, where at least 6,000 Irish expatriates were eagerly awaiting the plenipotentiaries. In an effort to lift the profile of the Irish Self-Determination League, and simultaneously advance the republican cause, Art O'Brien had organised an official 'reception' for the Sinn Féin delegation. He had hired, for the occasion, the ornate Victorian concert hall opposite Kensington Gardens, but the British authorities were nervous about the event's propaganda potential, particularly as it was scheduled for a day after the first anniversary of Terence MacSwiney's death. A week earlier, the manager of the famous building had abruptly revised the lease terms, stipulating that there was to be no 'speech-making' (except for O'Brien and Griffith) and that the concert was not to be turned into a 'celebration' of the 'late Lord Mayor of Cork'. Barred from staging an overtly political event, O'Brien laid on a night of Irish music, and invited representatives from the Egyptian, Indian and Scottish nationalist movements, in honour, as the brochure stated, and as the newspapers duly highlighted, of the 'Irish Republican Delegates'.[49] Yet the tribute to revolutionary unity could hardly have come at a worse time. It was only Griffith's pressure that persuaded Collins to begrudgingly add his signature to the letter; he would have preferred to throw in the towel, although his mood may have lightened when confronted with the rousing reception at the Albert Hall. The arrival of the delegates elicited 'a wild outburst of cheering, which lasted for nearly two minutes', according to one report, and, predictably, it was Collins who soaked up most of the attention. There were 'insistent' calls for him to speak, but the responsibility fell to Griffith, who praised 'the strength, the solidarity and the unconquerableness of the Irish race'.[50]

With the Irish reeling from the confrontation with de Valera, the British plunged into a crucial test of strength with the diehards. Lloyd George had decided to call their bluff by challenging them to a vote in the House of Commons. At the end of parliamentary questions on Thursday 27 October, the Prime Minister returned to the dispatch box to drop the bombshell news. 'It is quite clear we cannot proceed with this Conference,' he announced, 'unless we know the House of Commons supports us.' Arguing that the government was faced with what amounted 'to a vote of censure' against the peace talks, he declared that the House would have to decide whether they pressed ahead with the negotiations or not. His battle cry – Lloyd George that night laid down a debate and division on the subject – was met by stony silence from the Tory rebels. All around them, however, coalition backbenchers erupted into cheers.[51] Chamberlain thought that put 'A cold douche on the hotheads of some of our friends!'[52]

With the showdown in the Commons scheduled for the following Monday, Lloyd George now bore down relentlessly on the Irish, holding out the prospect of unity if Sinn Féin was prepared to swallow the Crown and Empire, and deliver assurances on defence. It was a strategy the Prime Minister had developed in response to the seemingly impossible dilemma that had confronted the British delegates earlier in the week. After the meeting with Collins and Griffith on the Tuesday evening, Chamberlain and Hewart told their colleagues the Irish 'could not recommend allegiance to the King unless they got the unity of Ireland'. Churchill reminded the delegation that on Ulster their hands were tied: 'We cannot give way on [the] six counties; we are not free agents.' Birkenhead echoed Churchill's thoughts, conceding that 'our position is an impossible one if these men want to settle, as they do'. Fearful of a rupture with the two most powerful players in his government, Lloyd George swiftly charted a different course. They should drop the discussion on Ulster for now, he advised. What they needed from Sinn Féin were definite answers to the 'vital' questions – meaning, the Crown, the Empire and defence. With these issues clarified, they could then offer to 'consider any machinery by which unity of Ireland should be reorganised' – a cryptic formulation which undoubtedly referred to a boundary commission.[53]

Before the meeting broke up, Chamberlain pushed the Prime

Minister to see James Craig, forcing Birkenhead to cut across him with a more realistic suggestion: 'Don't send for Craig,' he advised Lloyd George; 'see Carson' instead.[54] At 4 p.m. the following day, the Prime Minister duly touted the prospect of an all-Ireland parliament to the former leader of Ulster's unionists, who, in the words of one biographer, had been left 'isolated and impotent' by his elevation to the House of Lords the previous spring. The meeting proved fruitless and so Lloyd George tried again, this time at a dinner on Thursday 27 October, hours after his display of brinkmanship in the House of Commons. But as Stevenson noted in her diary, Carson was 'quite obdurate' and insisted that he could 'not possibly give in on Ulster'.[55]

With this early and unsurprising confirmation that Ulster's unionists were not prepared to cede an inch on the Government of Ireland Act of 1920, and with the clock now ticking on his premiership – a defeat on a vote of censure meant an instant fall from office – Lloyd George made sure to eliminate any lingering threats closer to home. At a lunch held at the end of the week with Churchill and Birkenhead, the Prime Minister solidified the bonds of allegiance with his main rivals by impressing on both that 'if he went out', then Bonar Law, who had always disliked and distrusted Churchill, would 'come in' – a move that would spell disaster for their own aspirations to the leadership. A reactionary Conservative administration was unlikely – even if Churchill switched political parties and returned to the Tory fold – to embrace two former ministers so closely associated with the Irish negotiations. In her diary, Stevenson recorded that this seemed to have done the trick, 'for they will not desert [Lloyd George] in order to put B. Law in'.[56] Of the two, it was Birkenhead who posed the bigger threat. The media baron Lord Beaverbrook claimed the Lord Chancellor was a 'formidable obstacle' because of his capacity to rouse 'the great bulk of the Tory Party against a projected settlement by a single speech'.[57]

While Bonar Law, beloved by the diehards, remained the more daunting prospect, Lloyd George calculated that he could be 'left to last because he was the hardest task'.[58] Since returning home from France, the former Conservative leader had kept an aloof presence in parliament, and yet still the Prime Minister squirmed in discomfort, conscious that his old friend's keen gaze now fell on him in intensified form as the negotiations threatened to recast Ulster's future. A recent meeting with Bonar Law had confirmed his worst fears. He was 'reasonable and moderate up to a point', Lloyd George confided to C.P. Scott, 'Then suddenly you touched something and he blazed up. At heart he was an Orangeman and the Orange fanaticism was there', and if he believed Ulster was under attack, he might at any time 'lead a Tory revolt'.[59]

Hemmed in increasingly by his Unionist flank, the Prime Minister began tightening the screw on Sinn Féin. On the morning of Thursday 27 October, as the Irish delegation recovered from a long night at the Royal Albert Hall, a memorandum from their British counterparts arrived at Hans Place. It embodied the strategy Lloyd George had suggested earlier that week. The Sinn Féin delegates were asked to declare, once and for all, whether or not they were prepared to accept Dominion status, in addition to the government's other demands on defence, trade and finance. With Ulster carefully sidestepped, the British presented the Irish with an ultimatum, insisting that if the conference were to proceed, they must have 'a definite understanding upon these vital questions'.[60]

To prevent such a full-frontal assault from backfiring, Tom Jones urged the Irish not to draft a reply before Collins and Griffith had met in private with the Prime Minister and

Birkenhead later that evening. No record exists of this hour-and-a-half discussion in the Lord Chancellor's office in the House of Lords, except for Griffith's letter to de Valera, which gives the 'gist' of the conversation in two sentences. Writing immediately afterwards and 'in great haste', Griffith told the President that 'if we ... accept the Crown they would send for Craig, i.e. – force "Ulster" in', as he 'understood' it. In response, they gave the standard line: 'We told them we had no power to do so. We might recommend some form of association if all other matters were satisfactory – above all Ireland unified.' Whatever transpired at that meeting, Griffith's letter to de Valera betrays a profound misunderstanding of the British position, or worse, a dangerous naivety, for there could be no forcing Ulster 'in' to anything, as Lloyd George had made clear to Sinn Féin on innumerable occasions.[61]

At some point during that day, possibly after the meeting at the House of Lords, the Prime Minister implored C.P. Scott to visit him at Chequers the next day as a matter of urgency. Meanwhile, Collins, Griffith and Duggan seized the opportunity for a night out at the theatre – Griffith had a particular fondness for *The Beggar's Opera*, an eighteenth-century ballad opera that mixed Rabelaisian humour with political satire. While they were gone, Childers received a telephone call from Cope, who asked to see Duggan or Barton straight away. As Childers recounts in his diary, everybody was out 'after dinner', so he went instead. At this curious nocturnal encounter 'near the Grosvenor Hotel', he learned that Lloyd George regarded the memo as 'too strong' but had sent it in an effort to placate 'the Tories'. Cope urged Childers to see Jones in the morning.[62]

The next day, in his office at Whitehall, the deputy secretary to the Cabinet duly offered a candid confession: the memo was not to be taken at face value, it was designed to keep Lloyd

George's Conservative adversaries off his back, because they were threatening 'to resign ... their tactics being [to] force a break on the Crown, Navy etc. and so safeguard Ulster'. This compelling news sent Childers hurrying back to Hans Place. A two-hour meeting ensued, and then another, for three hours, as the argument over how to respond to the British demands raged on. Finally, a draft response was hammered out by Childers and John Chartres, who laboured late into the night while 'All others', the former noted incredulously in his diary, disappeared 'to [the] theatre!'[63]

It was the conferences at Hans Place on Friday 28 October that caused Collins to run hours late for his above-mentioned appointment with C.P. Scott. Waspishly, the editor observed that 'precision' was 'not yet an Irish virtue',[64] though had he known the republican leader better, he would have been more understanding, for 'punctuality', as de Valera never failed to remind people over the ensuing decades, ranked as one of Collins' finest qualities – that and 'his amazing efficiency'.[65] At Chequers, Lloyd George had briefed Scott that Childers was 'the villain of the piece, always seeking to counter-work every approach to concession'.[66] But the following morning, as he listened to the details of the Collins meeting, the Prime Minister flared up again, denouncing the Irish leader as 'an uneducated rather stupid man'. Still, 'he liked him ... and if he had him and Griffith alone to deal with could settle in five minutes'.[67]

At 2.45 p.m. on Saturday 29 October, a day later than anticipated, the Irish provided an official response to the British memo. By 4 p.m., Cope was on the phone to Hans Place, summoning Duggan to an urgent meeting with Jones. The document 'was most unsatisfactory' and so hedged round with qualifications that Chamberlain had no idea what it meant. In fact, he had assumed, as Jones informed Duggan, that 'we were being fooled'.[68] The Irish reply had indeed been left as ambiguous as possible. Although it represented a slight advance on Sinn Féin's position, with some concessions on defence, the case for External Association was simply restated in a more convoluted manner. There was to be a 'Treaty of Association' with the 'Nations of the British Commonwealth' and the Crown would be recognised 'as symbol and accepted head of the combination of signatory states', but only if Ireland secured 'unimpaired unity' and the 'unfettered possession of all legislative and executive authority'.[69] Lloyd George's reaction was one of mingled excitement and relief, according to C.P. Scott, who was with the Prime Minister at Chequers when Jones read out the memo to him over the telephone. While 'not enough', it was 'better than he had feared'.[70] Yet if he had not already intended to exact more concessions from the Irish ahead of Monday's crunch vote, Chamberlain's attitude left him with little choice.

Back at Whitehall, Jones applied maximum pressure. Would 'it not be possible', he insisted, for Griffith to send 'a private letter to the P.M.' stating 'frankly that the official Reply did in fact mean acknowledgement of allegiance, common citizenship and Imperial Defence?' Then the Prime Minister could 'face [the diehards] with ... confidence'. Since the Sinn Féin delegates were wary of committing anything to writing, as Jones was all too aware, an uncomfortable Duggan instead suggested a private meeting between the Prime Minister and Griffith, 'with or without Collins'.[71]

At 7 p.m. on Sunday 30 October, Cope phoned through to Hans Place with details of the plan. Lloyd George and Birkenhead were dining that evening at Churchill's house near Hyde Park, and Griffith and Collins were asked to join them at 10 p.m. But there was a problem. Collins and Griffith distrusted

Churchill, seeing in him the worst of British militarism – an opinion shared by a large number of the future prime minister's colleagues, who continued to doubt his judgement right up until 1940. At this stage, there was not much warmth either for Birkenhead. So, before Lloyd George sat down to dinner at Churchill's, Jones telephoned and, in Welsh, warned him to speak to 'Griffith alone'.[72]

Most likely, the last-minute advice confirmed the Prime Minister's own instincts. He knew by now, thanks to C.P. Scott's intervention, that Collins remained unsympathetic to the British point of view, a realisation that coloured his perception of the IRA leader. Earlier in the day, over lunch at Chequers, he had confided to Riddell that he had changed his mind about Griffith, whom he now thought of as a 'pretty considerable man'; Collins, on the other hand, seemed 'quite a different sort of person – one with a simple sort of mind such as is often found in a great military commander'.[73]

Griffith reported to de Valera the next day that they had arrived at 9.30 p.m. and were greeted by Churchill in the hall, who asked if one or both would speak to Lloyd George in private first. 'After consultation with Mick, it was decided that I alone should see Ll. G.,' he wrote, and so, as Collins was ushered into the company of Churchill and Birkenhead, Griffith embarked on a forty-five-minute tête-à-tête with the Prime Minister.[74] No record of this discussion exists, other than what Griffith summarised in his letter to de Valera. But the conversation restored Lloyd George's spirits, and by the time Geoffrey Shakespeare collected him at 11.30 p.m., he was in a buoyant mood. 'The interview had been ... most satisfactory,' he declared, as they drove off, and it would now be 'necessary for him to recast his House of Commons speech'.[75]

6 · CASTING AND GATHERING
31 October–9 November

The lights were still blazing in Hans Place by the time Collins and Griffith returned at 11 p.m. Childers, always willing to work late into the night, sprang up to meet them, and with characteristic thoroughness insisted, there and then, on drawing up a memo of the 'Meeting at Winston Churchill's house'.[1] Alert to the growing suspicion, Griffith provided a more detailed account of the conversation in a letter to de Valera the following morning. The Prime Minister was frustrated, he explained, that on the eve of the House of Commons debate he remained unclear as to where the Irish stood on 'vital matters'. In language soon to be heavily scrutinised, Griffith reported that Lloyd George had asked for 'personal assurances' from him on the Crown, a 'free partnership' with the Empire, and continued access to Ireland's naval facilities, so he could 'smite the Die-hards' and 'fight ... to secure essential unity'.[2] Childers had captured the reply in his memo: Griffith had yielded, promising to 'recommend a recognition of the Crown', as long as 'we were satisfied on the other points at issue'.[3]

While this offer provided the Prime Minister with much-needed proof that a settlement with Sinn Féin was possible, it scarcely released him from his dilemma, for he could no more insist on Ireland's 'essential unity' than remain in power without the support of the Conservative Party. Throughout the negotiations, the perpetual threat of a revolt from this quarter circumscribed his every move. If he tried to force Ulster out of the United Kingdom and under the authority of a Dublin-based, all-Ireland parliament, he knew Bonar Law would go into battle against him. The former Tory leader's partially restored health had transformed the political dynamic, and his presence on the sidelines grew more menacing by the day. The diehards lacked the numbers to impose their will on the government, but Bonar Law, with his influence and popularity over the party, had the potential to turn a small-scale dissident protest into a fully fledged Tory rebellion.

Chamberlain, a weak and untested leader, had little room to manoeuvre. Like Lloyd George, he was in a delicate position. Embedded in the British government's 20 July proposals was the stipulation that any settlement 'must allow for full recognition of the existing powers and privileges of the Government of Northern Ireland which cannot be abrogated except by their own consent'.[4] This had been the price of Conservative support for the Treaty talks, and it left Craig and his colleagues with the assumption that, on Ulster, Lloyd George's hands were tied.

Chamberlain recognised the limitations of such lopsided diplomacy but remained trapped within its confines. Uncertain as to how far he could push the Conservative Party, and with no proof that it would abandon its usual radical stance on Ulster, he cleaved to a policy that jeopardised rather than enhanced the unity of the British Empire. In the pre-war era, Ulster unionism's militant opposition to Home Rule had been seen by the Tories as a source of strength – an essential defence against the fragmentation of the imperial heartland. In the autumn of 1921, however, those old loyalties looked more of a liability; an awkward impediment to an Anglo-Irish reconciliation based upon a united Ireland within the Empire.

Unable to plot a way out, Chamberlain lamented to his wife: 'F.E. [Birkenhead] and I are so pledged that we could not honourably alter the Ulster boundaries ... or powers without Craig's consent.' But he had no intention of defending partition to the death, since the 'six counties' were 'a compromise and like all compromises [it was] illogical and indefensible, and you could not raise an army in England to fight for that as we could for crown and empire. We should therefore be obliged to resign if [Lloyd George] proposed to force Ulster into a sacrifice.'[5]

Faced with a seemingly insurmountable problem, the Prime Minister went back to the drawing board. All options were on the table, even a potential reconciliation with Asquith's Wee Frees, as the Independent Liberals were known. In the weeks leading up to the showdown with the diehards, Lloyd George contemplated calling a snap election in order to run on an anti-Ulster ticket. That would have been one way of reviving his battered Liberal credentials, but equally he may have conceived of it as a means of blackmailing the Conservatives, since the Left disliked partition and an election waged on that front would likely leave the Tories divided and stripped of their considerable majority in the House of Commons. It is impossible to determine how seriously the Prime Minister weighed this strategy, which would have destroyed his long-cherished plans for a permanent Centre Party.[6] In any case, the economic conditions were not auspicious, and he soon dismissed the idea, telling Donald Maclean, chairman of the Independent Liberals, that it would be 'foolish to do so ... unemployment being as rampant as it was'.[7] Besides, his conversation with Griffith confirmed that if he could bridge the divide between Sinn Féin's demands for 'essential unity' and Ulster's insistence on a separate, six-county region linked to Westminster, he could persuade the Irish to remain within the Commonwealth, meaning the Crown's supremacy would be secured, and with it, the integrity of the Empire.

Lloyd George shed little light on how he planned to accomplish this feat. At Churchill's residence he appears to have made a glancing reference to three possible solutions, two of which he instantly cast doubt upon according to Griffith: 'Mr Lloyd George said that he could carry a six-county Parliament subordinate to a national Parliament. Alternatively he said he would try to carry a plan for a new boundary or a vote on the inclusion or exclusion of the whole of Ulster as a unit, but he was not hopeful of doing so.'[8]

Yet in many ways the more significant development that evening was the drastic warming in relations between the chief negotiators. The historian Margery Forester described it as a turning point, the moment at which Collins saw Churchill and Birkenhead as 'men rather than statesmen'.[9] And while his sentiments towards the former never fell into the realm of friendship, they famously did with Birkenhead. To those who witnessed this putative friendship at close quarters, the bond between the two appeared irrefutable. The artist John Lavery, who was a friend of Churchill's, and who painted all the Irish delegates' portraits, recalled how 'Many a morning before the Downing Street meetings Collins would be seen hurrying to meet Birkenhead', and marvelled at how the IRA leader and the Lord Chancellor 'took to one another'.[10] Later, the unlikely alliance came under suspicion; Collins, it was widely assumed, had been 'ruthlessly exploited' by the unscrupulous Birkenhead.[11] Others saw a relationship of convenience between two realists,[12] while in one altogether more misty-eyed account, it was a case of a 'fresh young man without finesse' in thrall to 'one [to] whom the ways of the world were well-tried indeed'.[13] And if the distinctions between the two were obvious, so too were the similarities. Pakenham noted that among the British and Irish delegates Birkenhead's 'Herculean physique' dwarfed all but Collins, and the ability to rapidly master complex information was recognised as a defining attribute of both.[14]

But perhaps, above all, their friendship developed out of a shared sense of humour; the robust kind that went far in Whitehall's 'irrefragably male' culture, as one historian characterised it, noting that 'the ideal of fraternity among men was fundamental to the way everything worked'.[15] Both Collins and Birkenhead saw politics as an emphatically male sphere. Neither promoted the participation of women in public life. The latter thought the Cabinet 'went mad' when it extended the vote to women above the age of twenty-one in 1927, while Collins is said to have looked upon 'female activists as the servant class of the revolution', seeing them less as 'colleagues or comrades' than as 'landladies, maids or cooks'.[16]

Along with a flair for bawdy humour, they were both prodigious imbibers – as was Churchill, of course. But it seems doubtful, despite the accusations slung at him later in the Dáil, that alcohol played a significant role in this much-advertised friendship. For a start, the Lord Chancellor, who eventually drank himself to death, embraced a vow of abstinence that year, encouraged by a £1,000 bet from Beaverbrook. In February 1921 Churchill noticed that self-restraint – at least when it came to hard liquor, the vow did not apply to wine, beer or cider – had produced a remarkable transformation in his friend: he looked 'ten years younger', and appeared 'vy [very] fierce and calm – a formidable figure'.[17] While Birkenhead's wit and mental agility could inspire awe even when he was hopelessly drunk, carousing, it seems safe to assume, rarely featured in this friendship. On the contrary, what captivated Collins was the quicksilver intellect. In private, undated notes from the conference, he wrote of the Lord Chancellor: 'If all the British delegation had his capacity for clear thinking, capacity for work and getting ahead, things would be much easier. Lawyer, but with a great difference. Concise. Clearness of ideas a great advantage. Refuses to be drowned by the might of others. A good man.'[18]

After the evening at Churchill's residence, it was not only Collins who recalibrated his perception of the British delegates, Griffith did too. In a letter to de Valera the following day, Monday 31 October, he related how, at the end of the night, Birkenhead, Churchill and Lloyd George showed a new sympathy towards the Irish position: 'They indicated that if they were certain of real goodwill on our side, they would take risks and fight. We parted on the understanding that they would go strongly against the Die-hard attack and go strongly for peace with Ireland in tonight's debate.'[19]

Not that the outcome of the vote in the House of Commons was ever in doubt. The opposition, as anticipated, declared support for the government, rendering the debate less a test of strength than a high-risk display of political showmanship. For as Lloyd George knew only too well, Westminster's gladiatorial encounters always brought with them unexpected eventualities; a misstep might prove fatal, particularly in the context of the coalition's crumbling support from the right wing of the Conservative Party. If he was to carry the country, and it was this wider appeal to the public that partly explains his compulsion to call the diehards' bluff, he needed to consolidate his support on both sides of the House and explain why it was necessary to negotiate with men once classed as murderers. In other words, he could not afford to lose the moral weight of the debate.

Victory on this front was all the more important because of the growing disenchantment at Lloyd George's leadership among the Conservative grass roots. For the moment, most MPs were unwilling to break cover, and few thought the diehard campaign worthy of their support, as the Duke of Northumberland had discovered at a regional Tory Party gathering in Newcastle two days earlier. He summoned the meeting in order to announce his long-expected secession from the coalition, hoping that this would trigger a wider stampede. But instead of stirring up a rebellion among northern MPs, his familiar refrain about the 'sinister forces' at work within the British Empire and the government's 'surrender' to Sinn Féin, merely confirmed him as an ossified outcrop of 'old-fashioned Toryism'.[20]

The diehards sustained another blow when it transpired, moments before the debate, that the Ulster Unionists intended to sit on the sidelines rather than align themselves with their loyalist colleagues. Their silence came at a price: the transfer of services – or the powers of local autonomy – to Northern Ireland's parliament. Under the Government of Ireland Act 1920, Home Rule was to be rolled out simultaneously on both sides of the border. And if the South proved recalcitrant, then the north-east would still gain limited autonomy, even as the rest of the island fell under Crown Colony rule. But the Truce threw all this into abeyance, leaving partition and political mastery of the six counties up in the air. Moments after he approached the dispatch box, Lloyd George pledged to 'put this right', asserting that it was 'unfair to set up a Parliament and deprive it of the only powers that enable it to work creditably'. Paralysing 'the necessary activities of the Ulster Government', he said, gave an 'unfair advantage to its enemies'.[21]

Hours earlier Lloyd George had reassured Griffith that he would go all out for Ireland's 'essential unity'. Now, in front of a packed chamber, and with the galleries overhead overflowing, so that 'many visitors', according to the *Daily Express*, were left with standing room only, he promised to finalise partition.[22] Little wonder the diehard offensive faded into a 'faint-hearted attack', as *The Manchester Guardian* crowed the following day. *The Times* judged it 'one of his greatest efforts', arguing the Prime Minister turned an inevitable parliamentary victory into a political triumph.[23]

Yet the diehard attacks were not entirely futile. The greatest moment of tension came as Lloyd George explained to the House that Sinn Féin was the one party to speak 'in the name of the Irish people'. Gwynne heckled him, accusing him of breaking his promise not to negotiate with the 'murder gang'. When Lloyd George denied the allegation, Gwynne leapt to his feet and, to shouts of 'order' and 'this debate is not over', he read out one of the Prime Minister's previous speeches, in which he had stated that 'there are certain individuals who are implicated in the commission of crime so serious that the Government cannot consent to abandon their intention to bring them to trial'. Lloyd George answered that those men had been convicted of murder. A voice shouted 'Michael Collins!' The Prime Minister replied, 'He has not been convicted', and, after expressing his dislike of the repeated interruptions, he resumed his speech.[24]

The moment of peril had passed and Lloyd George was once more in command of his audience, quickening pulses with a promise that an Irish refusal to accept Dominion status would be met with war. Having played upon entrenched prejudices, he just as quickly subverted them to his own ends. Lingering at length on the grisly realities of guerrilla warfare, he warned there would be 'unpleasant incidences', the enemy would have to be 'hunted over considerable tracts of territory', 'gigantic forces' would be required, and the terrain would be 'difficult', the population hostile. Nevertheless, he continued, 'If it has to be done, and the people of this country are convinced it must be done, it can be done and will be done.' After all, he said, his voice trembling with emotion, Britain had 'raised six or seven millions of men to fight for the liberties of Europe and is still quite equal to defending its own safety and maintaining its own honour'. The House roared its applause, and the Prime Minister finished by imploring parliament to trust its negotiators, so that they could strengthen 'this great Empire' and finally resolve 'a peril' that has always beset Britain 'in the hour of its deepest perplexity'.[25]

The result was a thumping victory, with the proposed vote of censure defeated by 439 to 43. Yet for all the acclamation from the press for his 'bravura' performance, the debate had highlighted the Prime Minister's limited room for manoeuvre. The Conservative Party, always the greatest obstacle to any resolution of the Irish question in the pre-war years, was willing to stomach negotiations with Sinn Féin, but that acquiescence came at a price. As *The Morning Post* sneered the next day, Lloyd George had been forced to 'buy off the Ulster vote', and had little choice other than 'to reaffirm his pledge not to betray Ulster'.[26]

More worryingly, there were signs of widening discontent at Chamberlain's leadership. The *Daily Express* noted that 'A pin drop might have been heard'[27] when he rose to speak, and this absence of backbench support spurred on the rebels, who heckled him constantly while he was on his feet. The next day, one Tory MP – not a diehard member – wrote in his diary that while the government had secured an 'enormous' majority, he thought Lloyd George 'not very convincing'. On the other hand, the 'faint hint' in his speech that he might resign rather 'than conduct a war with Ireland ... would create a very awkward situation'. But he took heart at the coalition's dwindling popularity, for while Chamberlain was 'losing ground', Bonar Law 'was back and well again': all in all, therefore, the chances of a 'pure Conservative government [were] getting stronger'.[28]

Immediately after the debate, the British delegates decided to step up the pressure on Collins and Griffith. The commitments entered into on Sunday evening were put to the test. At a meeting at Downing Street the next morning, Tuesday 1 November, Griffith was reminded of his obligation to provide personal assurances, in writing, on the questions of the Crown, the Empire and the ports. Although no records of this discussion between the chief Sinn Féin delegates and Lloyd George, Birkenhead and Chamberlain exist, Collins came away unhappy at what he perceived as a sudden shift in the British attitude. Later that day, when cornered by Jones, he admitted to feeling 'rather disappointed and flat' after the meeting and thought it 'very much more difficult than ... anticipated in view of what had taken place on Sunday night'.[29] But the British delegates, energised by their landslide victory in the House of Commons, were impatient and determined to capitalise on their gains, not least because fresh challenges loomed. Craig was due in London that weekend, while the annual Conservative conference (known then as the annual meeting of the National Union of Conservative and Unionist Associations) was scheduled for 17 November and looked certain to be overshadowed by another diehard revolt over Ireland. Jones, ever ready with his collusive charm, reassured Collins that unless a 'reasonable compromise was reached on Ulster ... the [Prime Minister] would resign rather than start a war of reconquest'.[30]

This appears to have assuaged Griffith's concerns, too. Confident that Lloyd George meant to uphold his pledge on Ireland's 'essential unity', he saw no reason to renege on his side of the bargain. That evening, at a meeting of the Irish delegates at Hans Place, he circulated a draft of the 'personal' letter he intended to send to the Prime Minister, emphasising that it should bear his signature only, so that he could 'shield' Collins' reputation if it ever became public. He explained that Lloyd George needed 'documentary evidence' of the conversation at Churchill's if he was to fend off Craig and avert a more bruising encounter with the diehards at the forthcoming Tory Party conference. But the accumulated grievances amongst Gavan Duffy, Barton and Childers had reached a tipping point. Convinced that Griffith was backsliding on an agreed negotiating position, all three 'strenuously opposed the sending of a personal letter', as Barton recorded in his post-dated notes on the conference, which were to provide crucial source material for Pakenham's 1930s' account of the Treaty talks.[31]

A row ensued, and Barton recalled that 'Griffith … made use of some very abusive language to [Gavan] Duffy'.[32] In the rancid atmosphere, old loyalties were dissolving, personal resentments and animosities became indistinguishable from diverging political perspectives, and, under the pressure of these conflicting perceptions, the delegation began to reform itself into two distinct groups. The reaction to Griffith's letter bears this out, for he gave nothing away. There was no capitulation. The promises to recommend 'recognition of the Crown' and a 'free partnership with the British Commonwealth' were diluted by statements deferring the precise definition of these relationships to a 'discussion at a later stage'. Above all, any adjustments on the Irish side were tied to a corresponding shift in the British position. As Griffith specified: 'on no account would I recommend any association with the Crown or the Empire, if the unity of Ireland were denied in word or in fact'. Nevertheless, Gavan Duffy, Barton and Childers 'objected vehemently to [the letter's] tone' and the meeting ended in a stand-off.[33]

Matters did not improve the following morning. At breakfast, Childers sidled up to Griffith and demanded to know when he wanted to have 'a meeting of delegates? He said, "What meeting? No meeting is required"', forcing Childers to whisper back, since 'others were present', that the 'delegates wished to make suggestions'.[34] In his diary, Childers noted that Griffith was 'much put out but consented to come to my room', where Gavan Duffy then read out to him a long letter of protest accusing the Sinn Féin founder of undermining 'the stand we have taken'. Barton recorded that he 'rose early' to compose this document, which delivered a turgid criticism of Griffith's negotiating tactics. In the dispute that followed, the letter to the Prime Minister was redrafted again and again, until eventually the text resembled the delegation's memorandum of 29 October, prompting Barton to conclude that 'our party won its points'.[35]

The sense of triumph soon faded. Within hours Collins and Griffith reversed course again, this time under pressure from the British. After handing the letter in to Birkenhead at the House of Lords, they were persuaded to reconvene that evening at 10 Downing Street. At this second gathering, attended by Lloyd George and the Lord Chancellor – Chamberlain joined partway through – the document underwent another exhaustive editing process and emerged out the other side with commitments that more closely approximated British expectations. Throughout this hour and a half session, Childers was confined to the hallway outside the Cabinet room. From his diary it appears that the time passed swiftly, with Jones and Edward Grigg, the Prime Minister's private secretary, there to engage him in a debate about the constitutional intricacies of Dominion status.

Afterwards, at Hans Place, the evolving power struggle within the Irish delegation temporarily subsided into an uneasy truce. Although Childers complained about the climbdown on defence, which afforded the British unimpeded access to Ireland's naval facilities, his was a lone voice. In his diary, he wrote: 'I protested at length but in vain. No-one supported me.' This isolation reflected an implicit understanding among the rest of the delegation that, for the foreseeable future at least, an independent Ireland would lean on Britain for the defence of the surrounding seas. Entrenched economic ties rendered this outlook a strategic necessity, since it would be an act of self-harm for a new Irish state to court military assistance from her neighbour's potential enemies.[36] From the outset, then, security issues were looked upon as a bargaining chip, to be exchanged in return for more important concessions. Far from 'weakening' on defence, as Childers put it, the Irish bowed to necessity; the question is, did they do so too early?

At 11 p.m. the debate was over and the Irish finally returned the much-edited document to Birkenhead, who was at his palatial Grosvenor Gardens residence dining with the Prime Minister. According to Barton, he and Gavan Duffy had 'very reluctantly' signed off on the British amendments, appalled at what they saw as an incipient slide towards Dominion status. But in his letter to de Valera the next morning, Griffith stressed that the 'wording' on the Crown and the Empire were 'consistent with external association and external recognition'. This does not quite cover it. There were in fact two changes that weakened the Irish position, although when de Valera received the latest version, he raised no word of protest. The first of the significant changes altered Ireland's 'free partnership with the

British Commonwealth' to 'within the British Commonwealth' – so clearly not External Association – while the second removed the iron-clad caveat on Ulster, which revoked all cooperation if 'unity were denied in form or fact'. Instead, Sinn Féin's compliance on other 'vital' matters now turned on the less specific and far vaguer demand for the 'recognition of the essential unity of Ireland'. This, as emphasised earlier, meant that an Irish administration would have legal sovereignty over the island of Ireland, but how this would be achieved was not thrashed out in any detail, allowing Lloyd George plenty of scope for opt-out clauses and other mechanisms that would ostensibly provide for Ireland's unity.[37]

Birkenhead was effusive in his gratitude. The following morning, at a meeting in the House of Lords, he told Collins and Griffith that the letter was '"hugely appreciated" as a weapon against Craig', adding that 'they would resign rather than make war if Ulster refused'.[38] On that same day, Thursday 3 November, Griffith gloried in the end of an era. England would no longer tolerate, he predicted in a letter to de Valera, the subjugation of Ireland by force. If the coalition fell, 'no English government is capable on a war policy against Ireland', validating, he implied, his long-conceived plan of pitting 'the question of Ulster against the questions of Association and the Crown'. He went on to tell of Craig's imminent arrival, writing that he had been summoned to Downing Street and was due in London on Saturday. For the moment, therefore, they were 'standing aside'. Finally, he urged de Valera to maintain the strictest confidence, because the British were 'anxious that their proposed way of dealing with obdurate Ulster should be kept … quite secret'.[39]

It was at about this time that Kevin O'Higgins, still a relatively minor figure in the republican movement, arrived in

London with his new bride. Although he played second fiddle to W.T. Cosgrave in the Department of Local Government, de Valera routinely brought him into the Dáil Cabinet meetings, and he attended his wedding on 27 October. A famous photograph of that day shows O'Higgins, as tall as de Valera, standing between the President and his best man, the diminutive republican hero Rory O'Connor. The image has become emblematic of the murderous divisions that blighted the separatist movement in the wake of the Treaty, for it was O'Higgins, Ireland's first minister for justice, who oversaw the execution of his erstwhile friend a little more than a year later. O'Connor and three other prominent republicans had been in custody for months before they were shot by the state in retaliation for the IRA's assassination of a pro-Treaty politician. Propelled into power by the deaths of Collins and Griffith, and convinced that the militarist opposition from the anti-Treatyites signalled a wider 'disintegration of the social fabric', O'Higgins championed a policy of ruthless suppression, believing that only overwhelming state force would crush the 'Irregulars', as the IRA faithful were termed.[40] The brutal measures blackened the Cosgrave government's reputation and established O'Higgins as the republicans' bête noire. Eventually, old adversaries decided to settle the score and, one summer's morning in 1927, O'Higgins was gunned down in Booterstown, County Dublin, not far from his home and on his way to midday mass.[41]

O'Higgins, like many of the revolutionary elite, came from a privileged middle-class background. In common with O'Connor, he was a pupil at Clongowes Wood, the exclusive Jesuit boarding school in County Kildare, and both later attended University College Dublin. While generally depicted as a reactionary, even a closet imperialist,[42] the historian Charles Townshend has more convincingly cast him as a pragmatist; a 'dedicated Sinn Feiner of the Griffith stamp', who believed the governance of independent Ireland should fall to 'responsible, professional people – like himself.'[43] Certainly, in early November 1921, when he arrived in London for a three-week honeymoon, few doubted his republican convictions. De Valera, above all, thought him a reliable ally, who, like Cosgrave, would provide support in the Cabinet for his policy of External Association.

It is impossible to determine to what extent, if at all, O'Higgins' trip to London altered his thinking. But according to his first biographer, who was writing in the late 1940s, O'Higgins was shocked at the mood within the Sinn Féin camp and 'became increasingly depressed by the deterioration in the relations between the delegates'. Childers wore the blame for these fracturing ties; his 'precise manner and air of aloofness gave an impression of conscious superiority'. He was also 'frail and coughed continually', and O'Higgins, a doctor's son, 'mistrusted the judgement of sick men'. Then there was Childers' discomfiting habit of writing memos late into the night, stoking fears among Collins and Griffith that he was relaying critical reports back to Dublin. For these reasons, O'Higgins thought Childers' presence in London was a mistake.[44]

By this stage, there was no doubt that the atmosphere within the delegation had turned toxic: resentments and mutual suspicions ran rife, and that evening, 3 November, Gavan Duffy, Barton and Childers weighed up whether to bypass their colleagues and appeal directly to de Valera over what they saw as a weakening of the Irish negotiating position. It would mean 'one of them going to Dublin', as Childers wrote in his diary, along with Collins, 'who goes tomorrow anyway'.[45] In the end, the role fell to Gavan Duffy.

Meanwhile, in the House of Commons, the diehards struck back at Lloyd George. Still smarting from the drubbing meted out to them in Monday's showdown, they rallied quickly and produced a more effective assault over the departure of Sir Basil Thomson, the egotistical, right-wing director of special intelligence. News of his exit had emerged earlier in the week, but the diehards knew Thomson had not gone willingly, and what infuriated them beyond measure was not only the realisation that they had lost one of their own – Thomson was regarded as a defender of Ulster – but that his prospective replacement was a Sinn Féin 'sympathiser'. Or at least that was the accusation hurled on the floor of the House by Admiral Hall, who earned his nickname 'Blinker' from the nervous tic he suffered in one eye.

The target of this outrage was the Liberal Home Secretary, Edward Shortt, and such was the ferocity of the diehard attack that *The Manchester Guardian* likened it to a 'tornado' breaking over the 'astonished' Minister's head, while *The Times* declared that for 'a few minutes there was pandemonium.'[46] Shortt, somewhat stunned, returned to parliament that evening to declare that the candidate for Thomson's job, General Sir Joseph Byrne, a former chief of the Royal Irish Constabulary, had turned down the post. The diehards were jubilant. At last, they had drawn blood. General Byrne had been in their cross hairs for years, ever since he dared to warn the former Irish Viceroy, Lord French, and the former Chief Secretary for Ireland, Ian Macpherson, of the dangers of proscribing an entire political movement. It was an indiscretion that cost him his job. Hounded out as a coward in December 1919, Byrne never regained his standing with the Anglo-Irish establishment, which held him in contempt for a perceived loss of nerve and for falling into sympathy with the rebels.[47]

But what was most remarkable about the Thomson episode was Lloyd George's willingness to parachute the vilified Byrne into a role of such strategic national importance, even as the Irish talks teetered on a knife-edge. As demonstrated by the historian Eunan O'Halpin, this was the work of the influential civil servant Sir Warren Fisher, who in the late 1930s played a key role in Britain's policy of appeasement towards Ireland.[48] On this occasion, however, the approach backfired, and Chamberlain brought the brawl to an end by forcing the diehard motion to a division, on the grounds that any government's 'administration of law and order' must have the confidence of parliament. The Tory rebels lost the vote again – 146 to 43 – but the narrower majority for the coalition showed that while an overwhelming number of Conservatives wanted a settlement on Ireland, they were not prepared to give Lloyd George free rein.

Two days later, at midday on 5 November, Craig strode in to Downing Street for what was to be his first meeting with the Prime Minister since the talks began. He and his wife had arrived early that morning at Euston station, where waiting reporters were told his business in London was personal. No political engagements were envisaged, just outings with his sons who were at school at Eton.[49] Weeks later, during a rousing speech to Northern Ireland's parliament, Craig described what happened that day as 'Black Saturday ... for it will always stand out in my memory as one of the darkest days that I have had to deal with since I have been associated with the Ulster question'.[50] With his imposing frame and ruddy complexion, the Northern Ireland Premier had always invited caricature – either as the straight-talking Ulsterman or the bull-necked epitome of Unionist intransigence.[51] For once, however, he appeared to momentarily lose his footing. Despite his public insistence that the London trip was long planned, he knew a summons from Downing Street was imminent, and when it came, he barrelled in, determined to hold the Prime Minister to account on the transfer of services to Belfast, without which Northern Ireland's parliament would remain a lame duck.

Craig distrusted Lloyd George. In July, when he and de Valera were in London and spoke to the Prime Minister separately, he had been amazed, according to Beaverbrook's account, by de Valera's willingness to meet Lloyd George alone, remarking, 'Are you mad? Take a witness.'[52] Now, he braced for some last-minute chicanery, convinced the Prime Minister would use the lure of local autonomy to 'manoeuvre us into a different position'. But instead, all was cheerful compliance. 'His Majesty's ministers wholeheartedly and energetically set to work to see that we were met in our just demands,' he recalled.[53] When they reconvened for a second meeting later in the afternoon, relief turned to rage as Lloyd George laid bare plans for Ulster to join an all-Ireland parliament. Incandescent, Craig insisted that 'such a thing was utterly impossible', and when he recounted this tale of defiance to a crowded sitting of the Northern Ireland parliament at the end of November, the echo chamber that was the Belfast assembly resounded with thunderous applause.

The reality, however, was considerably more complex. As Frances Stevenson's diary makes clear, Craig had at first signalled his agreement to the terms he would later denounce as an egregious outrage. Observing that Lloyd George anticipated nothing but obduracy from the Northern Ireland Premier, she wrote: 'However he talked to Craig on and off all day and by the evening … had extorted from him considerable concessions, the most important being an all-Ireland parliament.'[54] The situation was reversed the following day, Monday 7 November, after Ulster loyalists in Whitehall and Westminster's upper echelons closed ranks, unwilling to countenance a capitulation on 'everything for which they [had] been fighting for thirty-five years', as Bonar Law put it a week later.[55]

Among Ulster's Unionists' doughtiest supporters was Sir Henry Wilson, Chief of the Imperial General Staff, whose relationship with Lloyd George had been on the slide for some time. It was now close to breaking point.[56] So when Craig and Wilfred Spender, secretary to the new Northern Cabinet, turned up to a meeting at the War Office with Wilson and Worthington-Evans, they could be certain of a warm reception. Spender, an architect of the Larne gun-running incident, was also the former commander of the Ulster Special Constabulary, a civil defence force established by Craig's government in 1920. Billed as a supplement to the RIC, which the province's unionists regarded as too heavily infiltrated by Catholics, it was essentially a reconstituted Ulster Volunteer Force (UVF). Once unleashed, the notoriously ill-disciplined 'B Specials' proved every bit as violent and brutal as the Black and Tans. By aggressively targeting Catholic 'suspects', they inflamed communal rivalries and stoked the fires of sectarianism. As far as nationalists were concerned, the Specials were the UVF in 'state uniforms'.[57] The British government had turned a deaf ear to warnings about the dangers of this situation from the most senior ranks of its Irish administration. In 1920, both General Macready and John Anderson described the decision to deploy the Specials as 'madness' and tantamount to arming 'one side and not the other in civil war'.[58]

No such concerns troubled Wilson or Worthington-Evans. At the Monday afternoon meeting at the War Office, which lasted from 3.30 p.m. to 5 p.m., they listened sympathetically to Craig and Spender's security concerns, and agreed that Northern Ireland's executive could use its new powers to employ both the Specials and the RIC. In other words, Spender's ad hoc constabulary was to be regularised.[59] An emboldened Craig dashed back to Downing Street to reject Lloyd George's all-Ireland parliament proposal.

Members of the First Dáil, taken on 21 January 1919. In the front row (left to right) are Laurence Ginnell, Michael Collins, Cathal Brugha, Arthur Griffith, Éamon de Valera, Count Plunkett, Eoin MacNeill, W.T. Cosgrave and Ernest Blythe. Kevin O'Higgins is in the third row back, on the far right. Brugha would prove an implacable opponent of the Treaty, while Cosgrave was the deciding factor in its acceptance by the cabinet of the Treaty terms. (Courtesy of De Luan / Alamy Stock Photo)

Arthur Griffith and Éamon de Valera at the Mansion House Peace Conference, 4 July 1921. (Courtesy of Pictorial Press Ltd / Alamy Stock Photo)

Irish delegates to the Treaty talks (left to right), Desmond Fitzgerald, George Gavan Duffy, John Chartes, Robert Barton, Erskine Childers, unknown, Arthur Griffith, Éamonn Duggan and Fionán Lynch. (Courtesy of Pictorial Press Ltd / Alamy Stock Photo)

A sketch of the Treaty talks in the cabinet room of No. 10 Downing Street. (Courtesy of De Luan / Alamy Stock Photo)

Michael Collins wearing his famous trilby hat. The previously elusive IRA leader was already established in the public imagination as the hero of the guerrilla war, and when the Sinn Féin delegation arrived in London in October 1921, he was by far the most well-known of the Irish negotiators. Despite the glare of publicity, he remained a romanticised figure, his glamour and mystique enhanced rather than weakened by the constant exposure. (Courtesy of Pictorial Press Ltd / Alamy Stock Photo)

PUNCH, OR THE LONDON CHARIVARI.—January 25, 1922.

THE COLOSSUS: A TALE OF TWO TUBS.

Mr. Lloyd George. "GENTLEMEN, THE IDEAL CONDITIONS ARE THOSE DESCRIBED IN THE HALLOWED WORDS OF THE POET:—

'Then none was for a Party;
Then all were for the State.'

(*Aside*) L'ÉTAT, C'EST MOI."

A 1922 *Punch* cartoon satirising the mismatch between Prime Minister David Lloyd George's perceived desire for untrammelled power and the inherent instability of his position. The man who led Britain to victory in the First World War no longer inspired awe, and was detested by a majority of the Tory rank-and-file, partly for what many saw as his presidential style of leadership. (Courtesy of World History Archive / Alamy Stock Photo)

Lloyd George, Lord Birkenhead and Winston Churchill, three of the so-called 'Big Four' from the British delegation at the Treaty talks. (Courtesy of Fremantle / Alamy Stock Photo)

Austen Chamberlain (in the top hat), the fourth member of the 'Big Four', with Chancellor of the Exchequer Robert Horne, who had to be kept on side by Lloyd George if the Treaty was to be a success. (Courtesy of Fremantle / Alamy Stock Photo)

Sir Laming Worthington-Evans (left) and Attorney General Gordon Hewart, two of the less prominent members of the seven-man British delegation at the Treaty talks. (Courtesy of Alpha Stock / Alamy Stock Photo (Worthington-Evans) and Archive PL / Alamy Stock Photo (Hewart))

The final member of the British delegation was Sir Hamar Greenwood (second left), the hated Chief Secretary for Ireland, seen here with his wife (left), Lady Carson and Sir James Craig, leader of the Ulster Unionists, who staunchly opposed any suggestion of the six counties joining an all-Ireland government. (Courtesy of Smith Archive / Alamy Stock Photo)

Andrew Bonar Law, the former Conservative leader, was a constant source of anxiety for Lloyd George throughout the Treaty talks, and at the end of 1922 succeeded him as Prime Minister. (Courtesy of Alamy Stock Photo)

The signed copy of the Treaty. (Courtesy of De Luan / Alamy Stock Photo)

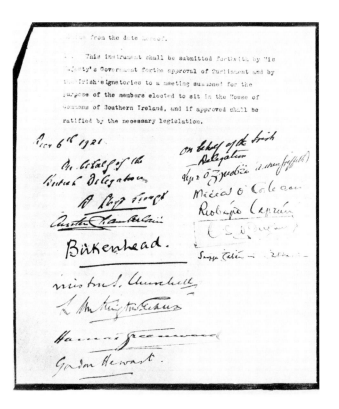

Group shot of pro-Treaty members of the Dáil outside Mansion House. (Courtesy of the National Library of Ireland)

THE TREATY GIVES IRELAND

1. A PARLIAMENT RESPONSIBLE TO THE IRISH PEOPLE ALONE.
2. A GOVERNMENT RESPONSIBLE TO THAT PARLIAMENT.
3. DEMOCRATIC CONTROL OF ALL LEGISLATIVE AFFAIRS.
4. POWER TO MAKE LAWS FOR EVERY DEPARTMENT OF IRISH LIFE.
5. AN IRISH LEGAL SYSTEM CONTROLLED BY IRISHMEN.
6. AN IRISH ARMY.
7. AN IRISH POLICE FORCE.
8. COMPLETE FINANCIAL FREEDOM.
9. A NATIONAL FLAG.
10. FREEDOM OF OPINION.
11. COMPLETE CONTROL OF IRISH EDUCATION.
12. COMPLETE CONTROL OF HER LAND SYSTEMS.
13. POWER AND FREEDOM TO DEVELOP HER RESOURCES AND INDUSTRIES.
14. A DEMOCRATIC CONSTITUTION.
15. A STATE ORGANISATION TO EXPRESS THE MIND AND WILL OF THE NATION.
16. HER RIGHTFUL PLACE AS A NATION AMONG NATIONS.

DUBLIN CASTLE HAS FALLEN !
BRITISH BUREAUCRACY IS IN THE DUST !
IS THIS VICTORY OR DEFEAT ?

SUPPORT THE TREATY

A pro-Treaty propaganda poster. (Courtesy of the National Library of Ireland)

Michael Collins' coffin leaving the Pro Cathedral. Collins prophetically declared on signing the Treaty: 'I have signed my own death warrant'; he was killed by anti-Treaty forces on 22 August 1922. (Courtesy of the National Library of Ireland)

The Northern Ireland Premier had every reason to feel bullish. Not only had he the backing of the War Office and the government's chief adviser on military matters, but he also carried with him the full weight of Bonar Law's support. Craig went to see the Ulster loyalist after the 5 November conferences at Downing Street, and although no records of their discussion exist, it is not difficult, as one historian noted, to 'surmise the tenor of the conversation'.[60] At any rate, from now on Craig resolved not to 'budge one inch'.[61]

Lloyd George promptly fell into despair. According to Tom Jones, he was 'more depressed than I had seen him at all since the negotiations began'.[62] Amid the panic, Chamberlain wrote to his wife that Bonar Law 'is rampaging ... [and] seeing red on the subject of Ulster'.[63] And yet this turn of events was all too foreseeable. After all, it was precisely because Bonar Law presented such a threat to Lloyd George's settlement plans that, back in September, he had considered dispatching the former Conservative leader to the Washington Naval Conference, for which occasion Arthur Balfour had just set sail. The trouble was that while the latter – always a rabid opponent of Irish nationalism – remained a member of Cabinet, Bonar Law, ostensibly, was on the sidelines.

Enraged at the weakness of his position, Lloyd George threatened to resign, again. He knew he could count on the support of Chamberlain and Birkenhead, but doubted Churchill's loyalty, fulminating that he 'never could rely on Winston in a crisis'.[64] Ironically for one who had gained power by prioritising his own political survival above that of his party's, he railed against the duplicity and base self-interest of Curzon, Worthington-Evans and Stanley Baldwin: 'My colleagues say they will stand by me and won't take office in an alternative Government but they did that at the last crisis ...

and within three days of their saying so I was putting the nose bags of office around their necks.' He was under no illusion, he told Jones later in another rant, that all three would 'go over to Bonar if the opportunity comes.'[65]

For all this sound and fury, Lloyd George had yet to play his trump card. With all other options off the table, he turned to Jones and said, 'There is just one other possible way out': a boundary commission. The Prime Minister had first raised this subject at the fourth plenary session on 14 October, after which it faded from view. On 25 October, he made a veiled reference to it at a meeting of the British delegates when he gestured to some 'mechanism' that might square Sinn Féin's demand for essential unity with the pledge not to coerce Ulster, and more recently he had touched upon it during the conversation with Griffith at Churchill's. Now he instructed Jones to 'find out from Griffith and Collins if they will support me on it; namely that the 26 Counties should take their own Dominion Parliament and have a Boundary Commission'. That meant Ulster could 'have her present powers plus representation' at Westminster, as well as 'the burdens of taxation, which we bear. I might be able to put that through if Sinn Fein will take it. Find out.'[66]

At 3 p.m. the next day, Tuesday 8 November, Jones met Collins and Griffith at the Grosvenor Hotel, where the Sinn Féin delegation kept two rooms as a third headquarters. He laid out the dilemma in stark terms, outlining the grim consequences that would follow unless some last-ditch alternative could be found, such as – and this he threw in as his own suggestion – a boundary commission. He noted in his diary that while Griffith was a 'closed book', Collins was 'obviously very much upset' and immediately rejected the idea, claiming it would sacrifice 'unity entirely'. To which Jones answered that he agreed, but 'what was the alternative? Chaos, Crown Colony Government, Civil War.'[67]

Hours later, in a remarkably phlegmatic account of the situation, Griffith informed de Valera that 'Craig is standing pat. Refuses to come under any All-Ireland parliament. Refuses to change six-county area.' This meant Lloyd George would have to resign by the end of the week, and 'Bonar Law would probably form a militarist Government against Ireland.' Then he sketched out Jones' alternative plan, which would 'delimit "Ulster"' and 'give us most of Tyrone, Fermanagh, and part of Armagh, Down etc.'. For the first time in the talks, Collins and Griffith had been told that a boundary commission would result in substantive territorial losses for Northern Ireland, and while the former was hostile to the idea and the latter showed no outward signs of enthusiasm, both men had come to the conference determined to uproot partition. For them, the issue carried far greater weight than for de Valera, whose chief concern during the Treaty talks, as the historian Kevin Matthews emphasises, was allegiance to the Crown. Furthermore, rather than present the prospect of territorial gains from a boundary commission as a promise from Lloyd George, Jones, who was acutely aware of nationalists' distrust and resentment of the Prime Minister, offered it up as his own improvised solution.

Significantly, Griffith did not reject the suggestion out of hand. He merely reassured de Valera that 'We did not give any definite opinion on the matter. It is their lookout for the moment.' In any case, he thought it 'partly bluff but not wholly', and if the conference were to collapse over the next few days, it would, at least, end 'on the note of "Ulster" being impossibilist'.[68]

The other delegates also bore the news with stoicism, and the meeting at Hans Place to discuss this latest development

passed off peacefully. It had been a long day for Collins and
Gavan Duffy, who had arrived back in London at 5.30 a.m.
As soon as the train pulled into Euston station, Collins shot
back to Cadogan Gardens and scrawled a letter to Kitty
Kiernan before breakfast, telling her that he was 'lonely and
very, very discontented.'[69] Gavan Duffy, meanwhile, reported
back to Barton and Childers. The meetings in Dublin had been
'peaceful' and all were at one on the issue of 'no allegiance'.[70]
Nothing, it seemed, could shake de Valera's confidence in his
own strategy. Seán T. O'Kelly, one of his faithful lieutenants
and the Dáil's representative in Paris, had dashed back to
Dublin that weekend to voice his own concerns about how
Collins and Griffith were conducting the negotiations. But the
President, as O'Kelly's friend later recalled, reacted 'coldly'
to the unexpected visit, and insisted that 'everything was safe
inasmuch as the delegates could not sign anything without first
submitting it to the Cabinet and getting their approval'. He
then instructed O'Kelly to return immediately to Paris.[71]

From de Valera's perspective, the negotiations were very
much running to plan: Gavan Duffy, Barton and Childers were
acting as a brake on Collins and Griffith, while Ulster looked
certain to become the wrecking ball of the conference, an
outcome that would guarantee a public relations coup for Sinn
Féin. With his Cabinet united behind him, de Valera would be
free to strike a compromise of his own with the British and,
as the historian John Regan argues, the inevitable republican
dissenters would be left to squabble ineffectually on the
sidelines, deprived of any political or moral authority.[72]

Reinvigorated, the President decided to break the silence
he had maintained ever since the row at the end of October,
when he had been forced into an embarrassing climbdown. He
began his first letter to Griffith in a fortnight by acknowledging

the string of missives he had received in the interim, the letters of 'October 27th, 31st, November 1, 3, 5 and 8th', then expressed his approval at the turn of events. The delegation had performed 'admirably'. They had not compromised on Sinn Féin's 'fundamental position' vis à vis the Crown and Empire, and had managed to steer the talks towards a break on Ulster, so he urged Griffith not to 'budge a single inch from the point where the negotiations have now led us'.[73]

In hindsight, it is difficult to believe Lloyd George took the all-Ireland parliament solution seriously. Nevertheless, he pursued it with vigour, perhaps hoping against hope that Ulster would compromise and accept Home Rule from Dublin if Sinn Féin jettisoned republicanism in favour of Dominion status. A more plausible explanation is that he drove this option as hard and as far as it would go, while simultaneously preparing the ground for his boundary commission strategy.

Craig had contemplated such a solution as far back as December 1919, when, most likely, he had in mind population adjustments rather than substantial changes to the six-county area. In the aftermath of the First World War, the concept of a commission tasked with ruling on national boundaries was not completely novel. The Upper Silesia question dominated foreign news coverage for much of 1921, and in October, this long-running territorial dispute between Germany and Poland was finally settled by an independent committee, which acted on the basis of its interpretation of a plebiscite. Griffith doubtless had this scenario in mind when the following day, Wednesday 9 November, during a second meeting with Jones, he effectively gave his consent to the proposal.

They had returned to room 125 at the Grosvenor Hotel, this time with Duggan rather than Collins in attendance. Jones began by describing 'the Boundary Commission as an absolute last card' and said the Prime Minister would play it if he was certain that 'Sinn Fein would take it, if Ulster accepted'. Griffith, who had yet to receive de Valera's letter, replied: 'We cannot give him a pledge but we will not turn him down on it. We are not going to queer his pitch.' He then added, 'We would prefer a plebiscite, but in essentials a Boundary Commission is very much the same.' That was enough for Jones, who reported back to a now 'perfectly satisfied' Prime Minister.[74]

The welcome news coincided with a demonstration of loyalty from Churchill, who, like the rest of the Cabinet, was unaware at this stage that Lloyd George was pursuing an alternative strategy on Ulster. Alarmed at the Prime Minister's loud threats of resignation, he wrote to reaffirm his support for the 'creation and recognition of an all-Ireland Parliament, subject only to the condition that no physical force must be used against Ulster from any quarter'. His mind was focused it seems – in precisely the manner Lloyd George hoped it would be – by the prospect of Bonar Law's unchecked ascendancy. For in a successor reactionary government, Churchill's ambitions were likely to be severely curtailed. Anxious to banish all thoughts of resignation from Lloyd George's mind, he asked, 'Why shd [Bonar Law] not succeed? Most men sink into insignificance when they quit office. Very insignificant men acquire weight when they obtain it.'[75]

But Lloyd George needed no reminders of the oblivion that awaited outside Downing Street. The coalition was certain to fragment at the end of its parliamentary term, if not before. Only an early election could reverse this fate. To persuade the Conservatives to renew the partnership, Lloyd George needed to shore up his political base and boost the government's standing: two eventualities that a successful resolution of the Irish question promised to deliver. His future, at this juncture, also depended on the cohesion of the 'inner cabinet'; he could not afford to lose the support of Chamberlain, Birkenhead, Robert Horne or Churchill. Nor could he afford to provoke Bonar Law, who stood ready to march against the government if Ulster's constitutional safeguards came under attack.

To ward off this challenge, and to mollify Craig and his colleagues, Lloyd George hastened the transfer of services to Belfast. On the day that Griffith agreed to the Boundary Commission, the King made two orders in council revising the 1920 Government of Ireland Act: partition was now legally complete.[76] For the moment, Ulster's Unionists were content, but it would not be long before Craig's 'Black Saturday' was overshadowed by a far greater crisis.

7 ▪ POWER AND INTENT
10 November–22 November

Emboldened by his successes, Craig prepared to publicly renounce the London peace talks in protest at the government's refusal to rule out an all-Ireland parliament. But even as he called in the cavalry, summoning several members of his Cabinet to an emergency meeting in London, Lloyd George was applying the finishing touches to an ingenious pincer movement, aimed at catching Ulster's Unionists in a trap of their own making. On Thursday 10 November, he ordered a meeting of all the British delegates – the British seven. He was in combative form and convinced that a more muscular approach to Craig and his colleagues would skewer the Ulster Unionists where it hurt most. In a burst of newfound confidence, he told Frances Stevenson that Sinn Féin would get an all-Ireland parliament, and if, after a year, Ulster remained resistant to Home Rule under Dublin, she could come 'back as part of the U.K.' and swallow the 'same taxes' as the rest of the country. That would stick in the craw, he predicted, with savage delight. 'They have their hands on their hearts all the time,' he said, 'but if it comes to touching their pockets they quickly slap their hands in them. "I know ... My wife is a Presbyterian!"[1]

The new plan, designed to coerce Ulster financially, was to be presented to the British seven later that day. In preparation for this meeting, Lloyd George gathered Jones, Grigg, Lionel Curtis and a civil servant from the Treasury at a breakfast at 10 Downing Street. They feasted on kippers in the company of the Prime Minister's two daughters, his son and his daughter-in-law, and if some of those present felt inhibited by this awkward assembly of Whitehall men and extended family, Lloyd George paid no heed. He remained as unselfconsciously lively as ever, veering between light-hearted banter with Megan (then nineteen), who was chided for 'her shyness and her pretty dress' at an event the night before, and a sustained grilling of the visiting Treasury official, who had been summoned to shed light on the finance section of the Government of Ireland Act. As Jones noted in his diary, the dilemma of how to bring 'pressure on Ulster through her pockets' had been troubling the Prime Minister for some time. True to form, however, he kept his ministerial colleagues in the dark about this latest swerve in direction.[2]

To his detractors, Lloyd George operated as a quasi-presidential Prime Minister. His style of leadership seemed to epitomise all that was wrong with a government prone to oligarchic tendencies. In 1922, Herbert Asquith noted venomously that 'there is not, and never has been, any Cabinet responsibility since [Lloyd George] became Prime Minister'.[3] Particularly deplorable, in the eyes of his critics, were the unprecedented powers afforded to individual advisers, who swarmed into areas once seen as the preserve of diplomats.[4] Orthodox politicians of all stripes frequently worked themselves into a frenzy over Lloyd George. It was not just that he lacked the gentlemanly reserve or statesman-like pomp of his predecessors; it was his undisguised contempt for convention, so breezily on show in the management of his personal finances, and his joyous adultery with Frances Stevenson – not since the Duke of Grafton had a Prime Minister lived openly with his mistress.[5] In October 1922, shortly before his downfall, Balfour could declare that Lloyd George 'is violently disliked by great bodies of his fellow countrymen'.[6]

He left office a diminished figure, his career marked by wild variations and a continual reversal of priories that remain difficult to reconcile even today. The economist John Maynard Keynes famously branded him a 'chameleon', devoid of a moral core and 'rooted in nothing'.[7] It proved as potent a myth as the one Lloyd George wove about himself as an impoverished 'cottage boy' who pulled himself up by his bootstraps.[8] In truth, he grew up among an educated, artisan family who spoiled him rotten. The hard times hit only after his mother and surrogate father, Uncle Lloyd, lavished all they had on the advancement of his legal career – and that of his younger brother, William, whose life was spent in the shadow, and often the service, of his elder sibling.[9]

But Lloyd George's background provides an explanation of sorts for his instinctive populism. His family's religious community – The Children of God, or the Campbellites as they were known – were so radical they were almost a cult. Even by the standards of Welsh nineteenth-century nonconformity, their 'severe' opposition to the laws and customs of the Church of England marked them out as 'a minority ... among the oppressed'. From an early age, then, Lloyd George was, in the words of Roy Hattersley, an 'outsider among outsiders'.[10]

He certainly felt unbound by the values that constrained his Conservative colleagues and threw himself with gusto into the new policy of discrediting Ulster's Unionists. After the breakfast table was cleared of dishes, he ordered Curtis to 'recast' a letter to Craig that was initially intended to be nothing more than a written confirmation of the proposals already discussed with the North's Premier. It invited Northern Ireland's ministers to a 'full and frank exchange of views'.[11] But by midday, when the British delegates arrived at 10 Downing Street, the missive to Craig had become an altogether different document, with large tracts on finance 'pitchforked into it'.[12] Worthington-Evans reacted first, insisting 'that Ulster was to get all her powers under the 1920 Act and therefore there could be no change in the matter of finance'. Immediately, an 'acute discussion' was underway. Lloyd George countered that if Ulster 'wanted to remain with Great Britain ... she must carry the same burdens as Glasgow, Liverpool and Birmingham'. His remarks came as a 'great and sudden revelation to his colleagues and the atmosphere was at once electric'. Chamberlain proclaimed himself 'disturbed' by the conversation, prompting Churchill to direct the delegation's 'attention to some drafting point in another part of the document'. Later, the still rattled Tory leader instructed Jones to 'defloridise' the letter, reminding Lloyd George, in a sulphurous aside, that 'we were now not writing to Celts but to Anglo-Saxons'.[13]

Another frantic rewrite ensued, and while Jones and Grigg retreated to the pub, Curtis laboured alone, fortified by port and sandwiches.[14] At 4 p.m. the redrafted letter was submitted to Cabinet, which was meeting for the first time since the start of the Irish Conference. There had been no need for an update before this point: 'We knew our instructions,' Lloyd George told his colleagues, before explaining that the conversations with Craig had changed everything.[15] Then he went on to deliver a dire report of Craig's negotiating style. The Northern Ireland Premier had been dangerously obstructive whereas Sinn

Féin were refreshingly progressive and collaborative. He had even brought them to the point where they were 'hauling down the Republican flag' and replacing it with 'the flag of Empire' as long as they could be assured of 'the unity of Ireland'. In this wholly overblown characterisation of the Irish position, traditional roles were reversed: Ulster and not Sinn Féin was the threat to the integrity of the Empire. Hammering home the point, Lloyd George declared that 'in this situation ... You could not begin to use force against the South.'[16]

Curzon, who liked to refer to Lloyd George as that 'little Welsh bruiser',[17] instantly leapt to Craig's defence, recounting how the Northern Ireland Premier had come to see him 'two days ago in a mood of extreme disappointment'. Craig felt 'betrayed', he said, and thought Ulster was being 'turned out of the British system'.[18] But in the Cabinet, imperial concerns choked back the old loyalties. And despite Curzon's exhortation to 'consider the susceptibilities of Craig and his men', it was Chamberlain's views that swung the Tory ministers into line. He would not contemplate coercion against Ulster but said that did not preclude him from exerting 'the greatest moral pressure on [them] if I think the settlement is satisfactory and vital to the Empire'. In any case, he concluded, Craig 'must desire a settlement. He has to govern a Sinn Féin population. The alternatives are peace or murder.'[19]

Within hours the Prime Minister's proposals were dispatched to Craig. The final text made plain the consequences of clinging to Westminster, and in a passage that resonates with fresh force post-Brexit, the government highlighted the 'inconvenience' of imposing a customs barrier on the island of Ireland. It was put to Craig that 'a jagged line of frontier' dividing North from South would disrupt the 'natural channels of trade' and alienate 'large elements of the population' whose 'sympathies' lay across the border.[20] The financial penalties attached to the status quo were also spelled out, forcing Ulster's Unionists to confront the unpleasant realities of the Government of Ireland Act. For while that legislation defined the geographical span of Northern Ireland and ascribed powers to the Belfast administration, it also established the devolved parliament as subordinate to the supreme executive authority of the King; meaning, as the Tory MP Leo Amery pointed out to Craig in 1924, that Ulster's status was no more than that of a province within the United Kingdom. She was not an equal partner.[21] So Lloyd George brought home the reality of Westminster sovereignty. Lower taxation privileges, a voluntary imperial contribution and free trade on the island of Ireland, all of which were among the benefits conferred on Northern Ireland by the 1920 Act, would be abolished if Belfast refused to participate in an all-Ireland parliament. On the other hand, if Craig and his colleagues consented to Home Rule under Dublin, they could retain all the powers and advantages of the 1920 Act. But as Lloyd George explained to his Cabinet, Ulster's Unionists 'can't expect to get all the benefits of both systems'.[22]

While the choice between Dublin and Westminster was spelt out with brutal clarity, the Boundary Commission, 'un-mentioned at breakfast, explicitly included by lunch, and out again by tea-time, was omitted'.[23]

The next day Craig retaliated with an explosive letter of his own. An all-Ireland parliament was 'precisely what Ulster' had been resisting 'for many years ... by all the means at her disposal', and her 'detestation' of it was undiminished. He countered that Northern Ireland should be made a Dominion too, on the grounds that 'equality of status' [between North and South] had been the overriding principle of the 1920 Act. British ministers, more accustomed to Ulster's 'passionate assurances of union' as Chamberlain scoffed, reacted with derision, and relations with Craig's government sank to a fresh nadir.[24]

The Northern Ireland Premier's letter reached Downing Street just as Churchill had embarked on a charm offensive towards the United States at an annual armistice day dinner. He was about to deliver a speech welcoming America's new ambassador to London, when an urgent summons from the Prime Minister forced him to abandon the event and entrust the overtures to his controversial relative, Freddie Guest, the Secretary of State for Air.[25]

Memorably described by Viscount Gladstone as Lloyd George's 'evil genius', Guest masterminded the expansion of the Prime Minister's election campaign funds. As the Coalition Liberals' Chief Whip from 1918 to 1921, he brought in Maundy Gregory, the Oxford-educated son of a clergyman, and a famously shady character who was later rumoured to have blackmailed Birkenhead, to head up the lucrative business of selling honours. Lloyd George lacked the revenue resources of a party machine, so to overcome this handicap, Guest and Gregory transformed the time-honoured trade in titles into a free-market system, complete with tariffs for the most coveted rungs of the social ladder: £10,000 for a knighthood, £30,000 for a baronetcy and £50,000 upwards for a peerage.[26] Inevitably, this entrepreneurial approach attracted the odd criminal, although the Conservative Party outcry that erupted in the summer of 1922 stemmed largely from the realisation that they were being muscled out of the market. As the Tories' chairman, George Younger, complained, 'Freddie Guest is nobbling our men'. But Lloyd George didn't care. 'He detested titles. This, no doubt,' wrote the historian A.J.P. Taylor, 'is why he distributed them so lavishly.'[27] Nevertheless, it proved a short-sighted move.

Although his campaign coffers were overflowing, the decision to debase the entire honours system so blatantly infuriated Lloyd George's political enemies and squandered what was left of his reputation among the Conservative base.[28]

During the Treaty talks, the trade in titles continued apace because Lloyd George had his eye on an early general election. And, as already mentioned, pivotal to this ambition was a successful resolution of the Irish question. Lloyd George reinforced the point when he reminded his colleagues at one stage during the conference: 'We are after a settlement – that [is] our objective.'[29] The dilemma was how to remove the Ulster obstacle from the negotiating table and steer the talks onto the Crown and Empire, for now that Craig and his colleagues had officially dispensed with the all-Ireland parliament plan, everything hinged on the Boundary Commission.

On Saturday morning, 12 November, Jones arrived at Hans Place for another private talk with Griffith. They had met the night before at the Grosvenor Hotel, but on that occasion Jones provided scant details about the Ulster position, merely confirming their rejection of an all-Ireland parliament. He dwelt instead on the recent Cabinet meeting, recounting how Chamberlain had rallied support for the Sinn Féin delegates by vouching for their 'straight and honourable character'.[30] This lifted Griffith's spirits, and in a letter to de Valera that Friday evening, he had signed off with a triumphalist flourish: 'The "Ulster" crowd are in the pit they [dug] for us, and if we keep them there we'll have England and the Dominions out against them in the next week or two.'[31]

Griffith's mood soared higher when Jones returned on Saturday morning with a copy of Craig's reply to Lloyd George. Revelling at the 'cloven hoof of Ulster's sordidness', he scoffed at their willingness 'to forego representation at Westminster [which would have been the price of Dominion status in the North] for the sake of a lower income tax'.[32] Urged on in this direction by Jones, who predicted that if 'Sinn Fein cooperated with the P.M. we have might have Ulster in' an all-Ireland parliament 'before many months had passed', Griffith may have felt, for a moment, as if he and Lloyd George were in common cause against Craig.[33] It was all a world away from those first, formal meetings around the Cabinet table when he and Collins had attacked the Prime Minister over partition, arguing that if only the British stood aside, Irishmen could settle the problem themselves. By the end of that conversation at Hans Place, Griffith had accepted an invitation to see the Prime Minister in private, so at three o'clock that afternoon, a short, sturdy man with a 'slightly swaying gait' turned up alone to the plush Park Lane mansion of Sir Philip Sassoon, where Lloyd George was waiting for him.[34]

According to Pakenham, without that 12 November meeting 'there might have been no Treaty'.[35] But Griffith arrived free of foreboding and, despite what unfolded, departed without dread. As far as he was concerned, the undertaking he gave that day went no further than what had been promised to Jones three days earlier, when, in consideration of the Prime Minister's 'tactical manoeuvre' against the Ulster Unionists, he agreed not to publicly repudiate the Boundary Commission. In his mind, there was a sharp distinction between this and an acceptance of the scheme as the answer to the Ulster problem. Perhaps because he felt the Boundary Commission was no more than a bargaining ploy, Griffith dropped his guard; alternatively, he may have assumed that Jones had explained his attitude to the Prime Minister already.[36] Whatever the reason, Griffith failed to clarify his position. And since he was engaged in hand-to-hand combat with, arguably, the most agile and ingenious politician of the age, this, not unsurprisingly, turned out to be a foolish move. In A.J.P. Taylor's view, Lloyd George was 'devious even at his greatest moments'.[37] In 1924, Birkenhead reflected that the 'man who enters into real and fierce controversy with Mr. Lloyd George must think clearly, think deeply, and think ahead. Otherwise he will think too late.'[38] The morality of his methods did not concern him. What mattered, as one biographer noted, was achieving the result he thought right for himself and the country.[39]

Lloyd George began by showing Griffith the exchanges with Craig, explaining that, aside from himself, 'all the principal members of the Cabinet', and even Bonar Law, had been 'a bit knocked out by it'. The plan, he told Griffith, who later recorded the scene in a letter to de Valera, was to send 'a further reply to the Ulstermen – refusing their Dominion proposal, but offering to create an All-Ireland Parliament, Ulster to have the right to vote itself out within 12 months, but if it does a Boundary Commission to be set up to delimit the area'. He added that once the border had been decided upon, whatever was left of Northern Ireland – or to quote Griffith's letter verbatim, 'the part that remains after the Commission' – would, as a region, bear 'equal financial burdens with England'.[40]

Lloyd George then lapsed into a familiar routine. The diehards, he said, were 'mustering all their forces' for the impending Conservative Party conference, which threatened to turn into a 'crucial' test of the Tory Party leadership. With the stakes so high, it would be unconscionable for Chamberlain and Birkenhead to enter the line of fire uncertain as to whether Sinn Féin was going to 'cut the ground away behind them by repudiating the proposal'. Griffith reassured him that 'we would not do that'; there would be no 'decrying it' in public. 'And if the Ulstermen accepted it, we would have to discuss it with him in the privacy of the Conference.' But he could not, as he stressed in his letter to de Valera that evening, guarantee 'acceptance' of the Boundary Commission. The promise he gave, he explained to the President, was that while Lloyd George 'was fighting the "Ulster" crowd we would not help them by repudiating him'.[41]

Before signing off, he swore de Valera to secrecy, instructing him to tell no one outside the 'inner cabinet' about the 12 November meeting, since Lloyd George was fearful that Craig's men or *The Morning Post* might accuse him of 'conspiring with me against "Ulster".'

Having coaxed Griffith into acquiescence, Lloyd George wasted no time consolidating his advantage. The next evening, Sunday 13 November, Jones paid Griffith another visit. This time Hans Place barely stirred. With the negotiations at a virtual standstill, most of the delegates had returned to Dublin for the weekend. Even Childers felt he could relax and take his eye off the ball for a while. On Saturday, Cope had advised the delegation that until 'the pro and anti Ulster parties test their strength' at the following week's Conservative Party conference, there would be no further progress in the talks.[42] This proved a wildly inaccurate prediction, but it removed the hyper-vigilant Childers from the scene. Within hours he and Barton were en route to Dublin. Had they remained in London, the Treaty talks might have turned out very differently.

It was not just that Childers recorded every meeting in his diary; he assiduously monitored all interactions with the British, so that Collins and Griffith were forced to account for each encounter. No private conversations escaped his notice, nor did he overlook the failure to provide documentary evidence of a meeting. This scrupulous approach undoubtedly fuelled the atmosphere of mutual suspicion, and left Griffith feeling harried and on the defensive, without any freedom of manoeuvre. He had not forgotten the long arguments and tortuous revisions that accompanied his previous letter to the Prime Minister, all of which, in his view, were entirely unnecessary. So, when he met Jones that Sunday evening at about 7 p.m., he took matters into his own hands. There were no racking doubts. Far from it. All the Welsh secretary had asked him to do was approve a document summarising the previous day's discussion with the Prime Minister, which he had recounted in detail already to de Valera. He merely looked it over briefly, agreed to its contents and then thought no more about it. In his estimation, it was a singularly inconsequential meeting, which was why nobody learned of Jones' memo until it was too late.[43]

An unwitting Griffith had been spectacularly outmanoeuvred by the Prime Minister. But the extent of his blunder would become apparent only in the dying hours of the talks, when Lloyd George played this trump card to perfection. Had Griffith properly scrutinised the memo, he might not have been so blasé about it, for this version of the Boundary Commission fundamentally differed from the one he had been discussing with the British for the past week. It did not simply 'delimit' the six-county area, which was how Griffith described the commission working in his reports to de Valera; instead, if Ulster chose to retain local autonomy within the United Kingdom, a tribunal would 'revise' the Irish boundary, and 'adjust the line by both inclusion and exclusion'.[44] In other words, territorially, Northern Ireland now stood to gain as well as lose from the Boundary Commission.

It was an accommodation that placated Chamberlain. He arrived at Sassoon's Park Lane mansion on Saturday as soon as Griffith had left, and was told by Lloyd George that, effectively, the chairman of the Sinn Féin delegation had promised not to break off negotiations over partition.[45] Griffith thought his pledge meant something completely different, but the lapse into ambiguity sealed his fate. Now, a 'jubilant' Lloyd George, eager to head off for his weekend break at another of Sassoon's magnificent properties – Trent Park on the outskirts of London – asked Chamberlain to check over Jones' memo before it was shown to Griffith.[46] This apparently casual approach was nothing of the sort. By inviting Chamberlain to rework the document to his own satisfaction, which he promptly did, since he felt Jones' version was not entirely accurate, the Conservative leader not only put his own stamp on the agreement, but became an accomplice to it. And this meant that what Griffith approved the following day was ultimately Chamberlain's understanding of the compromise.[47] By such subtle manoeuvres Lloyd George transformed an insuperable obstacle into a stepping stone from which he could leapfrog his way to a settlement.

Frances Stevenson, who also spent the weekend at Trent Park, thought she had never seen Lloyd George 'so excited about anything before'.[48] And yet, even in this first flush of triumph, the tension scarcely dissipated. On the sidelines, Bonar Law remained a menacing figure. If he intervened against the Irish negotiations at the upcoming conference, Lloyd George's administration was finished. With parliament prorogued on 10 November, the diehards directed all their efforts at this decisive battle. And while the Prime Minister was adept at exploiting the threat posed by the Tory rebels, much was genuinely at stake at this annual gathering of the party faithful for, despite the 31 October debate in the House of Commons, Conservative Party members had yet to manifestly detach themselves from the radical Ulster policy of the pre-war years. And with Bonar Law hovering in the wings, the leadership knew that there was no guarantee they would do so.[49]

The diehards had also struck it lucky in terms of the location of that year's conference. It was to be held in Liverpool, a stronghold of Protestant, working-class Toryism. In the days leading up to this critical event, newspapers continued to bang the drum about Bonar Law's impending return, and to the Tory rebels it seemed as if their hour had come. With the whiff of victory in the air, a fevered far-right press piled on the vitriol towards Lloyd George. The *National Review* sneered that 'our beloved Premier' can always be trusted to sit down with murderers, for with 'him it is simply a case of "the dog has returned to his vomit"', a reference to the Prime Minister's trade talks with the Bolsheviks.[50]

As the date of the conference approached, Chamberlain and Birkenhead became increasingly jumpy. For the former, the constant speculation about Bonar Law brought back bitter memories of the pre-war leadership race, and he complained to his sister about the 'troubles' heaped upon him by that 'ambitious ... Ulsterman'. He believed Bonar Law was targeting the 'first place' in politics out of a conviction that it 'might & ought to be his'. With mounting anxiety, he declared, 'I am fighting for my political life.'[51]

But Chamberlain misunderstood his rival's motivations. Bonar Law's animus sprang from the fear that the battle for Ulster had been lost: the heartland of Protestant Ireland would be cast out of Britain, with all ties to Westminster severed, rendering her, as he put it, nothing more than 'a province of a Dominion'.[52] He found this intolerable. In a written statement to the editor of *The Scotsman*, J.P. Croal, dated 12 November, he vowed to lead a Conservative Party revolt against the coalition unless they abandoned this policy. At a dinner with the Prime Minister two days earlier, Bonar Law had set out his concerns in the same stark terms. He recounted this conversation to Croal, describing how he had urged Lloyd George not to confine your bullying to Ulster. Try it on the Sinn Feiners too. 'Say to them, Ulster in spite of all the pressure I have put on is immovable, and not only so but the party on which I rely will be hopelessly broken up. However much I wish it, it can't be done ... I therefore make this proposal to you – For your own part of Ireland frame your own constitution, and if it is within the Empire we will accept almost anything you propose.'

If they refused that, the government should 'say to them "Very well go to the devil in your own way – govern your own part of Ireland as you please ... we will spend no more British blood in Ireland. We will fight you by an economic blockade. We will allow no intercourse of any kind between Ireland and the United Kingdom."'53

Evidently, then, Bonar Law was no diehard. As long as Northern Ireland's security and existence were guaranteed, he cared little about the terms of a settlement with the South. At the end of 1922, when he finally succeeded Lloyd George in 10 Downing Street – a transition that horrified Irish nationalists – his indifference proved essential to the fledgling Irish state's survival.54

Despite the clash of views over Ireland, Bonar Law maintained to Croal that his friendship with Lloyd George had been unaffected. But the events of the following evening suggest that this was an exaggeration. According to Frances Stevenson, the subject led to 'unpleasantness' between the two men at a dinner at Trent Park on Sunday 13 November, although Lloyd George 'talked [Bonar Law] round' and afterwards they sat up talking into the early hours. These frequent private conversations with the former Conservative leader afforded the Prime Minister vital leverage over his Conservative colleagues. At a meeting of the British seven on 12 November, convened to discuss Craig's reply, Lloyd George claimed that Bonar Law supported the Boundary Commission and thought Ulster should pay the same taxes as the rest of the United Kingdom. 'That is coercion,' he concluded. 'It is fair but it is fiscal pressure.' In typical fashion, Lloyd George had distorted the meaning of Bonar Law's words. His point was simply that Irish unity must be abandoned if Ulster's unionists rejected the lure of lower taxation.[55]

By the end of that weekend, if the skies had not quite cleared for the coalition, the position certainly looked less precarious. In virtually the blink of an eye, obstacles that might have felled or fatally weakened the government were swept away by the sudden turn of events. Griffith's undertaking had removed the threat of a break on Ulster, or at least it had in the eyes of the British delegates; Bonar Law had retreated back into the shadows, declining even to attend the Liverpool conference, although a letter he wrote on the eve of that event showed that he remained vigilant; and with the diehards' baying for blood, the top ranks of the Tory Party threw all their resources at a last-minute campaign for unity.[56] None of this, however, dispelled the mood of nervous expectation among senior Conservatives. The party's members were gathering in almost unprecedented numbers, an ominous sign, given the depth of discontent felt by the grass roots towards the coalition.

As the week of the conference dawned, Lord Derby, a Tory Party elder statesman, and accurate barometer of Conservative opinion, warned Chamberlain about how 'difficult ... our meeting is going to be'.[57] The diehards' motion condemning the government's Irish policy represented the main item on the agenda at Liverpool, raising fears that it would become a lightning rod for dissatisfaction at the coalition in general. Much depended on Chamberlain's performance, and the Conservative leader was so worried that he enlisted the help of his half-brother Neville – no friend of the coalition or of Lloyd George. Birkenhead also leapt into action, badgering Archibald Salvidge, Liverpool's leading Conservative, into abandoning his publicly declared neutral stance on the resolution. At a private meeting between the two on the morning of Tuesday 15 November, the staunchly pro-Ulster MP promised to actively support the government. After Lord Derby lent his formidable influence too, it was no surprise that on 17 November, the Tory rebels suffered another humiliating defeat, one that knocked them out of the fray for some time.[58] But what astonished most Conservatives was the transformation in Chamberlain. The usually grey, uninspiring leader transfixed the party with his impassioned defence of the Irish negotiations and, in a speech that briefly restored faith in his leadership, assured his adversaries that the government would give Ulster a 'free choice'. He finished by reminding delegates of the grim alternative facing them if the talks collapsed.[59]

The result sent Lloyd George into an effusion of delight, and, according to Jones, he marched 'up and down the Cabinet room pretending to play "See the Conquering Hero comes" on a cornet'.[60] Celebrations were more muted among the Tories. Lord Derby claimed that considerable disquiet lurked beneath the surface; in the *Manchester Guardian*'s view, the Liverpool vote was 'a nervous and somewhat hesitating rally to the leaders of the party.'[61] In the short term, it provided yet another boost for the Prime Minister. There was now, though, only one option left for a settlement, and that left the Sinn Féin delegation buckling under the familiar weight of British coercion. In fact, by this stage, the Irish delegates were already reeling from what Pakenham described as the 'sudden turning of the tables', the rapidity of which was 'too staggering to be comprehended easily'.[62]

While the British delegates faced into the storm of the Liverpool conference, the week was also one of tension and conflict for the Irish delegation. It started quietly enough. On the morning of Monday 14 November, Childers was quietly at work in the garden of his south Dublin home, certain that nothing of significance, given Cope's reassurances, would occur at the peace conference until after Liverpool. But by nightfall, he and his cousin Barton, who raced into Dublin on his motorbike from Wicklow, were back on the boat to England, having received an urgent summons from the British to return to London at once. George Russell (Æ), the poet, mystic and philosopher, hurried into the city to see them off; at that point he still believed that Sinn Féiners who 'laid claim to the legacy of 1916 were "our Irish Boers"'.[63]

Back at Hans Place the next day, Childers snapped into his old routine, noting in his diary that although Jones and Griffith spoke at 3 p.m., there 'was no report verbally or in writing to see'.[64] His anger intensified when Collins and Griffith then traipsed off to Sassoon's Park Lane mansion for a private meeting with Lloyd George. They returned to Hans Place at 6.15 p.m. and informed Childers and the other delegates – except Duggan who remained in Dublin for another day – that the British were preparing a draft Treaty. When it transpired that Gavan Duffy was expected to lend his legal expertise to this venture, Childers hit the roof. A furious argument ensued, exposing the familiar fault-lines within the group. Sassoon, a doyen of London high society, who continued to cherish hopes of a front-line position in politics (Lloyd George appointed him Parliamentary Private Secretary in 1919), had arranged for a car to transport Gavan Duffy to Park Lane after dinner, so that work could begin immediately. Instead, an irate Childers shot around to Mayfair to explain that Gavan Duffy 'was unavailable', at which news Sassoon appeared 'downcast'. After Childers returned to Hans Place, he, Barton and Gavan Duffy sat up late discussing 'this astounding situation'.[65]

The following day, the Prime Minister's failed gambit was quickly forgotten in the drama generated by the draft Treaty. It arrived at lunchtime and looked more like an anonymous memo than an official document.[66] But if the presentation came as a surprise, so too did the content. Ireland was to remain within the Empire and assume Dominion powers along the lines of those possessed by Canada. Its army would be limited to 40,000 men and the responsibility for coastal defence would fall to Britain until the two countries mutually agreed an alternative arrangement. There were to be no trade restrictions, although both governments were free to impose duties to prevent dumping and unfair competition. In essence then, the draft differed little from the 20 July proposals except in one important respect: the accommodation on Northern Ireland. Craig's government would have up to a year to opt out of the new Irish state but faced higher taxes and a share of the imperial debt burden if they pursued this path. The frontier between the North and the South would be redrawn by a boundary commission. Crucially, though, and in a stipulation that assumed renewed significance years later, these alterations were to be made 'in accordance with the wishes of the inhabitants'.[67]

In the radically different political climate of spring 1924, John Chartres, a principal secretary to the Sinn Féin delegation, pointed out that the draft Treaty had imposed 'no limitation whatever' on the commission's remit, and maintained that Griffith would never have warmed to Dominion status if he believed only 'minor rectifications' to the border were possible.[68]

But it was the compromise on the Crown and Empire that infuriated the delegation's hardliners. Childers, Barton and Gavan Duffy demanded a delegates' meeting, with Gavan Duffy insisting that Lloyd George must be written to at once and informed that his Treaty was 'unacceptable'. He told Griffith, 'We shall draft another.' Griffith dismissed the suggestion, reminding his agitated colleagues that it was the eve of the Liverpool conference, so there was not much point in kicking up a fuss at this stage. That triggered another round of bickering, with Barton hurling accusations about their ill-treatment; how they had been frozen out of the talks, and 'not told enough'.[69]

Collins, meanwhile, retreated to the relative calm of Cadogan Gardens. The boredom and discomfort of sitting most of the day for Sir John Lavery, who was painting his portrait, had soured his mood. 'Absolute torture' was how he described the experience to Kitty Kiernan in a letter that afternoon, for he had been 'expected to keep still ... a thing I cannot do'.[70] Lavery never complained though; in fact, quite the opposite. Leo Whelan, who painted Collins in 1922, characterised him as the 'worst sitter he ever had'.[71] Perhaps that explains why neither artist captured their subject's restless energy, let alone anything approaching his nature or essence. The Collins who emerges from Lavery's portrait is an insipid, uninspiring figure; fleshy-cheeked, dew-eyed and one-dimensional, devoid of soul, character or presence.

Yet given the pressure of events, it is hardly surprising that Collins felt conflicted at idling away his time in an artist's studio. It was there that he met the beguilingly beautiful Hazel Lavery and the friendship that sprang up between them ensured her name became indelibly linked with his. After his death, those close to Collins dismissed Lady Lavery as a 'fantasist'. More recently she has been cast as a fearless manipulator, a siren who promoted and then profited from the salacious interest in their putative affair. The historian Peter Hart labelled her a 'super groupie' and presented her as someone who fed off Collins' celebrity status. Regardless of the truth, the rumours of a sexual liaison between them thrilled and titillated London's high society, and over the decades the nature of their relationship has remained a source of enduring fascination.[72]

In his letter to Kitty that afternoon, Collins made no mention of Lady Lavery. But he also omitted any reference to the more pressing matter of the day: the fatal shooting of Cork alderman Tadhg Barry at Ballykinlar internment camp. News of his death ignited a firestorm of outrage in Ireland after it transpired that the thirty-nine-year-old republican had been shot by a British sentry for venturing too close to the wire. Collins instantly made preparations to attend the funeral, to be held that weekend in Cork city. Meanwhile, the British, anxious to ease tensions, promised an independent inquiry to follow the inquest. As it turned out, however, there was no inquiry, and the inquest into Barry's death, which apportioned no blame, was adjourned until after the Treaty, when all internees in Ireland were released.[73]

The next day, Thursday 17 November, with the Ballykinlar incident still dominating the Irish media, the Sinn Féin delegates attempted to turn up the heat on the British by firing off a formal letter of protest to Lloyd George, condemning the conditions at another internment camp in County Kildare, where two prisoners were bayoneted while attempting to escape. Childers, who drafted the missive, called for 'immediate action'.[74] But by this stage both sides felt they were moving into the endgame. Collins had said as much in a recent letter to Kitty Kiernan, declaring that 'they were getting into the heart of things now and I don't suppose we will be here much longer'.[75] The renewed pressures strained the feuding delegation to breaking point.

Earlier in the day, as Childers noted witheringly in his diary, he had gone through the draft Treaty 'paragraph by paragraph [with the delegates] ... slowly disillusioning' them, and yet throughout, Griffith 'affected indifference ... to its demerits'.[76]

Back in Dublin, de Valera's patience was wearing thin. In his view, there had been too 'much beating around the bush' and he urged Griffith 'to get down to definite business and send them ... our final word'. In a letter written in response to the draft Treaty, he underlined how important it was to maintain 'the consistency of our position'. That meant presenting the British with draft Treaty A, 'modified somewhat to meet the exact position'.[77] He wanted the delegates to serve up another offer of External Association. But by this point, Collins had virtually reconciled himself to Dominion status, seeing it as 'beneficial', if only as a temporary settlement. In a letter to his friend John O'Kane, written in early November, Collins categorised it as a 'first step', arguing that, for the moment, more 'than this could not be expected'.[78] His views must have been partly influenced by the rapport established with Birkenhead, and the close ties forged with Griffith, although he also read widely on the subject, particularly Smuts' pioneering arguments in favour of a 'decentralised Commonwealth of Nations'.[79] He pored, too, over a memorandum Curtis had produced earlier in the conference, which purported to show 'how Dominion status actually works'. From this, Collins concluded that the Commonwealth states were moving gradually, but inexorably, towards full independence; meaning that what Dominion status offered was the freedom to achieve freedom.

His chief problem, and Griffith's, was not so much the dissent in the delegation but the attitude in Dublin. Collins constantly blamed the Cabinet for its inadequate and confusing instructions, and frequently complained about the futility of their task, knowing that any settlement opened them up to accusations of apostasy. In a swipe at de Valera, he told O'Kane at one point that he had been 'warned more times than I can recall about the ONE [i.e., de Valera]. And when I was caught for this delegation my immediate thought was how easily I walked into the preparations. But having walked in I had to stay.' On 17 November, he wrote in a similar vein to his friend, describing Griffith as 'particularly dour today. He said to me – "You realise what we have on our hands?" I replied that I realised it long ago. He meant [the] Dublin reaction to whatever happens here' – adding that Griffith told him, 'We stand or fall in this together.'[80]

After more than a month of talks, the old allegiances within the delegation had been obscured and twisted out of all recognition. Meetings at Hans Place had become more of a forum for vituperative attacks than for productive debate, making the formulation of a response to the draft Treaty a lengthy ordeal. On the afternoon of Friday 18 November, a four-hour discussion ended without consensus on any counter-proposals. In the evening, when Collins left for Dublin, Griffith wrote back to de Valera, urging him not to consider the British proposals as a draft Treaty. They were no such thing, he said, merely 'tentative suggestions' which required a reply 'with a similar document'. Yet even as he wrote these words, the British, who, as usual, were in command not only of the pace but the course of the negotiations, were busily reworking the draft into what eventually would form the basis of the final discussions. Curtis was selected for the task, or at least the vast bulk of it. When asked to undertake the responsibility, he replied modestly that he was 'no legal draftsman'.[81] Instead, he suggested a friend of his, the British-born South African judge Richard Feetham, who was also a Milner protégé. But it would be another three years before Feetham, who was as committed an imperialist as Curtis, would have the opportunity to leave his mark on Ireland's history – in his capacity as Chairman of the Boundary Commission.

Yet despite the anti-partitionist fervour that dominated Irish politics in the decades ahead, the delegation's rows rarely centred on Ulster: the supremely divisive issue, as Childers' diaries show, was always Ireland's sovereignty. And when Collins returned to Hans Place on the morning of Monday 21 November, hostilities between the two distinct groups within the delegation intensified. Over the weekend, Childers, aided by Gavan Duffy and Barton, had produced a rough counter-response to the draft Treaty. According to Barton's post-dated conference notes, they decided to present this document to Collins and Griffith as Barton's work, since Griffith reacted with 'animosity ... to any proposals put forward by Childers'.[82] But it was a futile exercise judging by what happened next. At 11.30 a.m. the delegates assembled in a belligerent mood, with the suggested defence and trade proposals immediately encountering what Childers described as 'strong opposition ... from the other side'. Amid the constant back and forth, Griffith snapped. Childers, he ranted, had started 'the last European war' with his spy novel, *The Riddle of the Sands*, and now he was hell-bent on causing another. A 'hot argument' ensued and the meeting broke up in disarray. When they reconvened some time later, enmities were as vicious as ever, and it was not until 11 p.m. that Chartres began typing out counter-proposals 'from a tangled mass of papers', and when he was finished, 'both sides' discussed the document separately. The bickering continued until well after midnight, and as Barton and Childers kept up the protest over trade and defence, Griffith, full of inchoate rage, directed a steady stream of insults at his adversary, until at some point, in the small hours of the morning, Childers snapped. He threatened resignation, a jolt that caused Griffith to 'climb down'. They agreed to resume the discussion at 9.30 a.m., although the counter-proposals were due at Downing Street at 11 a.m. 'Impossible now,' Childers wrote, ending an unusually long diary entry that day with the words, 'Bed at 3AM'.[83]

The next morning the delegates reassembled wearily; Barton appeared unwilling to go another round on trade, but Childers continued to express dissatisfaction at defence. The previous day, he thought Collins had shown 'complete ignorance' of the delegation's position on the subject, and now listened incredulously to Griffith's admission that he had 'read no defence documents'.[84] With the clock ticking, there was little time for debate. Jones had phoned earlier and demanded they submit the counter-proposals no later than 12.30 p.m.

On this occasion Sinn Féin's response arrived at 10 Downing Street on deadline, and after digesting it, the Prime Minister flew into a rage. '"This is no use", he cried. "They are back on their independent state again."' Jones recalled how 'he started walking up and down instructing me to go to the Sinn Fein leaders and tell them that unless they withdrew their document he would have to break off the negotiations'. Then he said, 'Fetch Chamberlain.' In the presence of the Conservative leader and Birkenhead, Lloyd George wheeled out the familiar threats. Jones was to relay to the Sinn Féiners that 'Ministers were busy men, they had spent weeks on this matter and apparently made no progress whatever', and with calculated menace warned that if 'they are not coming into the Empire, then we will make them'. This drew 'accompanying remarks of approval' from Chamberlain and Birkenhead.[85] Yet despite the threats and bluster, the counter-proposals had reduced Lloyd George to despair. As Frances Stevenson observed in her diary, 'things seem very shaky. [Lloyd George] is worried & irritable. There seems to be so many snags and he is almost worn out with these protracted negotiations.'[86]

8 ▪ CROSSINGS
22 November–30 November

It took Jones less than forty-five minutes to corner Griffith and convey the gravity of the situation to him. They were nearing the end, he warned. Unless Sinn Féin's counter-proposals were 'withdrawn or explained away', the Prime Minister 'would have no option' other than to break off the negotiations. Griffith reacted with terse impassivity. He 'said very little', Jones recorded in his diary, 'and most of the little he did say I had to extract from him'. But he thought the Irish leader 'unprepared for my message'. Privately, he even sympathised with Griffith's restrained protests, noting that the document marked an advance on previous offers, and the safeguards on Ulster 'went further … than we had asked'. But it was External Association that brought out the gall and brimstone in No. 10, so 'in the most conciliatory manner' he begged Griffith 'to use "within" the Commonwealth and drop "associated"'.[1]

Tom Jones was a shrewd, energetic man, who once characterised his role within the Cabinet secretariat as that of 'a rather fluid person moving amongst people who matter'. His position at the centre of government was the result not of a steady ascent through the civil service ranks, but the strength of his Welsh connections. Launched into Lloyd George's orbit in 1916 by David Davies, a wealthy industrialist and Liberal MP from South Wales, Jones, like so many of the mavericks with whom the Prime Minister surrounded himself, was no 'born bureaucrat'. Brought up in a Welsh-speaking, working-class family, he funded his degree in economics from the money he earned as a Calvinist preacher, although he had lost his faith by the time he graduated. After first trying out a career in academia, he moved into philanthropy, before being propelled into Whitehall, where he developed an unswerving loyalty to Lloyd George.[2] Indeed, it is hard to imagine his free-wheeling approach – he loathed office hours – would have been tolerated by a less orthodox premier. Jones thrived because Lloyd George revolutionised the Cabinet secretariat, radically expanding its powers so that it became, in the words of the historian Kenneth O. Morgan, an 'ancillary department to the Prime Minister'. This helped him dominate his government from within, for although Lloyd George showed little interest in the details of the machinery of government, he was, as Morgan observed, 'an artist in the use of power'.[3]

And what made Jones indispensable to him in the Irish negotiations was the Welshman's ability to inspire trust. He made friends easily and, unlike his wooden superior, Cabinet Secretary Maurice Hankey, who had been parcelled off to the Washington Conference, Jones moved freely within different political and social circles. Above all, he radiated integrity, to the extent that the Sinn Féin delegates took him at his word.[4] When he repeated Lloyd George's threats, they resonated with full force, and later Curtis would claim that the Prime Minister's technique was 'to put the wind up so badly with Tom Jones that T.J. put the wind up with the Irish', convincing them that a rupture in the talks presaged war and certain military annihilation.[5]

At these moments of crisis, a buttoned-up Griffith tended to become more reserved and inscrutable than usual. And on this occasion, he conceded nothing. Instead, with outward equanimity, he levelled his own accusations at Jones, complaining that the British had played into Craig's hands by first extracting concessions from Sinn Féin. He predicted the leader of the Ulster Unionists would concede nothing and would accuse Sinn Féin of betraying their followers, adding that Irish nationalists had long experience of these tactics. Part-way through this conversation, Collins arrived and, after another debate, Jones asked, 'What was to be done?' How could they prevent a breakdown in the negotiations? The Irish were reticent, so Jones suggested they take the rest of the day to reconsider the memo 'in light' of the Prime Minister's message. In the next breath, he offered detailed instructions: the Irish were to ring him 'later in the evening' and state that it 'would be useful' to arrange a meeting for the following morning with the Prime Minister and Birkenhead.[6] Then he left them.

After lunch, Jones returned to 10 Downing Street where he found Lloyd George 'resting on a couch in the drawing room'. He sat down 'by his side, and beginning in Welsh and passing into English, spoke ... quietly and soothingly ... about the interview [with Collins and Griffith], moving rapidly over their explanation and telling him that they had gone off to consider his message with their colleagues' and that they should hear back from them 'during the day'.[7] But to the chief British delegates – 'the Big Four' as Pakenham called them – Sinn Féin's silence that afternoon was a cause of acute concern. At a Cabinet meeting held in the Foreign Office so that ministers could consider 'the artistic merit' of the building's partially completed 'mural decorations', they struggled to concentrate on Curzon's denunciations of the artworks, which depict the triumphs of Britannia in a racially ordered Anglo-Saxon empire. Curzon thought their Bacchanalian scenes were out 'of harmony with the architecture of the Foreign Office', and on another occasion, disparaged the paintings as best suited to a German beer hall.[8] Amid the debate, Birkenhead, then Chamberlain, and finally the Prime Minister, peppered Jones with anxious enquiries, each passing him a note asking after the 'interview with Griffith'. When Lloyd George asked whether they were very truculent, Jones 'scribbled back "Nervous, rather firm, not at all truculent."'[9]

Some hours later, the Welsh secretary spoke to Andy Cope, Assistant Undersecretary to Ireland. He urged his colleague to use his influence with the Irish delegates, and impress upon them the importance of giving 'categorical assurances on fundamentals like allegiance and the navy'. Cope dashed off, found Duggan at the theatre, and 'hammered' away at him.[10]

At Hans Place, the parlous state of the talks precipitated another tempestuous meeting. Griffith, told his colleagues that 'Jones says [the] fat is in the fire', and after some debate, the delegates agreed to the suggested follow-up meeting with the Prime Minister, 'but only to explain [the] document' as Childers wrote in his diary. More angry exchanges followed when Gavan Duffy insisted on Barton attending too. Griffith, now overflowing with frustration, 'broke out about Allegiance saying he was willing to give it to save [the] country from war – personally willing'. Emotions reached such a pitch that he threatened to march straight over to Lloyd George and proclaim his position at once. When Barton challenged him to do just that, he retreated, and the meeting was brought to an abrupt end.[11]

In the evening, the delegates drifted off to the theatre, but Childers had no time for such pursuits. He 'worked late' on another memorandum, one that explained at length why the latest proposals were a bridge too far.[12] In the first line he asserted that 'Ireland's full claim is for a Republic, unfettered by any obligations or restrictions whatsoever.'[13]

The next morning, he presented this paper, entitled 'Concession Memo', to his colleagues and recorded in his diary that an 'unpleasant incident' followed. Griffith 'exploded and said he hoped it was not supposed to represent [the] Delegation as he strongly disagreed with it'. Childers countered that it was 'a personal memo [and] asked him what he disagreed with ... he said a "great deal"'.[14] Agitated, Griffith set off for Downing Street, accompanied by Collins and Barton. Waiting for them was an equally unsettled Prime Minister, flanked by Chamberlain and Birkenhead. Yet, with both sides keen to avoid a rupture, the tensions subsided into a 'long and not unfriendly discussion', which, in Jones' judgement, removed 'certain misunderstandings'.[15]

From the Irish perspective, however, nothing could have been further from the truth. On the subject of Ulster, the encounter embedded rather than dispelled confusion, because Griffith once again failed to properly articulate the Irish position. In their response to the British proposals, Sinn Féin made no mention of the Boundary Commission, promising that in exchange for 'essential unity', Northern Ireland could retain its local parliament and powers, along with any other safeguards that it felt were necessary.[16] The omission irritated Lloyd George, because he was due to see Craig in the coming days and wanted to know why the Sinn Féin delegates had not 'embodied' the scheme in their memorandum. Griffith replied that he stood by his earlier 'assurance' but reminded the Prime Minister that the Boundary Commission was 'his proposal –

not ours'. This 'satisfied' Lloyd George, Griffith wrote to de Valera that evening. 'He had misunderstood us in this instance and said ... He would put his proposals to Craig from himself only.'[17] What this implied to the Prime Minister, however, was that Griffith would accept the Boundary Commission even if the Northern Ireland Premier rejected it. To the Sinn Féin leader, Craig's refusal was a foregone conclusion, and for this reason, he perceived no threat to the fallback plan of collapsing the talks on Ulster. What escaped him was that Lloyd George was prepared to implement his alternative proposal, whether Craig agreed with it or not.

At this point, the Prime Minister suddenly called a halt to the meeting, declaring that he needed to confer in private with Chamberlain and Birkenhead. When they returned, Lloyd George forced matters to a head, and warned the Irish that time was running out: he 'must know where he stood on the fundamentals' before seeing Craig. As he quickened the pace, the language became correspondingly more aggressive. He reiterated remarks made at the start of the discussion: that 'on the Crown [the British] had no alternative. They must fight.' But he wished to avoid the 'tragedy' of a break-up 'on any verbal or technical misunderstanding' and was therefore advising a follow-up conference in the morning, between Collins, Griffith and Birkenhead. That way they could review the assurances Griffith had given in his 2 November letter to the Prime Minister and establish once and for all what the Irish position was on the Crown and Empire. With this agreed, Lloyd George lapsed into a 'much milder mood'.[18] Jones noted afterwards that he 'hardly referred to the question of a rupture but asked rhetorically "Why did they bring that pip-squeak of a man Barton with them? I would not make him a private secretary to an Under Secretary."'[19]

That evening, at Hans Place, Childers, still smarting from the earlier exchanges with Griffith, extolled Barton's superior note-taking skills, writing that his cousin's record of the meeting at 10 Downing Street 'added much & shamed AG's [Griffith's] minutes of such conferences'. These, he thought, were not to be 'relied' on even when Barton was 'present'.[20] Attention now focused on who was to accompany Collins and Griffith to the sub-conference with Birkenhead at the House of Lords. The Lord Chancellor had told them to bring along a 'constitutional lawyer'. Collins suggested Chartres, but Childers also wanted Gavan Duffy to attend, on the grounds that he was the 'legal member of the Delegation'. The row flared up again in the morning and this time Gavan Duffy declared, in his cut-glass English accent – he was educated at an elite Jesuit school in England – that there 'should have been a [delegates'] meeting to decide' the issue. Griffith 'lost his temper and exploded', then 'had the face', Childers wrote in his diary, 'to say that GD had "let him down" on neutrality at an early conference', when, 'in reality', he seethed, it was 'the opposite'. The mood deteriorated further when Gavan Duffy and Barton argued that Childers 'ought to' attend too. As Griffith grew 'very angry', Collins 'remarked smilingly' that he had no idea that Childers 'knew anything about the constitutional side', a slight that did not go unregistered. Finally, Chartres made a 'perfunctory offer not to [attend]', since Collins and Griffith were apprehensive about the Irish turning up en masse to a sub-conference with two British delegates. But Childers thought the gesture 'absurd' and immediately seized the opportunity to assert that he 'would go away anyway' just to be 'officially in attendance'. It took a conciliatory overture from Barton to end the debate. He suggested that Griffith enter Birkenhead's office first, so that he could check the British had no objections to Childers' presence.[21]

Griffith did just that, and 'needless to say', Childers wrote, 'arranged that I should be left out!'[22] But he was not to be bored. Curtis, his old schoolfellow joined him, and before long the 'two yogis' were locked in a debate about imperial citizenship and External Association. Their discussion grew so animated it distracted others, and although they 'asked for an empty room', none was available. So, in the presence of two of Birkenhead's secretaries, they sat out the rest of the meeting in silence.[23]

Progress proved elusive, too, in the more spacious surrounds of the Lord Chancellor's room, as both sides became bogged down on the question of allegiance. Birkenhead, in the company of the Attorney General, Gordon Hewart, tried to persuade Collins, Griffith, Gavan Duffy and Chartres that the Crown represented nothing more than symbolic British suzerainty. There would be no interference in Ireland's internal affairs, he said, 'except on the advice of Irish ministers'.[24] Chartres answered that Ireland would never accept the 'sincerity of that proposal'. He had submitted a memorandum in advance of the meeting characterising the English as an occupying force; an endemic evil that Ireland wanted rid of so that her people could control their 'own affairs free from the dictation or control of another nation'. And if the Crown was to be reduced to a mere symbol, the Irish would demand written guarantees to this effect, exposing 'the monarchical principle' to 'ridicule and contempt'.[25] For this reason, he argued, an associated republic offered the sole solution. Griffith struck a similar line, arguing that External Association bridged 'two apparently irreconcilable positions', while preserving the 'honour and interests of both peoples'. Unmoved, Birkenhead repeated that the 'issue was vital' – words that conveyed the unmistakable menace of war.[26]

The Sinn Féin delegates were then asked to formulate

a proposal for recognition of the Crown and submit it to Downing Street in writing. In the car back to Hans Place, Griffith apologised to Gavan Duffy, and later that evening, accompanied by Collins and Barton, boarded the train for the first leg of the overnight journey back to Dublin.[27] The delegates were under instructions not to make major decisions without first consulting the Dáil Cabinet, and so the meeting with Birkenhead made a precipitate journey home unavoidable. But their departure unnerved the British, who discovered the three Irishmen were crossing back to Ireland only an hour before the train pulled out of Euston station. Cope learned the news first and, in a panic, rang up Jones, who, in turn, dashed round in the dark to 10 Downing Street, where the Prime Minister was on the phone to Birkenhead. He had heard a 'rumour' about their plans and was riled that Scotland Yard appeared to be in the dark, which suggests a routine knowledge of the Irish delegation's movements and deliberations.[28] Most likely, it was the disruption of this information flow that caused such agitation, particularly for Cope, who believed the belated discovery left them unable to influence public opinion in Dublin. He worried that this raised the risk of the hardliners triggering a 'break on allegiance'.

It has been known for some time that there was an informant in the Irish camp, but the extent of British surveillance during the Treaty talks remains a mystery: a conspicuous knowledge-gap in what is otherwise well-excavated terrain. Professor Eunan O'Halpin has beaten the drum about this issue for decades, arguing that it 'beggars belief that [Sir Basil] Thomson, who made almost a fetish of snooping on foreign diplomats, would not have made a sustained effort to collect intelligence on Griffith, Collins and their comrades during their time in London'.[29] The Soviet Trade Delegation was immediately put under close surveillance after arriving in the capital in May 1920. Indeed, the Russians' legal adviser in England, the solicitor and Conservative MP Sir William Bull, who was close to senior members of the government, including the Prime Minister and Bonar Law, routinely passed information about his Bolshevik clients back to the security services.[30] It is not a great leap to imagine that the British achieved a comparable level of covert access to the Irish delegates during the 1921 Treaty talks, but until whatever remaining evidence of the intelligence-gathering during this time comes to light, it is impossible to assess how these tactics affected the outcome of the negotiations. O'Halpin believes it is 'highly likely' the British 'listened in on phones used by the Irish ... and probably tried to bribe servants in Hans Place'. In his view, there remains an outside chance that Sinn Féin's London headquarters were bugged, although he admits the available technology would have been rudimentary and 'cumbersome to use'.[31]

Home Office files indicate there was at least one informant in Hans Place. On 1 November, a still unidentified source passed details of the Irish delegates' views and negotiating tactics to the British; information that was so extensive – albeit not very insightful – it stretched to a two-page report.[32] Over the decades, despite a paucity of substantiating evidence, an accusatory finger has been pointed at Chartres, on the grounds that he was English and associated with the security services during the First World War. However, if Thomson had run surveillance operations on the Sinn Féin delegates, his influence was now at an end. By the time Collins, Griffith and Barton were hurrying back to Dublin on the evening of 24 November, Thomson was out in the cold, with his fiefdom at Scotland Yard scrapped, and his old adversary, Commissioner of the Metropolitan Police William Horwood, once more in the ascendant.

Lloyd George, it appears, could do nothing other than sit tight and await the delegates' return. In a fit of despondency, he told Frances Stevenson that 'a break may occur at any moment', and on the same day, he wrote to his wife, Margaret Lloyd George, explaining that he could not make it back to Wales that weekend as the 'Irish negotiations have taken a turn for the worse – seriously. This time it is the Sinn Feiners,' he said. 'Last week it was the Ulsterites. They are both the sons of Belial!'[33] His anxiety was made more acute by the realisation that the Liverpool conference had left him as unpopular as ever among the Conservatives. In the show of strength against the diehards, a newfound confidence was at work: a belief, still maturing among the Tory ranks, that the electoral Elysian fields were theirs again provided they remained united. The renewed stridency alarmed Liberal members of the coalition Cabinet. Edwin Montagu of the India Office warned Jones on 25 November that, after Liverpool, it was clear 'the Tories would desert the P.M. given the slightest chance'. Lloyd George's political future hinged on the outcome of the Irish peace conference, Montagu argued, and the Prime Minister could 'not afford to let the negotiations fail'.[34]

On that same day in Dublin, a momentous row engulfed the republican leadership. As the talks hung in the balance, de Valera pressed ahead with a long-planned overhaul of the IRA. The army was to be subordinated to civilian control, its chain of command overhauled and the Minister for Defence installed at its apex. For Cathal Brugha, this was to be his hour of triumph, a moment of vindication. He would no longer suffer the 'daily humiliation', as the historian John Regan put it, 'of holding an emasculated portfolio as a sinecure, while real power remained outside his influence in GHQ and by inference with the IRB and Collins'.[35] As part of the reorganisation, the inexperienced Stack was to occupy the second most powerful position in the army hierarchy, replacing Eoin O'Duffy, Collins' protégé, as Deputy Chief of Staff. Brugha had been insisting on this appointment since September, when he and de Valera first embarked on the 'New Army' project. In his view, Stack's entitlement to the role stretched back years and he remained impervious to sustained objections from Mulcahy, resulting in an ill-timed stand-off between the Minister for Defence and the IRA's Chief of Staff. A protracted exchange of letters between the two men widened the rift, and, although Mulcahy appealed to de Valera in October, a meeting of the three failed to ease tensions and the dangerous dynamic was left to fester.[36]

These altercations failed to suppress Brugha's determination to press ahead apace with the army reforms, which had the full support of de Valera. Yet although the Dáil Cabinet agreed on 15 September to subject the IRA to civilian control, it was not until mid-November that Brugha formally notified GHQ of the decision 'to issue fresh commissions to Officers, and to offer re-enlistment of all other ranks'.[37] When the divisional commanders received the Defence Ministry memorandum, they reacted with a mixture of surprise and outright opposition. Liam Lynch, Commander of the 1st Southern Division, flatly rejected the plan, while Frank Aiken, O/C 4th Northern, replied tartly that the 'circular was the first we ever received from the Minister for Defence'. Dan Hogan, commander of the 5th Northern Division, was similarly unimpressed, commenting that as this 'was the only intimation' he had received of the changes, he could not accept the new commission until he had the chance 'to communicate with the chief of staff on the matter'.[38] In an effort to resolve the difficulties, Mulcahy suggested a meeting on 25 November between the Cabinet and the entire GHQ staff. From the outset the proceedings were marred by a tone of bitter intensity. O'Duffy had fired in a missive the day before declaiming his reduction in rank as a 'personal slight and grave dishonour'. And when he repeated this complaint at the meeting, Mulcahy recalled that his 'voice became a little bit shrill'. O'Duffy was among the last in the room to voice an opinion, and predictably all GHQ staff before him vehemently rejected the changes. This apparently proved the last straw for de Valera, with O'Duffy's 'slight touch of hysteria' provoking an extraordinary reaction from the President. Confronted by GHQ's united opposition, he 'rose excitedly in his chair, pushed the small table in front of him, and declared in a half-scream, half-shout, "ye may mutiny if you like, but Ireland will give me another Army"'. According to Mulcahy, he then 'dismissed the whole lot of us from his sight'.[39]

To some historians the wrangling over the army signalled the 'beginning of the slide into civil war'.[40] It certainly exacerbated the long-standing feud between Mulcahy and Collins on the one hand, and Brugha and Stack on the other. Yet as Bill Kissane has written, the post-Treaty fratricidal strife cannot be attributed solely to the complex power struggles among the revolutionary elite.[41] An abiding perplexity, though, is why de Valera pursued such a destabilising policy at such a sensitive time. Was it to embed 'his people' in the post-IRA army, a school of thought that casts de Valera as a craven figure, eager for greater influence and personal prestige.[42] John Regan argues persuasively that while the New Army plans could have waited until the London negotiations were concluded, 'settlement reached and war averted', there is no evidence that de Valera had slipped into a 'partisan role'. His overriding concern was 'cabinet unity' so that he could ram through his compromise, an outcome that hinged on a 'hierarchy of responsibility for the settlement', meaning the Cabinet would carry the Dáil, and the Dáil the army.[43]

As far as de Valera was concerned, Collins and his circle within the IRB had indicated they would accept a compromise; therefore, the most important militarist-republicans he needed to placate were Brugha and Stack. The former had tacitly accepted External Association as the basis on which talks could be entered into, but, as Regan emphasises, throughout the negotiations he and Stack 'remained stubbornly non-committal in defining precisely what they would accept as a settlement other than de facto recognition of the republic'.[44]

If Brugha was bargaining his principles – rowing in behind de Valera in exchange for the ability to assert his authority over the army and usurp Collins' power base – the events of 25 November proved a disappointment. GHQ's hierarchy remained effectively untouched, except for the deputy chief of staff role, which was split between Stack and O'Duffy, with the former forced to assume a nominally inferior position to the latter. As the Dáil Cabinet minutes for that day attest, the minister for defence was established as the 'Administrative Head' of the army. He possessed the power to sanction all appointments, along with the rights of nomination and veto. Mulcahy meanwhile retained his chief of staff role, with his duties, as the 'professional or technical head of the army', to be defined by de Valera at a later date.[45]

The upshot was that, within the IRA, Brugha's de facto position remained unchanged and Collins' influence undimmed. As if to reinforce this, Mulcahy issued a circular a few days later, explaining to divisional commanders that 'while it might be inferred from this document [the Ministry memorandum] that a New Army is being formed, this is not really so'.[46] Given the strength of feeling within GHQ, de Valera refrained from forcing the issue any further, and ultimately, the New Army plan was never put to the test, for within a fortnight the old certainties had shattered. The world turned upside down and nothing was ever the same again.

After the meetings over the draft Treaty, Griffith was the first of the delegation's three Cabinet ministers to make it back to Hans Place. He returned on Saturday morning, 26 November, and Childers noted dourly in his diary that 'He told us nothing.' He rang up Jones to ask when 'they expected to receive' the formula on the Crown and was told, breezily, that 'Monday would do'.[47]

Dense fog enveloped London that weekend. It became so impenetrable that at times the traffic inched forward 'only with the help of flares', while on the Strand, as *The Manchester Guardian* reported, fog 'blotted out the lamps on the opposite side of the street and ... descended from the roofs in swirls of soot-laden smoke, making eyes ... smart and heads ... ache'.[48] It was, perhaps, the implacable November weather that inspired Childers to produce what Pakenham lauded as the delegation's 'ablest' defence of External Association.[49] Marooned at Hans Place, he worked all day and, while the others played whist, laboured on until 2 a.m. The resulting, skilfully crafted polemic retrod familiar terrain: the Crown was a symbol of historic repression in Ireland; distance afforded no protection from its powers; if it remained, the risk of British interference also remained, so it was 'incompatible with the independence and dignity of our country, incompatible with real peace' and could not 'be accepted'.[50]

The Irish were advancing their claim for External Association for the fourth time. At the Cabinet meeting in Dublin, Collins and Griffith, despite their misgivings, had agreed to stand over the strategy again and present it as the maximum concession on offer. On the formula, the unanimous decision was that: 'Ireland shall recognise the British Crown for the purposes of the Association as symbol and accepted head of the combination of Associated States'. By 28 November, this had been reworked into an ostensibly more palatable version: 'Ireland will agree to be associated with the British Commonwealth for all purposes of common concern, including defence, peace and war, and political treaties, and to recognise the British Crown as Head of the Association.'[51] To cushion the blow further, the Irish offered to make an annual voluntary contribution 'to the King's personal revenue'; proof, Jones noted with a droll air, that 'Their antipathy is not to the King.'[52]

Childers had expected to discuss the document early that morning, but Griffith, whose energy and health were flagging, deferred the meeting until lunchtime. It nonetheless turned into another volcanic encounter. Childers objected to Griffith's 'redraft' of the memo, particularly the passage on defence, provoking 'the usual explosion' from the latter about this constant 'waste of time'. In his diary, a piqued Childers noted that there was 'Little help from anyone else.'

The frequency and vehemence of these rows lay bare a curious dissonance between Griffith's public and private personas. To the British he was an inscrutable character, a man of few words; 'sphinx-like' as Jones put it. His followers in Ireland formed a similar view. The Belfast-born essayist Robert Lynd recalled that 'one only had to look at his abnormally developed jaw muscles and his square, powerful shoulders to realise the strength of will that lay behind his habitual quietness'.[53] Readers of his forceful and accusatory journalism often found the first encounter with Griffith a shock, for it was impossible to reconcile the imperturbable figure in front of them with the man 'who wielded', as Piaras Béaslaí wrote, 'so brilliant, so trenchant, nay, sometimes so savage a pen'.[54] His detractors could be equally lavish in their condemnation, with the doomed revolutionary Patrick Pearse producing this diatribe of him in 1912:

> You were too hard. You were too obstinate. You were too narrow-minded. You were too headstrong. You did not trust your friends enough. You trusted yourself too much. You over-estimated your own opinion. You distrusted people who were as loyal as yourself. You would follow no one's advice except your own. You preferred to prove to the world that no one else was right except yourself.[55]

Pearse's damning judgement, written in Irish, appears to have served as a final word on Griffith in the public's imagination, for while the martyrs of Easter 1916 were swept into the republican pantheon, he slipped into relative obscurity. And little has changed over the past century: Pearse remains an object of mass veneration; Griffith has all but faded from view. He died in a Dublin hospital in August 1922, a lonely and embittered man, 'with nothing more auspicious uttered over his head than "take up that corpse at once"'.[56] Anti-treatyites imprisoned in Portobello Barracks reportedly cheered the news of his death, and years later his widow, Maud, complained, in anguish, that her husband was remembered solely for calling Erskine Childers 'a damned Englishman'.[57]

There was a state funeral and for a time, a shabby cenotaph of 'peeling wood and plaster' occupied the Irish parliament's Leinster Lawn, in part tribute, as the historian Anne Dolan documents, to the first President of the Irish Free State.[58] But the awkward commemorations of the 1920s were a far cry from the adulation showered on dead republican heroes. The choices Griffith made in that last dramatic year of his life defined his legacy; yet, at the start of the century, it would have been incomprehensible to speak of him as a moderate. Back then he was the extremist, the embodiment of a new, uncompromising independence movement. For years, as the historian Patrick Maume observes, Griffith told the Irish people that they 'could liberate themselves if only they had the will, and denounced those who thought otherwise as degenerate traitors'.[59]

By the time of the Treaty talks, the erstwhile icon of Irish nationalism, aged fifty, had become something of a revolutionary embarrassment to republican hardliners. They eyed him with suspicion, none more so than Childers, who on 28 November came to the conclusion that Griffith, assisted by Duggan, had double-crossed him in what he saw as their reckless determination to meet with Lloyd George. To Childers' mind, the delegation had a duty to unite behind External Association. Until the British responded to what he, Gavan Duffy and Barton regarded as the final restatement of this demand, there was nothing to be gained from another encounter with the Prime Minister.

The Irish delegation's response to the British proposals had been dispatched to Jones at 5 p.m., who handed it to the Prime Minister at Chequers almost three hours later. Lloyd George read it aloud and said, 'This means war.'[60] But Chamberlain, equally exasperated, displayed more moderation. Before departing for Chequers, Jones showed the Sinn Féin memo to the Conservative leader, who, overcoming his consternation, dashed off a letter to Lloyd George, insisting that while 'We cannot make peace on these terms ... we must not break on this document.'[61]

Jones had spent much of the day in pursuit of Griffith. The Prime Minister wanted the Irish delegation's two leaders, together with Birkenhead and Robert Horne, to join him at Chequers that evening. But the plans were thrown into disarray by Childers. He answered the phone at Hans Place that afternoon, relayed the

message to Griffith, then rang back informing Jones that Collins
was away, and Griffith 'did not much care for the proposal'.
A short while later, Jones called again, spoke to Griffith and
the invitation was accepted. Appalled, Childers accused his
colleagues of going behind his back, writing in his diary that it
was 'pretty clear' that Griffith and Duggan 'took steps to reopen
this matter ... Why I don't know.'[62] Both men had, in fact,
met Cope and Jones, shortly after 5 p.m. when the External
Association document was submitted. Although he assumed
that Childers 'had done his best to block' the proposed meeting,
Jones ultimately attributed the delegates' initial reluctance to
a misunderstanding about whether the invitation to Chequers
was an official one or not. 'They wanted to be sure that the P.M.
was asking them down,' he wrote in his diary.[63]

Almost an hour later, in a hastily convened meeting in
Childers' room, it was clear there was far more at stake. As
Childers insisted there was no need for the Chequers gathering,
Griffith openly advocated for Dominion status, arguing that
the 'whole country wants peace' and would 'surrender on the
Crown'. A 'plebiscite on war,' he asserted, 'would not get two
seats'. Duggan expressed his support for this position, while
the others confined their reaction to 'mild remonstrances', as
Griffith, despite his frustration, had reassured his colleagues
that when he spoke to Lloyd George, he would 'insist on "no
Crown"'.

At Chequers, meanwhile, the Prime Minister was concentrating on creating as threatening an atmosphere as possible. He
wanted the Sinn Féiners shown into the 'famous' Long Room, a
gallery which runs along the north side of the sixteenth-century
manor house, where they would be surrounded by the relics of
Cromwell. On the mantelpiece above a vast fireplace lay the
Lord Protector's great sword and in a glass-topped bureau at

the end of the room was his death mask. According to Jones, he thought it an appropriate room for such a 'historic interview'.

Anxious to avoid British hospitality, Griffith and Duggan set off for Chequers immediately after dinner. They arrived at 10.10 p.m. and declined an offer to stay overnight. Later, after they had left, Jones recorded that Lloyd George 'went off to bed with the remark in Welsh "Gwell" (Better)'. Childers merely noted that the two delegates returned to Hans Place at 2 a.m.[64]

According to Griffith's report to de Valera the following day – the sole account of this meeting – Lloyd George began the discussion on a belligerent note, deploying the sort of aggressive rhetoric that had been his stock-in-trade since his early days as a backbencher. No British government, he told the Irishmen, 'could … propose to the British people the abrogation of the Crown. It would be smashed to atoms.' But having vented his anger, Griffith recalled how he then 'knocked out' the Irish argument on the Crown. The Sinn Féin delegates could insert any phrase in the Treaty they 'liked to ensure that the function of the Crown in Ireland should be no more in practice than it is in Canada or any Dominion'. And if it helped the Irish, he would, despite the 'immense difficulty', try to 'modify' the traditional oath of allegiance. Finally, he declared that the Crown's representative in Ireland would be appointed only in consultation with the Irish government.[65]

With these concessions ringing in their ears, Lloyd George began to march Sinn Féin to the precipice. Another meeting was arranged at Downing Street for 4 p.m. the next day, Tuesday 29 November. Childers was again consigned to Curtis' company, and joined by Jones; while Lloyd George, Birkenhead and Chamberlain confronted Collins, Griffith and Duggan in the Cabinet room. They retraced the main points of the Chequers conversation before the Prime Minister brandished an alternative form of the oath of allegiance. The Irish were wary. They conferred in private for ten minutes, before declaring that they needed more time to consider the matter. Then, towards the end of this hour and a half discussion, Lloyd George announced that he intended to send Craig the final terms of the Treaty by Tuesday 6 December. Sinn Féin would receive it at the same time. Griffith, thoroughly alarmed, protested that Ulster's people might learn what had been agreed in advance of the rest of Ireland. That 'would make his course very difficult', he warned. In response, Lloyd George promised to send the Treaty to the Irish by Thursday evening – in two days' time.[66]

Back at Hans Place, Griffith wrote immediately to de Valera: 'It is essential a Cabinet meeting should be held. I shall return to Dublin on Friday morning and hope to see you on that evening. Please have a Cabinet meeting arranged for Saturday morning, when we shall be all there.'[67] Meanwhile, in Belfast a nascent triumphalism took hold, as Craig told the Northern Ireland parliament that by 'Tuesday next either the negotiations will have broken down or the Prime Minister will send me new proposals for the consideration of the Cabinet.' Having ruled out any participation in the Irish Conference until the British government abandoned its pursuit of an all-Ireland parliament – or the 'Sinn Fein surrender terms', as *The Morning Post* put it – Craig declared that, whatever the outcome, 'the rights of Ulster will be in no way sacrificed or compromised'. He hinted, too, at renewed warfare in the South, proclaiming that every 'inch of ground in the Six Counties was sacred, and must be a harbour of refuge for those who might be driven over the borders in search of safety of life and limb.'[68] Prolonged cheers greeted this hour-long speech, and the next day *The Morning Post* reported with satisfaction that Craig's delivery had been characteristically 'blunt and straightforward'.[69]

At Hans Place, as they awaited the draft Treaty, the sudden lull in activity sharpened anxieties and heightened tensions. Barton, fed up with the confinement, wanted to return to Dublin immediately, but acknowledged to Childers that this would be seen as 'too much like a personal affront' to Griffith.[70] On Wednesday 30 November, Collins wrote to Kitty Kiernan, admitting that he was in a 'very troubled state of mind', plagued by all the 'Little wrongs I may have done people'; while Childers laboured away on part two of his memorandum entitled 'Law & Fact in Canada'.[71] He was still working on this when Jones called to convey that they were running ahead of schedule, and that the Articles of Agreement, later known simply as the Treaty, would be delivered to Hans Place by 10 p.m. As the rest of the delegation engaged in an after-dinner game of roulette, Childers retreated upstairs to his room to rest, having finally finished his 'Law & Fact' memo. He heard Jones arrive with the draft Treaty and noted in his diary that he did 'not ask for me'. Instead, the Welshman spoke to Duggan, and shortly afterwards, Childers heard the voices of Griffith and Collins in 'the room below'. At 11 p.m., Griffith 'opened the door & handed me an envelope of documents'.

Almost immediately Barton, Gavan Duffy, Chartres and Childers grouped together and, after a 'long talk', agreed that it was 'impossible to accept'. To Childers, the British had scarcely advanced on their 20 July proposals: it was the Crown 'in practice' and, aside from the Boundary Commission, and 'safeguards to Ulster', the 'Oath [was] as before', and 'Defence [was] hopeless'.[72] They focused not so much on the freedoms gained but rather on what would be lost with a settlement of Dominion status and the renunciation of the self-proclaimed Republic. And if this group represented a distinct political constituency, unwilling to concede what the British regarded as the bare minimum, so, too, did the IRA, 'the fighting men, the men who count' and 'who are ready', as Brugha would later put it, 'to make sacrifices'.[73] For as the historian Peter Hart wrote, the 'guerrillas thought of themselves as sovereign'. And they

> were not just defending the national republic declared in 1916 and launched in 1919, they were also defending the 'Cork republic' and the innumerable little parish 'republics' ... proclaimed during the Tan War wherever the I.R.A. writ ran unimpeded. From the moment of the Truce onwards, each unit was in effectively undisputed control of its territory and the reality of local power was as difficult to surrender as the ideal of a pure and untrammelled Ireland.[74]

These multiple, conflicting visions of Ireland rendered agreement on the terms of any Treaty an unlikely prospect.

In the Cabinet in Dublin, attitudes were hardening. At the end of November, de Valera, writing to Harry Boland in Washington, declared that as 'things stand to-day it means war. The British ultimatum is allegiance to their King. We will never recommend that such allegiance be rendered.' He expected that 'my view will be that of the Cabinet as a whole', but explained, in stark recognition of the travails ahead, that 'if I appear with those who choose war, it is only because the alternative is impossible without dishonour'.[75]

Collins, too, succumbed to a fatalistic mood. He told John O'Kane that the 'only names worth considering after this will be the names of those who have kept away from London. Integrity of purpose', he wrote with bitterness, 'is defeated at all times by those whose star rests elsewhere.'[76]

9 ▪ LAST DAYS
1 December–6 December

In the days that followed, events unfolded at a frantic rate. The British, still in control of the pace and flow of the talks, and aware of the divisions within Sinn Féin, now rushed the conference to its close, narrowing the options by presenting the Irish with what they described as their final terms. With less than a week to accept or reject these terms, the Sinn Féin delegation, weakened by weeks of jarring acrimony, rancorous divisions and intense personal rivalries, was in no state to hold its ground. To the Cassandra-like Childers, it appeared as if his worst prophecies were coming true: the fate of Ireland was 'being settled hugger-mugger by ignorant Irish negotiators', and the worst of it, he wrote with despair in his diary on 1 December, was that Griffith showed 'genuine sympathy with many of the English claims'.[1]

At midday, a meeting at Hans Place had turned into another ill-mannered debate. Griffith asked his colleagues to voice their objections to the proposed Treaty so that 'it might not ever be said afterwards that all arguments had not been fully heard'. But as they ran through the eighteen Articles of Agreement, which proposed to establish Ireland as a self-governing Dominion operating on the same constitutional lines as Canada, with a governor general to represent the Crown and members of the Irish parliament to take an oath of allegiance to both the new state's constitution and the British monarch, tempers frayed. Childers accused Griffith of flaring out at him with some 'vague' charge, and Collins, rather than remain on the sidelines as he usually did when these two crossed swords, waded in with his own criticism. Indignant, Childers demanded Griffith put his accusations of him in writing, and in this tense state of affairs, the discussion ended abruptly, although Childers noted that, afterwards, Collins made a 'ghost of a suggestion of an apology'.[2] At just after 6 p.m., all three took off to Downing Street for a meeting with the Prime Minister. In the Cabinet room, Collins and Griffith presented Lloyd George with an alternative oath of allegiance, one that described the King as the head of the Commonwealth rather than the Irish state, before launching an attack on the Treaty's defence and finance provisions. Outside in the hallway, Childers found himself surrounded by a heavy contingent of the Prime Minister's secretariat, along with the ever-reliable Curtis. The 'whole place', he noticed, was 'in a hum'. Philip Kerr, a Round Table stalwart, and Lloyd George's former private secretary, was circulating, as was Lord FitzAlan, Ireland's Lord Lieutenant, together with numerous civil servants and 'a swarm of Cabinet ministers'.[3]

Once the Sinn Féin leaders left at 7.45 p.m., the British delegation filed into the Cabinet room. This was a moment of reckoning for Britain's imperialists. If they were to safeguard the Empire, securing British global power and prestige, then the settlement with Ireland needed to be water-tight. There could be no gash in the hull of the 'great liner' (Churchill's metaphor)[4] since that risked sinking the entire enterprise. For a start, it would have immediate consequences for the ongoing and difficult discussions with nationalists in Egypt and India, which were at a critical juncture; particularly in the case of the former, following the collapse of the latest round of negotiations with the country's moderate nationalist Prime Minister, Adly Pasha. He had just left London, and was now en route to Cairo, having rejected Curzon's proposals for a settlement. The Foreign Secretary was in a fluster, and furious with Lloyd George and Churchill for their refusal to countenance indirect rule in Egypt. A blueprint for this power-sharing arrangement had been laid out by Lord Milner back in February, but Churchill, once characterised as a 'Kipling imperialist',[5] had worked himself into a lather over the issue, and told Curzon that he had no intention of watching 'the loss of this great and splendid monument of British administrative skill and energy'.[6] While the politicians bickered, Egypt languished under British martial law, administered by the High Commissioner, Lord Allenby.

The Irish were intimately acquainted with these developments, thanks in part to the efforts of Art O'Brien. Still surly at having been frozen out of Sinn Féin's talks with the British, he had been busy courting the company of the Egyptian delegation, and was on familiar terms, at this stage, with their spokesman, Makram Ebeid Pasha, the Oxford-educated scion of one of Egypt's noblest families. Ebeid provided O'Brien with a full rundown of the Curzon proposals and predicted that Adly would resign as soon as he arrived back in Cairo on 6 December, a move he looked forward to with relish because of his close association with Saad Zaghlul, Egypt's radical nationalist leader, who led the '1919 revolution' and who continued to command broad popular support.

O'Brien, equally excited by the prospect of a renewed challenge to Britain's imperial authority in the Middle East, readily acceded to Makram Ebeid's request for an official reception of the Egyptian delegation in Dublin. After much back and forth, they arranged that on 8 December, between twelve and fifteen of Zaghlul's supporters would lunch with de Valera at the Mansion House, and that 'the Press' were not to 'be notified [about the meeting] in advance'.[7]

Meanwhile, an exultant O'Brien told Childers of the Foreign Office's disappointment at the failure of the Curzon proposals, which he correctly characterised as 'less than the Milner plan'. He believed the British were 'without knowledge of what Adley [sic] will do', and were counting on the situation simmering along until 'the Irish crisis ... and Washington conference were out of the way', at which point they would return to the 'Egyptian question ... with ... force'.[8]

The diehards, eagle-eyed, were monitoring both sets of negotiations closely, while simultaneously scanning the horizon for signs of imperial slippage in India. Partway through the Irish conference, Lloyd George fired off a bracing missive to the viceroy, Lord Reading, reminding him that 'Our course in India is being watched in many other quarters, and we cannot afford to be misunderstood.' The British Empire, he argued, was 'passing through a very critical phase, and it will not survive unless it shows now in the most unmistakable fashion that it has the will and the power to stand by its policies and to deal conclusively with any who challenge its authority.'[9]

A Sinn Féin-style campaign of resistance could not be allowed to take root in either Egypt or India. This was the nightmare vision for the British; the fear that shadowed the self-styled image of a beneficent, civilising empire which, at the Commonwealth level, had been transmuted into a 'community of nations', a putative model for world government – or so its propagandists, the likes of Curtis or Kerr, chose to believe.

Dread of a rupture in the broader imperial fold forced a focus on the strategic imperatives, on the economic, technological and social links that bound together the British world-system. And if global pre-eminence was to be preserved, there was no room for a republic at the imperial centre. Throughout the talks, the Irish delegation had been told over and over that the Crown was 'one and indivisible'. Little wonder then that the British delegates, with their deeply embedded imperial mindsets, rejected the alternative oath of allegiance submitted by Collins and Griffith that evening.

At 9.30 p.m., the two Sinn Féin leaders returned to the Cabinet room at No. 10 to be confronted by the Prime Minister, Chamberlain, Churchill, Horne and Hewart. Although they struck down the suggestion on the oath of allegiance, the British agreed to review the defence question in ten years, opening up the possibility that Ireland would be responsible for her own external defence after this transition period. They agreed a handful of other minor amendments, including no pension liabilities for the Auxiliaries and Black and Tans.[10] As Jones scrawled in a note to Lloyd George during the afternoon, it would be 'Difficult to get [Collins and Griffith] to swallow pensions for B. and Tans.'[11]

Meanwhile, Childers, consigned to his usual position in the hallway, found himself chaperoned on this occasion by Cope, who 'urged' him to 'support peace'. It was another two hours before the Irish delegates were back in the car to Hans Place, with Collins trumpeting the ten years 'won' on defence. But when the redrafted Treaty was delivered to the delegation's headquarters at 1 a.m., Childers dismissed the concession as a 'fraud', convinced that the naval occupation of four strategic ports, one of which was in the North, would undermine Ireland's sovereignty and make her a party to future British wars. Now at the end of his tether, he noted snidely that these latest drafts of the Treaty were addressed again to Griffith, who was 'muzzy with whiskey', although he had 'succeeded in getting some copies from him'. The diary entry ended with 'Bed at 2.30 a.m. What a day!'[12]

Some hours later, not long after sunrise, Griffith and Duggan embarked on the first leg of the journey home. They were the advance party; the other delegates and Childers were to follow that evening. Griffith carried with him a copy of the second redraft of the Treaty, which he kept in a closely guarded battered briefcase. The founder of Sinn Féin remained a poor man throughout his life. He spent his childhood in some of Dublin's notorious slum districts and always spurned more lucrative journalistic pursuits in favour of his nationalist newspapers. He reassured his wife that if he died, she and the children would 'be looked after as he'd given up all ties to work for Ireland'.[13] Instead, the new Irish state handed his impoverished widow a modest pension and taxed every penny of it. Yet on that cold, wintry morning, as the train sped towards Holyhead, Griffith, to divert his thoughts from the crushing pressure of the present, threw himself into several rounds of chess. He played mostly with one of the young legal advisers to the delegation, who later became a judge, and it was he who recalled the mishap that might have derailed the talks altogether. Griffith had brought the old attaché case containing the Treaty to breakfast, and afterwards, accompanied by Duggan, returned to his own carriage. Half an hour later, on a train 'swarming with journalists coming over to Dublin to report on the result of the Cabinet meeting', Cope, who had been sent to monitor events for the British, spotted the case in the dining car 'reclining on the rack'. The young legal expert handed it to Griffith, who had come bustling back into the carriage 'in a state of excitement'. But aside from this 'entertaining incident', the rest of the journey passed off uneventfully.[14]

The same cannot be said for the others, who had an ordeal in store. There was to be no opportunity to recover from the day's gruelling schedule, which for Collins and Childers had revolved around two tortuous, long-drawn-out encounters at the Treasury and 10 Downing Street on the subject of financial safeguards for Ulster. The issue ultimately had no impact on the Treaty, but, as Pakenham wrote, the discussions showed 'Collins at his versatile best. How many clerks trained in the lower walks of the Stock Exchange and the Guaranty Trust could have held their own in financial interchange with two ex-Chancellors of the Exchequer and the most bewildering of contemporary economists?' (The reference is to R.G. Hawtrey, whom Pakenham considered 'already competent to dazzle and befog beyond the common run of economists'.) And while he observed that Collins leant heavily on Childers, and 'warmly acknowledged the debt', he neglects to mention that in Childers' diaries, to which Pakenham had access, the entry for that day is riddled with barbs about Collins' ignorance and incompetence.

In the evening, at Hans Place, the *Manchester Guardian*'s editor, C.P. Scott, arrived. During a 'hasty' dinner, he asked the Sinn Féin men 'how far they could go on the question of allegiance' and recorded in his diary how 'Childers asked Collins if he might say and Collins nodded consent. It appeared,' he wrote, that 'they were not prepared to admit the Crown in Ireland at all.' This came as a shock to the editor, for as a progressive Liberal, he passionately believed in the value of the British Commonwealth and the League of Nations. To him and his ilk, these institutions stood as the guardians of a new global order and underlay the whole concept of collective security. When Scott pointed out that the Crown could act only on the advice of Irish ministers, 'as in the parallel case of the Dominions', he was told 'the Dominions were a long way off and it would be quite different in the case of a country only a few miles away'. Horrified, he asked, 'you mean to have a Republic in Ireland in association with the British Empire'? When Collins 'assented ... I said you expect the negotiation to break down', to which Collins replied, 'with emphasis: "I do."'[15]

The British delegates had guessed as much, which was why Scott was summoned to London early that morning in the first place. In preparation for his lunchtime meeting with the Prime Minister, he had caught up beforehand with two like-minded friends – one of them the political theorist Harold Laski. As Scott wrote in his diary, they updated him on the dismal state of affairs. The situation, they complained, was 'almost desperate', with Churchill at his worst, 'full of threats of John Bull laying about with a big stick. We had utterly broken rebellion in the sixteenth century. Why not now with vastly greater power? Yes ... Laski [had replied], but the condition of Ireland today is the result of our policy then.'[16] At 10 Downing Street, Scott found Lloyd George 'looking tired'. He was in one of his black moods and bemoaned the inferiority of Sinn Féin to J.B.M. Hertzog's nationalists, who had 'made no difficulty about' the oath. 'The fact was the Boers were a finer people,' he said, adding that if 'there was no settlement there must be coercion'. Reminded of the vast army required to fulfil that threat, he fell back onto Bonar Law's solution of simply laying waste to the economy instead, meaning 'no great numbers will be needed. We could blockade.' But this too gave rise to doubts and he pondered aloud about the 'punitive expeditions' needed if 'there were any outrages on loyalists', prompting Scott to conclude 'that [Lloyd George] had evidently not in the least made up his mind what he would do'.[17]

Nor had Collins for that matter, despite his forthright comments to Scott that evening. Amid the intensifying pressure on the delegation, he continued to play his cards close to his chest on what, ultimately, he would accept or not accept. Griffith, by contrast, left no one in any doubt where he stood.

Shortly after his arrival in Dublin, he presented the draft Treaty to de Valera at the President's new quarters on Kenilworth Square, an elegant corner of the city's well-heeled south suburbs. He turned up at the door at 11 p.m., just half an hour after de Valera's return from an inspection of the troops in Limerick, Clare and Galway – a 'grand tour' designed to increase his influence and standing with the IRA. With his eye for propaganda, the President had the inspections recorded by a 'film man', so that, in the public's mind at least, he was established as the head of the army. The tour itinerary was dominated by meetings with local dignitaries, and as de Valera was hosted in the 'big houses' of the bishops, with various entertainments laid on to fête and honour him, the visit appeared more a state procession than a simple marshalling of the troops.[18] And yet that was its primary purpose – and with it, the opportunity to send another unmistakable signal to the British that Ireland was readying for war.

According to his official biographers, de Valera deeply regretted what happened next. Weary from the long drive home, he found himself unable to 'argue satisfactorily' with Griffith, and after a two-hour debate, in which the Sinn Féin founder reminded the President that he would not break on the Crown, the unresolved questions were held over until the Cabinet meeting in the morning. In 1970, de Valera claimed to regret bitterly this 'adjournment', maintaining that he 'missed his most favourable chance of persuading Griffith of the consequences of acceptance'.[19] This scarcely credible observation should be seen as more of an exercise in crafty self-exculpation than a flash of insight into the dynamic of those last days. It neatly pins the blame for the Treaty on Griffith, while ignoring the fact that at this point, the delegates were being asked, in the apparent absence of any contingency plan, to embrace war as the alternative to the collapse of the talks. And while historians differ about the IRA's capacity to renew the fight, there was no question that if the British threw more resources at the problem, the separatist movement faced certain military defeat, and the corollary to this onslaught would be the loss of its fragile political hegemony. The historian Sheila Lawlor wrote that despite 'the inspections, the pictures [and] the exhortations ... de Valera had no definitive policy to meet the event of war'; facts not lost on Collins, who was all too aware of the republicans' military capacity. He trod more carefully as a result, always favouring conciliation and pragmatism over the President's complex game of brinkmanship. For as Lawlor emphasised, the Irish could never match the menacing prospect 'of thousands of British troops converging on Ireland from across the globe, with all the appurtenances of modern warfare'.[20]

By the 3 December Dáil Cabinet meeting, all the key decision-makers were exhausted, but none more so than Collins. While Griffith and de Valera stayed up late arguing, the other delegates endured a night of high drama, after the mail boat ferrying them back to Dublin collided with a schooner, splitting the small vessel in two and killing three of its crew. In the days that followed, the newspapers lavished attention on Collins' reaction, reporting that he had helped lower the steamer's lifeboats in the rescue of the schooner's four surviving crew members and, after they were hauled on board, offered them the delegates' saloons to recover. This was the Collins the public knew well. Predictably then, when handed a lifebelt, he replied mischievously and with a 'smile', that 'I have been in tighter corners than this, and got out of them'.[21]

Curiously, despite the excited reaction of the press, Childers, an experienced yachtsman, made no mention of Collins' gallant behaviour in his detailed diary entry of the incident.

The accident at sea left the delegates substantially behind schedule and by the time they arrived at Dún Laoghaire there was little more than half an hour to spare before the 11 a.m. Cabinet meeting. According to Childers, they shared a taxi to the Mansion House, but if there was any camaraderie during that confined journey, it rapidly evaporated, for this gathering between the Irish delegation and the Dáil Cabinet, the first since the talks began, was mired in bitterness and acrimony almost from the outset. Divergent opinions, vehemently expressed, soon gave way to vituperative attacks. The President invited the delegates to air their views first, and Griffith began by declaring that the terms on offer were the best that could be won and the only alternative to 'fresh war'. Barton disagreed. 'England's last word had not been reached,' he insisted, and there was no chance she would wage 'war on [the] question of allegiance'. He vowed to vote against the Treaty on the grounds that it offered neither Dominion status nor unity. His position was warmly endorsed by Gavan Duffy, who believed that 'England was bluffing' and that, with pressure, 'the Irish proposals, with small reservations on Defence, etc., could [still] be obtained'. Up next was Duggan, who sided with Griffith, for he could not bear the 'responsibility of saying "No"'.[22]

But this version of events, laid down in the Dáil Cabinet minutes – and apparently recorded after the fact – is at variance with Childers' recollection. In his diary he notes that Duggan's reaction was the 'same' as Collins; that is to say, 'difficult to understand', even though the latter was 'repeatedly pressed' by de Valera. So reluctant was he to stake out a definitive position that Childers had no idea 'what his answers amounted to'.[23] There is no doubt that Collins was evasive, as the Dáil minutes – taken by one of his loyalists, Colm Ó Murchadha – attest. At first, he warned that a rejection of the Treaty was a 'gamble' since 'England could arrange a war in Ireland within a week', but then, with a few supple twists, undermined this position by establishing himself as an agnostic on the vital issue of the oath of allegiance. Pointing out that 'it would not come into force for 12 months', Collins implied that he might renegotiate it during this period, or even ditch it altogether if the provisions proved onerous. In the same breath, he advised putting the Treaty before the Dáil with a recommendation of 'non-acceptance' on the oath, a scenario that heightened the risk of the Treaty's rejection.[24] More evidence of his ambivalence can be found in Stack's account of the meeting. Collins, he recalled, 'did not speak strongly about the document at all', yet later described the oath as nothing more than 'sugar-coating to enable the English people to swallow the pill' of Irish independence.[25]

According to the Cabinet minutes, it was not long after Childers denounced the Treaty's defence proposals that the conversation took an abrupt turn for the worse. Without warning, Brugha lobbed in a grenade, demanding to know who had split the 'Delegation so that [Griffith and Collins] did most of the work', while the others were deprived of 'full information'. Endlessly combative, he followed this up with a claim that the British had 'selected its men', an accusation Griffith angrily insisted he withdraw. But the damage had been done, and from then onwards, the discussion continued in a volatile, ill-tempered atmosphere.[26]

Partway through this marathon six-hour meeting, the delegates who were not Cabinet members withdrew and de

Valera made it plain that he 'personally could not subscribe to
the Oath of Allegiance nor could he sign any document which
would give N.E. Ulster power to vote itself out of the Irish Free
State'. But he thought the plenipotentiaries should return to
London and 'secure peace if possible'. They were to press again
for External Association, although he reassured them that even
if this could not be achieved, 'the Delegates had done their
utmost and it now remained to them to show that they were
prepared to face the consequences – war or no war'.[27]

Later in the afternoon, when the non-Cabinet members of
the delegation rejoined the meeting, Griffith repeated that he
would not 'take the responsibility of breaking on the Crown'.
Brugha rounded on him with uncomprehending fury. 'Don't
you realise', he barked, 'that if you sign this thing, you will split
Ireland from top to bottom?' In a dramatic exchange recalled
by Stack more than a year after the event, Griffith answered:
'I'll tell you what I'll do. I'll go back to London. I'll not sign
that document, but I'll bring it back and submit it to the Dáil,
and if necessary to the people.' This mollified Brugha and the
other opponents of the terms, although earlier in the meeting
Griffith had warned that if the negotiations foundered 'on the
question of allegiance' that too would 'split' the country.[28]

In Pakenham's account, during this discussion, and in the
days afterwards, Collins' 'spirits flagged ... [and] his volubility
dried up'.[29] He became 'reticent, morose' even, behaviour
that contrasts with the renewed magisterial assertiveness of
de Valera. The plenipotentiaries were reminded again of their
original instructions to refer all matters back to the Cabinet,
and were told to foist the blame for a break on Ulster. When
Barton implored de Valera to accompany the negotiators back
to London on the grounds that 'it was unfair to expect us to
get the best terms without his assistance', his efforts met with a

familiar response. There was no reason, the President retorted, for him to reverse 'his earlier decision'.[30] All of which affirms the historian John Regan's argument: that from de Valera's perspective, 'the negotiations were only the overture to the main performance he would deliver'.[31]

But at this penultimate Dáil Cabinet meeting, arguably the most significant in modern Ireland's history, the President's resolute inflexibility was outshone by Brugha's remorseless obduracy. He stood as the sole dissenter to de Valera's suggested amendment of the oath: 'I ... do solemnly swear true faith and allegiance to the constitution of the Irish Free State, to the Treaty of Association and to recognise the King of Great Britain as Head of the Associated States.'[32] Even Stack agreed to accept this, but Brugha held firm to his republican principles and refused 'to consider any form of oath' whatsoever.[33] The crushing disappointment of the botched army overhaul was surely not far from his mind, raising the question, as Regan has argued so persuasively, as to whether Brugha 'was still awaiting his opportunity to demand full control' of the IRA.[34] If his republican convictions struck that deep, he could have resigned at any point from August onwards, when the compromise of External Association was explicitly on the table. Instead, as Regan highlights, he chose to fight his corner, possibly arousing Collins' suspicions that he was playing his own game and that he had pegged his support for any settlement to the fulfilment of a long-held political ambition: full control of the IRA.[35]

Ultimately, it is impossible to establish whether the army formed the subject of fraught negotiations between de Valera, Stack and Brugha in those last days before the Treaty was signed, but, either way, Collins continued to guard his territory. Throughout the talks, he strove to keep the IRB informed, giving them the impression that they were part of the consultative process. He handed the Brotherhood's Supreme Council a copy of the draft Treaty so that they could discuss the document on the same day, and during a break in the Cabinet meeting, discovered their concerns centred on the oath of allegiance. In the evening, as he prepared to leave for London, he met Seán Ó Muirthile and Gearóid O'Sullivan, two members of the council, to gauge the mood again, and was heartened by the response of 'the lads'. For their part, they worried that he was too optimistic about the Brotherhood's appetite for such a settlement and 'agreed it would not satisfy the fighting men'. Ó Muirthile later recollected that he even considered following Collins to London to 'clarify things'.[36]

From this, it appears Collins embarked on that final pre-Treaty crossing under the impression that, aside from the oath and a number of other specified amendments, the document would pass muster with the IRB. With the endorsement of the Supreme Council, he could, as Regan puts it, circumvent the Cabinet and achieve a consensus in the Dáil.[37] While the strategy's success hinged on the Brotherhood's capacity to hold together and 'withstand the duress' of a settlement, it reflected an approach to civil and military powers that by now were second nature to Collins. For as Tom Garvin has highlighted, throughout the guerrilla war 'he bypassed the formal Dáil government structures and was running the finances and much of the military campaign himself.'[38] Such secretive behaviour lay at the heart of de Valera's mistrust of his younger, more captivating rival.

At this time, while the Irish concentrated their attention on the draft Treaty, fresh waves of paranoia were sweeping through Britain's security services as reports piled up about the IRA's growing strength and the campaigns of destruction supposedly in an advanced stage of development. One intelligence chief predicted that the new dirty war would involve the deployment of poisonous gas that was already 'being ... manufactured in laboratories owned by the Christian Brothers and other like institutions'. He warned of wide-scale hostage-taking of members of the military and police, as well as leading loyal citizens, 'so that for every I.R.A. [combatant] shot two loyalists will be shot'. The republicans would cripple communications and transport links, and there would be coordinated attacks on small RIC barracks. The vision of violence and mayhem was made all the more nightmarish by predictions of a second front opening in Northern Ireland, as a 'reliable informant' disclosed that 'fifteen thousand I.R.A. men' were massing on the border, and were 'ready and equipped' to attack the North at a 'moment's notice'.[39]

Exaggerated intelligence reports of this sort had the potential to fatally undermine the negotiations, but were limited in impact by the inflated counterclaims emanating from the civilian authorities in Dublin Castle, as Cope and his boss, Sir John Anderson, Senior Undersecretary to Ireland, repeatedly vouched for the bona fides of Sinn Féin and the outlook for peace.[40]

Yet now that the talks were in the balance, the unremitting alarmist assessments began to take effect. Anxiety mounted within Whitehall and Westminster, and by Sunday 4 December, the mood verged on outright panic, amid confirmation that the British proposals had been 'rejected' by the Dáil Cabinet. According to the records in Britain's National Archives, the delegates 'learned privately' of this development – most likely from Cope, who characteristically overstated the case, describing Collins, Griffith and Duggan as advocates of the settlement, while Gavan Duffy and Barton opposed acceptance.[41]

A meeting between the two sides had been scheduled for 5 p.m. that evening, an indication that the conference was reaching a crisis point – the make-or-break moment had arrived.

As usual, the Irish delegation spent the hours leading up to this encounter locked in bitter combat. That morning, back at Hans Place, Childers, Barton and Gavan Duffy had compiled a list of proposed amendments to the draft Treaty, so the revised terms effectively restated the demands submitted at the end of November, with the original oath of allegiance supplanted by de Valera's version. It was to be External Association for the fifth time.

At the delegates' meeting at 3 p.m., Collins, Griffith and Duggan immediately objected, insisting the Cabinet had not authorised a full-scale return to the previous proposals. But since no agreed document had emerged from the six hours of talks the day before, it proved impossible to resolve the conflicting interpretations. Predictably, the terms of the oath, which de Valera had not written down, produced the most explosive exchanges, with Childers, Barton and Gavan Duffy arguing that the King was to be acknowledged as 'Head of the Association', not the 'Associated States', the wording that Collins, Griffith and Duggan claimed the President had used. This furious spat over detail – a mere phrase – brought into question the entire principle of External Association, for the first title excluded the monarch from Ireland, while the second implied that he was head of the Irish state – a formulation evidently aimed at placating the British.[42]

Childers' account shows that Collins led the charge, while Griffith took a back seat, remaining, for the most part, unusually subdued. In what appears, principally, to have been a duel between Childers and Collins, the former stood his ground while the latter resorted to 'sneers and bluster'.[43] By the time it came to discussing who was to attend the meeting at Downing Street – always a contentious subject – Collins' frustration had reached a tipping point and he refused to go.

This extraordinary decision has long divided historians. To suddenly withdraw from the field of battle when peace and war, and the fate of Ireland hung in the balance has struck some as 'bizarre, even childish'.[44] To Peter Hart, it seemed to mirror de Valera's behaviour; Collins wanted to steer clear of failure and avoid wearing the blame. Others have attributed it to exhaustion and the realisation that there was little point in pushing proposals that on four previous occasions had received an unequivocal rejection.[45] A more logical assessment is that Collins stood aside knowing full well that this would avert a break: that Lloyd George would view his abstention not as a sign of belligerence and opposition, but as precisely the opposite, seeing in it a signal that Collins remained open to compromise.

In the midst of this debate, Jones arrived, wanting to know who would attend that afternoon's Downing Street conference. Roused from his silence, Griffith suggested that Barton and Gavan Duffy should go. A 'major wrangle', as Childers put it, ensued, until eventually Griffith backed down and braced himself for a fifth and final fight for External Association. Childers tagged along, too, but at Downing Street, found himself shunted into the hallway again, surrounded by a phalanx of civil servants and the ever-present Curtis.[46] In the Cabinet room, the assembled British representatives – Lloyd George, Birkenhead, Chamberlain and the Chancellor of the Exchequer, Sir Robert Horne – had already been told not to expect Collins, who was apparently '"fed up" with the muddle'.[47]

The meeting began with a short discussion about the future structure of the new Irish parliament, before Griffith, diving into the breach, attacked the British on their Ulster proposals. Steering clear of any mention of the Crown, he focused instead on the claim for Ireland's 'essential unity', for if de Valera's plan had any chance of success, if they were to force the British to the brink on External Association, yet prevent them from waging all-out war, then the break had to come on Ulster, so that domestic and international opinion, particularly in the Dominions and the US, could be rallied to the Irish cause. But the six-hour Dáil Cabinet meeting had been dominated by the debate over the oath of allegiance, and in the counter-proposals to the draft Treaty, there was no mention of Ulster, reinforcing Lloyd George's belief that the Northern question no longer posed an obstacle to a settlement.

Treading warily, Griffith tried to 'work Ulster in to its proper place', as he phrased it in his letter to de Valera that evening. He told the British that although he stood by his 'personal assurances' on the Boundary Commission and would 'not let them down' on the matter, Sinn Féin could not shoulder responsibility for a solution involving partition. In a transparent attempt to prepare the ground for a break on Ulster, Griffith asserted that his earlier letter to the Prime Minister, in which he 'conditionally accepted association with the British Empire', called for a reciprocal response from the North's Unionists. Craig, too, he argued, should write to Lloyd George 'accepting essential unity'. But it was a clumsy advance and he was brought up short by a sharp riposte. 'Craig would not write such a letter', they countered and if the Treaty was signed, they would implement the Ulster proposals regardless.[48]

The discussion moved on to Sinn Féin's proposed amendments, and in the midst of these exchanges, with seemingly well-practised abruptness, the British announced that they would have to confer in private. When they returned, Lloyd George assumed a menacing tone. The 'Irish proposals were wholly inadmissible', and while they 'might have considered some form in the change of the oath this was a refusal ... to enter the Empire and accept the common bond of the Crown'. Now at his most aggressive, Lloyd George barked that if this was 'their last word, their answer meant war'.[49]

For some time, the Sinn Féin delegates sat in silence as the Prime Minister vented his fury at their conduct, for if Griffith's line of attack had been all too obvious, so, too, was Lloyd George's. Finally, as a parting shot, he declared that he could not understand what the difficulty was; why could the Irish not accept Dominion status? Blindly, Gavan Duffy rushed in: 'Our difficulty,' he declared, 'is ... the Empire [given] ... all that has happened in the past.' With orchestrated outrage, the British delegates leapt to their feet, while Lloyd George snapped, 'in that case, it is war'.[50]

Out in the hallway Childers waited. He had not moved for the full hour and fifteen minutes it took for the talks to collapse, and when it was over Gavan Duffy walked up to him, and in his ear whispered, 'C'est fini.'[51]

As they drove away from Downing Street, a jarringly chipper Barton told Griffith: 'Well I admired the way you stuck like a bull-dog to the Ulster issue'; and for added reassurance remarked, 'it may all be for the best yet'.[52] Convinced the British would cede more ground if pushed, Childers, Barton and Gavan Duffy appeared to embrace the brinkmanship, but Griffith was incandescent. In Pakenham's account, he tore into Gavan Duffy, excoriating him for a misstep that had stripped the delegation of its leverage and propelled them towards chaos.[53] He had no way of knowing, of course, that it would not be Gavan Duffy who was remembered for these mistakes. That would be his own legacy.

As soon as they returned to Hans Place, another dispute erupted. The delegates, now operating under extreme pressure, bickered over the wording of the letter to de Valera, no trivial matter given that their account of that meeting in Downing Street was likely to be made public once the talks had officially ended. Collins and Griffith objected to a phrase that implied that they 'had been giving way' to British demands, while Childers thought Gavan Duffy's mention of the Empire a mistake; 'we should have said [there could be] no Crown in Ireland', he wrote in his diary. After the letter had been typed and dispatched, the belligerence and posturing gave way to despair. Gavan Duffy and Barton, embittered and 'much depressed', felt they 'had been jockeyed by Griffith and made fools of' but took some consolation from the thought that the draft Treaty amendments would make 'good propaganda'.[54]

Meanwhile Griffith appeared to be living through his worst days. Before leaving Downing Street that evening, he and the other delegates had been told, with crushing finality, that 'a formal rejection' would be sent to them in the morning, and Craig would be notified that 'the negotiations were broken down'.[55] The accumulated strain of the past six weeks had already begun to take its toll on him physically; his wife, Maud, claimed that when she visited him in London, 'the first thing' she noticed was that 'his hair was turning white'.[56] And in an undated letter to John O'Kane, Collins revealed that his ailing colleague had asked him 'to assume leadership of our party even if [it was] unofficial ... [as] further burdens would grossly exaggerate his condition.'[57] But Gavan Duffy's ill-judged intervention seemed to have pushed him over the edge. When Jones turned up at Hans Place at midnight, in an effort to drag the talks back from the brink, he was struck by the stark change in Griffith's demeanour. 'He was labouring under a deep sense of the crisis and spoke throughout with the greatest earnestness and unusual emotion. One was bound to feel that to break with him would be infinitely tragic,' Jones declared in a hastily scribbled three-page memorandum to the Prime Minister, dated 1.30 a.m. on Monday 5 December.[58]

He spoke to Griffith alone for an hour, and during this time, the Sinn Féin founder pleaded for the Prime Minister's help. Although 'he and Collins had been completely won over to belief in [Lloyd George's] desire for peace … their Dublin colleagues' had not. They were 'told that they have surrendered much ("the King" and "association") and [had] got nothing to offer the Dáil in return. Cannot you – and this was the burden of his appeal,' Jones wrote, 'get from Craig a conditional recognition, however shadowy, of Irish national unity in return for the acceptance of the Empire by Sinn Fein? … The upshot of the whole talk,' he explained, 'was: "Will you help them get peace".'

Clearly, to a negotiator as ruthless and crafty as Lloyd George, this was, as others have highlighted, a confession of weakness. But Griffith was under no illusion as to whose opinion counted most. For there to be any chance of a settlement, the Prime Minister needed to convince Collins: that was who the 'gun-men will follow', he told Jones, before urging him to 'have a heart to heart talk' with the IRA leader. 'I said yes – 9.15 a.m. … so [Griffith] went over at [one o'clock] to hunt out Collins to fix this up.' Evidently much affected by the midnight encounter, Jones concluded his memo to the Prime Minister with an impassioned appeal of his own: 'Peace with Ireland is worth that effort with Craig. War is failure at home and at Washington.'[59]

But already the wheels of the British state were grinding in the opposite direction. At 7 a.m. Curtis deposited a draft statement for the Prime Minister with the watchman at 10 Downing Street. It explained why after 'five months of negotiation and nearly two months of conference' the British were ending the talks.[60] A code-worded message was also sent to the British army in Ireland, warning of an imminent resumption in hostilities. Craig, too, was bracing for the conference's collapse. At some point during the day, his brother, C.C. Craig, the Ulster Unionist MP for South Antrim, wrote to him and told how he had been summoned to Downing Street as the talks had broken down 'on the question of Allegiance'.[61]

Collins, too, appeared reluctant to re-engage. Griffith and Jones both pleaded with him, but he turned up uncharacteristically late for the scheduled meeting with Lloyd George, and by his own admission, made up his mind to see the Prime Minister only at the last minute. The memo that he wrote, after this private conversation with Lloyd George at 9.30 a.m., has persuaded some that this pivotal meeting marked the moment at which Collins 'irrevocably moved away from ... the self-sacrifice school of Irish separatism'.[62] But the document is no smoking gun, and the point at which Collins made up his mind to sign the Treaty remains an open question.

In his memo, Collins claims that he only grudgingly agreed to the Lloyd George meeting, and emphasises that he had avoided the previous evening's conference because he had 'argued fully all points'. Intimating that, at this dire extremity, he was in no mood for any further diplomatic gamesmanship, he recounts how he told the Prime Minister, with customary bluntness, that he was 'perfectly dissatisfied' with the British proposals, in particular 'with the position as regards the North East'. When Lloyd George replied that Collins himself had acknowledged 'on a previous occasion that the North would be forced to economically come in', Collins insisted that he wanted 'a definite reply from Craig and his Colleagues', adding that he was as 'agreeable to a reply rejecting as accepting. In view of the former,' he argued, 'we would save Tyrone and Fermanagh, parts of Derry, Armagh and Down by the Boundary Commission.'

He then pressed Lloyd George to accept the IRB-approved oath of allegiance, but the Prime Minister, while indicating his willingness to compromise on this issue, refused to discuss it further until the Irish accepted Dominion status. There were more exchanges over trade and defence, then Lloyd George, snatching at the opportunity that now beckoned, suggested a further meeting of the two delegations that afternoon at 2 p.m. Collins, still wary, 'tentatively' agreed.[63] He left Downing Street at 10.15 a.m., conscious that the Prime Minister had not contradicted his interpretation of the Ulster proposals and had let predictions of large territorial gains by the South pass without qualification. He could take comfort, too, from the prospect of a compromise on the all-important oath of allegiance. But whether these assurances led to the fateful decision that was to be made in the hours ahead is unclear. At any rate, the conversation served its purpose: it kept the conference alive, and, amid the deepening gloom, provided hope that a settlement remained within sight.

Not that this was the impression formed by C.P. Scott, who had been waiting patiently outside the Cabinet room for the past quarter of an hour. As Collins had turned up late, the Prime Minister was running behind schedule and at that very moment was due at Buckingham Palace for an audience with the King. George V was travelling to his favourite estate, Sandringham, later that day and, before he left, he wanted an update on the negotiations with Sinn Féin. In his diary, Scott recalled how after the meeting with Collins, Lloyd George had come rushing out, 'laid hold of me and pulled me in. He was excited and angry, said the Irish had gone back on everything – allegiance, naval securities, in fact all along the line. Agreement on these terms was impossible ... then he hurried off to see the King.'[64]

It was a consummate performance by the Prime Minister and confirms that for much of that day – one of the most dramatic and consequential in modern Anglo-Irish history – Lloyd George dealt in half-truths, resorting to Machiavellian wiles whenever the occasion called for it. The talk with Collins had strengthened, not weakened, his hand, for the IRA leader's dissatisfaction was focused on the North-East, not the more vital matter, as far as the British were concerned, of Ireland's constitutional status. He offered no objection to the Crown's overarching sovereignty, or membership of the Empire, allowing Lloyd George to act upon the assumption that Collins, like Griffith, and by implication Duggan – in other words three of the five Irish delegates – would not break upon the Treaty's first three clauses, which defined Ireland as a new British Dominion.

Scott knew nothing of these developments. He had been summoned to Downing Street that morning, 'at the unusual and curiously exact hour' of five minutes to ten, because the Prime Minister, acutely aware of the risk to his own political life, was racing to control the fallout.[65] If the talks failed, he wanted his narrative to prevail. Less than two hours later he changed tack again, indicating at a full Cabinet meeting that a settlement remained within grasp. He emphasised that Collins and Griffith seemed willing to accept Dominion status; and in a pivot that entirely repudiated Collins' earlier interpretation of the Ulster clauses, reassured his colleagues that a Boundary Commission would provide for nothing more than a 're-adjustment' of the border between Northern Ireland and the rest of the country.[66] From this it can be seen what a spry and subtle practitioner Lloyd George was. The conversation with Collins, when he had been at his most conciliatory, enabled him to present the Cabinet with what looked like a dramatic turnaround in the negotiations. After the grim state of affairs that had prevailed earlier in the day, when it appeared that only Griffith might be willing to compromise, the renewal of hope encouraged his colleagues to strain every sinew in the search for an accommodation. At the end of the meeting, it was decided that, as long as the Irish accepted Dominion status, 'the precise terms of the Oath were immaterial'. Three resolutions were then agreed upon: the British delegation would press for a Dominion settlement at the afternoon session; Churchill would attempt to persuade Sinn Féin to swallow the substance of the defence clauses; and the remaining members of the Cabinet would 'hold themselves in readiness' for another emergency meeting.[67]

Over at Hans Place, where nerves were considerably more frayed, the Irish delegates also prepared for the final round. They did so in increasingly chaotic conditions. As the *New York Times* correspondent recorded, 'all was apparently confusion' at the delegation's headquarters: 'There was much going and coming, much banging of doors and telephoning galore. None of the Secretariat appeared to know whether they would have to make a hurried departure from London before the day was over.' The morning's newspaper headlines contributed to the sense of an impending crisis; Beaverbrook's fiefdom, the *Daily Express*, went out on a limb with: 'IRISH CONFERENCE FAILS'; while *The Manchester Guardian* solemnly announced that the talks 'had reached the most critical point', before urging readers to oppose 'entering a new war with men of our own speech and partly of our own blood'.[68]

Over the weekend, tensions had been ratcheted up by a succession of bellicose speeches from de Valera. He had left Dublin after the Cabinet meeting and, with Brugha and Mulcahy in tow, resumed his propaganda tour, heading west for Galway, where he told the people to stand firm and brace for more mayhem. 'We are not going to quail now,' he declared in a widely publicised speech. 'Freedom was never won without sacrifice, and the country must be as prepared now to face sacrifice as it has been in the past.'[69] In Limerick, on the final day of the London talks, he issued a blunt diatribe: 'Never – not till the end of time will they get from this nation allegiance to their rulers.'[70]

At 3 p.m. on 5 December, the world's press watched as the Sinn Féin delegates clambered out of a car and walked, stony-faced, into 10 Downing Street. As the *New York Times'* reporter observed, unlike the first day, when hopes were riding high, there were no cheering crowds to 'shout them a welcome'; no 'patriotic songs' were sung, or prayers 'recited'. And whereas they had arrived in luxury cars back in October, cost-driving measures now forced them to cram into one small vehicle, which appeared to 'have some difficulty in carrying them all'.[71]

Earlier in the day, at a lunchtime meeting, they had decided to accept Lloyd George's offer of another conference. On this occasion, there was no dispute, or at least Childers made no mention of one in his diary, over who should attend, and it was agreed that Collins, Griffith and Barton – Gavan Duffy presumably being ruled out on the basis of his dismal performance the previous day – should argue the case one final time. In one of the enduring mysteries of the talks, no resistance surfaced at this point, or indeed any other, to the British deadline of 6 December, and as the clock ticked down, the psychological pressure and accumulated exhaustion began to take its toll.

And so the closing act of the conference was a slimmed-down affair. In the Cabinet room, the 'Big Four' – Lloyd George, Birkenhead, Chamberlain and Churchill – confronted the three Irish delegates across the Cabinet table, while outside in the hallway, Childers assumed his familiar post. Anticipating a protracted wait, he delved into his book, the writings of Abraham Lincoln, turning a blind eye, it seems, to his hero's open-mindedness and flexible statesmanship. He would not witness what played out over the next four hours, nor could he guess at the significance of the scenes unfolding close by. Over the past century, the story has been told and retold to the point where the outcome seems almost predestined, and yet nothing that happened on that whirlwind day was predictable, least of all to the protagonists, who were swept up in a fast-moving chain of events that left them facing the worst of all moral choices: peace or war.

The sources for these final hours are punishingly familiar. Churchill's recollection, although one-sided, is perhaps the most memorable. Published almost a decade later, he describes how 'after two months of futilities and rigmarole ... unutterably wearied Ministers faced the Irish Delegates, themselves in actual desperation and knowing well that death stood at their elbow'.[72] But the popular dramatic reconstructions in print and on screen are underpinned by Barton's account, which was written the following afternoon on the instruction of Griffith. Chamberlain kept a record for the British, and although his notes are more detailed than Barton's, they are curiously devoid of drama and emotional chiaroscuro.

Both accounts show the meeting began with a discussion of the Ulster issue, and Griffith again tried to make Sinn Féin's acceptance of Dominion status conditional on Craig's government accepting Irish unity. Lloyd George and Chamberlain countered this with indignant protests, accusing him of backtracking on previous pledges. Griffith persisted. It was irrelevant whether Craig agreed or not to the Boundary Commission; they merely needed to know where they stood. Collins entered

the fray at this point and put up an uncompromising front: he
could not contemplate a settlement unless Craig also signed
up to the proposals. To do otherwise, he claimed, 'would be
to surrender our whole fighting position'. Furious, the Prime
Minister reminded him of all the political sacrifices that had
been made; the risks they had taken to quell the diehards.
Griffith, more emollient, said he would 'accept inclusion in the
Empire if Ulster comes in'.

But Lloyd George was now working himself into a rage.
Barton's endlessly replayed account has the Prime Minister
shaking 'his papers in the air', ranting that the Irish were trying
to stage a break on Ulster because their Cabinet had refused
membership of the Empire. He levelled an accusatory finger at
Griffith, and, much to the amazement of Collins and Barton,
declared that the Sinn Féin delegation's chairman was going
back on a personal pledge he had made earlier on the Boundary
Commission. Out came the note that Griffith had so blithely
approved – but not signed – on 13 November; in the shock of
its reappearance, and with his honour under attack, Griffith
suddenly dried up, his mind went blank and in the strained
silence, he stated, 'I said I would not let you down on that and
I won't.'

Having raised the temperature, Lloyd George, just as
unexpectedly, lowered it. He became conciliatory; a series of
concessions were trotted out, starting with the Irish version
of the oath of allegiance, which Collins had supplied to
Birkenhead earlier in the day. After some minor alterations,
it was promptly approved, and they moved on to defence.
Here too, after a lengthy discussion, the British abandoned a
previously unyielding stance: Ireland would have a stake in her
own coastal security in five rather than ten years' time, and in the
meantime, could patrol her surrounding seas for the purposes

of 'Revenue and ... Fisheries'. Then came trade, Barton's great crusade. On this front, all British opposition crumbled. After months of debate, fiscal autonomy was conceded without a murmur of dissent, leaving the new Irish state free to impose industry-protecting tariffs and restrict British imports. And in the last of these concessionary moves, Northern Ireland's government was given one month, rather than six months to a year, to decide whether it wanted to join the new Dominion. The Sinn Féin delegates thought Craig and his Cabinet should give their 'answer at once', and not surprisingly, in light of their more conservative expectations of the Boundary Commission, the British readily agreed.

At this point, both sides took a break to reassess the position. When they returned at about 7 p.m., the Prime Minister was back in pugilistic form. Impatiently, he demanded to know whether the 'Irish were prepared to stand by this agreement whichever choice Ulster makes?' Griffith answered that he would, but he could not speak for his colleagues, and in a last-ditch effort to salvage the delegation's badly damaged Ulster strategy, 'said it was not fair to demand acceptance from them before Craig replied'. For some time, he clung desperately to this position, before Lloyd George cut him dead. 'He said he had always taken it that Arthur Griffith spoke for the Delegation' and told them that they 'were all Plenipotentiaries and that it was now a matter of peace or war'. Every delegate, he insisted, must 'sign the document and recommend it or there was no agreement'.

With the art of a conjuror, he suddenly produced two letters, one of which was to be sent to Craig that evening. The first contained the Articles of Agreement and news of Sinn Féin's acceptance of the terms; the second was a declaration of failure. It meant 'war – and war within three days'. In the charged atmosphere, he told them they would have to choose

'Which of the two letters I am to send', because a special train and destroyer were on standby, ready to carry one 'or the other to Belfast'. At this moment, Griffith capitulated. He would sign, he declared, rushing to add that 'this was his personal pledge only'. But Lloyd George waved him away. If there was to be peace, the Irish delegation needed to offer 'a united obligation'. He wanted their answer by 10 p.m., giving them just under three hours to decide whether or not to sign the Treaty.[73]

Collins, who sat in silence throughout these exchanges, 'rose looking as if he was going to shoot someone, preferably himself,' according to Churchill's account, which describes how the British 'went off ... had some food and smoked, and discussed plans of campaign'.[74] Outside, in the cold, as Childers and the three delegates clambered into a taxi, reporters bombarded them with questions: 'Were they returning to Downing Street that night? "I don't know", Collins replied. "Has the Conference finished? I don't know that either", he answered.'[75]

And yet within minutes Collins had made up his mind. On the way back to Hans Place, he declared that he would sign the Treaty, as Barton recalled in a later account.[76] Up until this point, the rest of the delegation had been unaware of his intentions, but the shock disclosure meant that the final meeting would run along a familiar divide, with Collins, Griffith and Duggan on one side, and Childers, Barton and Gavan Duffy on the other. They reassembled at 9 p.m. in an atmosphere of profound anger, despair and panic. Griffith spoke first and, in his diary, Childers recorded how he argued 'almost passionately for signing', while Collins 'said nothing'. Barton and Gavan Duffy, on the other hand, stood their ground. Unwilling to give up the fight, they 'refused to sign'. A 'long and hot argument' followed 'all about war and committing our young men to die for nothing. What could [Gavan Duffy] get better? Etc etc.'

At this precarious moment Barton turned to Childers, who reassured his cousin that it was a matter of 'principle', and in a somewhat surreal exchange, said he felt that 'Molly [his American wife] was with us'. Molly Childers' legendary charm usually exerted a tight hold over Barton. As one historian observed, their relationship 'was so warm and passionate that it threatened to transgress the boundaries of Victorian propriety'. But if Childers hoped the mere mention of her name would be enough to stiffen Barton's resolve, he was in for a rude shock. For, instead, his cousin declared, 'Well I suppose I must sign.'[77]

The choice of peace or war, as the delegates saw it, then fell to Gavan Duffy, but as Pakenham observed, 'his position was now impossible' and minutes later he, too, relented.[78] In the 1950s, Barton gave a more graphic account of this last debate, describing it as 'a most frightful battle' in which the 'most terrific things were said to Gavan Duffy and to me by Collins and Griffith and Duggan. They called us murderers, stated that we would be hanged from lamp-posts, that we would destroy all that they had fought for.'[79]

Much has been made of why the delegates failed to pick up the telephone and consult Dublin. Yet de Valera deliberately removed himself from the line of communication at the critical moment, and as Nicholas Mansergh highlighted, on the night in question, he 'remained conspicuously remote and uncontactable'.[80] In any case, Collins and Griffith were weary of the obstructionism in the Dáil Cabinet, and likely concluded that to consult anyone back home would result in no settlement. Why then did Barton, who was also a member of the Cabinet, not alert his colleagues in Dublin? The answer to this question is less clear, though as Regan argues, even if another minister, such as Stack or Cosgrave, could have been located, the only decision they could refer to, in the absence of de Valera, was the one reached two days earlier. In other words, the delegates were still faced with the dilemma of whether to accept the Treaty or reject it and risk renewed war.[81]

At 11.15 p.m., more than an hour over schedule, Griffith, Collins, Barton and Childers traipsed back into Downing Street to deliver their decision. In Churchill's account, the British were braced for failure. They expected that no one other than Griffith 'would agree, and what validity would his solitary signature pose?'[82] Despite the tension, the 'room rang with laughter' and Chamberlain recalled that the 'talk was of the merriest'; an outburst of hilarity he attributed to the day's 'unrelieved strain'. 'There is a limit', he opined, 'to human endurance.'[83]

Childers experienced the next few hours as if in a waking nightmare. Dazed, he sat down in the hallway, while the others walked into the Cabinet room. After a 'long pause', or so it seemed to Churchill, Griffith announced: 'Mr Prime Minister, the Delegation is willing to sign the agreements, but there are a few points of drafting which perhaps it would be convenient if I mentioned at once.' And so with the 'easiest of gestures,' Churchill wrote, 'he carried the whole matter in to the region of minor detail'.[84] Still, it took another two hours to hammer out the various amendments, in which time the British agreed that the office of the governor general could be renamed; the word 'local' was also removed from the description of the new Irish state's 'military force' – redefining it, effectively, as a regular national army.

After a lengthy discussion, Lloyd George turned to Griffith and asked whether the Irish delegates were now prepared to 'accept these Articles of Agreement'? Griffith replied: 'We do.' Both sides then separated for an hour while the Treaty was retyped. During this time, Childers watched 'Churchill in evening dress [move] up and down the lobby with his loping stoop [and] long strides', a 'huge cigar' protruding from his mouth 'like a bowsprit'. He found himself repulsed by the minister's 'coarse, heavy jowls', and thought him nothing but a 'brutal' militarist.[85]

At ten minutes past two on the morning of 6 December – according to Chamberlain's watch, Barton recorded it as ten minutes later, at 2.20 a.m – the delegates returned to the Cabinet room and signed the Treaty.[86] Gripped by a fraternal spirit that would be sorely tested in the months and years ahead, they shook hands for the first time, then said goodbye.

Outside in the freezing fog, a large crowd of journalists were predicting the worst. They had spent most of the evening exchanging bets on the chances of a settlement, and, at first, the odds of failure heavily outstripped those of peace. But by 'two o'clock evens were laid'. And when the 'Sinn Fein delegates emerged looking much more cheerful than when they went in, it was realised that if a settlement had not been reached, any possibility of warfare was appreciably further off.' Yet Collins remained tight-lipped as he climbed into the car. Asked what the news was, he replied, 'Not a word.'[87]

It was only when Birkenhead appeared 'in crumpled evening dress ... smoking one of his ... inseparable long cigars' that the situation became clear. He greeted 'the political journalists whom he knew well', then reassured the rest of the pack that the news was 'good'. Moments later, amid calls for an official statement, Churchill, 'also with a big cigar', emerged onto the Downing Street doorstep. 'Sorry you've had such a long wait out here,' he said, before drawing Birkenhead into a 'whispered conversation under the lamp'. Turning back to the reporters, and speaking in a voice that conveyed 'so much more than ... his prosaic words', Churchill announced that an 'agreement has, in fact, been reached'. And with that the 'press representatives promptly jumped into their waiting taxis for a sprint to Fleet-street'.[88]

10 · AFTERMATH

Erskine Childers woke later that morning still in a state of shock, and to his diary confessed to feeling 'desperately dreary and lonely'.[1] For him, the Treaty was no stepping stone to freedom, as Collins would soon characterise it, but an abject surrender of the republican cause, and by signing it, the Sinn Féin delegates had left his world in ruins.

Over at 10 Downing Street, the mood was euphoric; even the secretariat was seized by a giddy triumphalism. The *New York Times'* correspondent spotted one of the 'staidest Cabinet officials … skipping about the corridors … to the infinite delight of the Prime Minister's grandchildren', while Lloyd George was said to be 'the most relieved and happiest man in the Empire'.[2] At just after 9 a.m., the King telegraphed his congratulations from Sandringham, declaring that he was 'overjoyed to hear the splendid news', before going on to praise Lloyd George for the 'patient and conciliatory spirit which you have shown throughout'.[3]

The wave of jubilation swept through the London stock market, too, as ebullient investors sent share prices soaring, and the next day, newspapers reported on the 'electrifying effect' of the Irish settlement on financial markets. Fittingly, the celebratory atmosphere was accompanied by a sudden change in the weather, with one journalist noting how sunshine and a 'benign temperature ... succeeded the bitter blast of the last few days'.

At 12.30 p.m., at a Cabinet meeting in Downing Street, the Prime Minister, basking in the afterglow of his success, told his colleagues that the signing of the Treaty in the early hours of that morning, marked 'one of the greatest days in the history of the British Empire', a sentiment enthusiastically seconded by Curzon, who described it as 'an astonishing victory' which would remove a 'dark cloud' hanging over Britain's relations with the United States. The Cabinet then unanimously endorsed the Treaty, before debating whether the government would come under fire for failing to reach a similar settlement 'some time ago'. But all agreed that 'Sinn Fein would not have entertained or even agreed to discuss' such proposals a year before, and that only the 'rough treatment' meted out to Ireland's extremists 'had brought home to the men in the field the need for some equitable compromise'.[4] In other words, without coercion, and the threat of coercion, there would have been no Treaty. This unwavering belief in the value of violence as a tactical ploy, or the oscillation between 'criminalisation and accommodation', as the historian Alvin Jackson put it, influenced the resolution of later Irish disputes.[5] For there could be no doubt that Lloyd George's threat of immediate and terrible war, levelled when the talks had reached a point of unparalleled pressure, pushed the Sinn Féin delegation over the edge and ultimately ensured compliance. One Liberal member of the Cabinet wrote in his diary that day that the Irish 'would never have signed, as Collins admitted, without the coercion'.[6]

So was the threat of war a colossal bluff, and if it was, does it matter, given the outcome? The late historian Ronan Fanning argued this line in his book *Fatal Path*, dismissing what he described as an 'essentially meaningless debate', since from the perspective of the British delegation, 'all that mattered, was that, bluff or not, it worked'.[7] And yet, over six months later, when it looked as if the sanctity of the Treaty – and the British always insisted on a rigid interpretation of its terms – was about to be violated, Lloyd George's government rolled in the guns. This rapid recourse to coercion suggests that the Prime Minister was prepared to carry his threat to extremity. Had he done so, there would likely have been strong support from the Dominion governments. Australia, which clung fervently to the apron strings of the mother country, welcomed the news of the Irish settlement, but as Melbourne's *Age* newspaper made plain, it was seen as a necessary victory for Britannic nationalism. Irish extremism risked undermining imperial cohesion, and 'Sinn Fein's militancy', and the 'fight for the complete separation of Ireland from the British Empire', had left the British government with 'no alternative but to maintain its authority by force of arms'.[8]

On a practical level, however, Lloyd George's threat of war 'in three days' had little chance of success. As others have highlighted, more time was needed to restore the British army in Ireland to a state of wartime rigour, and, most likely, the 'result of an Irish refusal on 5 December would have been an indeterminate period of militarisation and manoeuvre before any shooting began'.[9]

Not that anyone in Downing Street lingered over these considerations as plaudits poured in for Lloyd George's 'resourceful genius', in the words of *The Manchester Guardian*.[10] Some even thought the Treaty had applied the last rites to the Conservative Party, with one newspaper describing it not merely as 'vindication' of the coalition government, but as the 'funeral of

Unionism'.[11] Meanwhile, from Washington, Maurice Hankey, the Cabinet Secretary, cabled that 'even the French ... crowded round with tributes of admiration' when news of the Treaty broke.[12] It would be another week before the disarmaments conference in the American capital registered a second diplomatic victory for the Prime Minister, who had reached, unbeknownst to him, the zenith of his post-war premiership. Within twelve months, the weeks ahead would seem little more than the prelude to a remarkably swift decline and fall.

As Lloyd George soaked up the glory for settling the long-standing Irish question, where the powers of 'Pitt, Parnell and Gladstone had failed', as Birkenhead put it in a speech that afternoon,[13] Collins played up to his status as the elusive revolutionary hero. The press had been gathered outside 15 Cadogan Gardens since the early morning, and although the IRA leader had been spotted up and about before 11 a.m., the *Pall Mall Gazette* reported that he was proving 'shy', and had become locked in a game of cat and mouse with Fleet Street's photographers. Eventually, a message was sent down to the assembled press that 'Mr Collins won't pose ... but he doesn't mind the camera men having a pot shot at him. He is accustomed to that sort of thing.'[14]

The laughter that rang out found no echo in Dublin. De Valera felt personally betrayed by the delegates' decision to sign and initially seemed incapable of absorbing the news. The President, together with Brugha and Mulcahy, was still in Limerick on the morning of 6 December, when the IRA's adjutant-general, Gearóid O'Sullivan, called to relay the news from London. Mulcahy recollected that he passed the message on to de Valera, who answered '"no" to my query as to whether he would like to speak to Gearoid on the phone'.[15] Rather than establish the facts and find out exactly what had been agreed, de

Valera went straight home to his house in the County Wicklow suburb of Greystones before travelling back to the city later that evening to chair a symposium commemorating the Italian poet Dante.

At the Mansion House, he met Brugha and Stack, brandishing a copy of the *Evening Mail*. When de Valera asked whether the news was 'good or bad', Stack replied 'bad'. Just then, Duggan and Desmond FitzGerald arrived, the first two members of the delegation to make it back to Dublin. The former handed the President an envelope containing a copy of the Treaty and asked him to read it. 'What should I read it for?' de Valera retorted. Duggan informed him that the terms were to be published in London and Dublin within the hour. Incredulous, the President replied 'What ... to be published whether I have seen it or not?'[16]

His rage intensified the next day, as the major Irish newspapers joyfully endorsed the settlement, with *The Freeman's Journal* hailing it as a compromise that secured 'every essential ... freedom which the Irish people have sought for over seven long and sorrowful centuries'.[17] Although popular support for the Treaty throughout the twenty-six counties was never in doubt, the reaction in Cork was tepid, almost hostile, compared to the more prosperous east, where attitudes tended to be more pragmatic, and the terms were looked upon as the best that could be expected. General Macready witnessed little 'outright enthusiasm', but people were willing to make a virtue out of necessity. As the *Kilkenny People* noted drily, 'the alternative to ... Self Determination is ... Self Extermination.'[18]

De Valera, on the other hand, had already launched the resistance. At 11.30 a.m., the Cabinet ministers then in Dublin – the President, Brugha, Stack, Cosgrave and Kevin O'Higgins – gathered at the Mansion House for an emergency session.

In a haze of anger, de Valera announced his intention to call for the immediate resignation of Collins, Griffith and Barton, but Cosgrave objected, insisting that the three plenipotentiary ministers should have the opportunity to tell their side of the story. And since de Valera needed Cosgrave's support to secure an inner Cabinet majority against the Treaty, he agreed to hold fire. Afterwards, though, he issued a public summons to the delegates to return home at once, and the statement's peremptory tone, as Desmond FitzGerald pointed out with dismay, left no one in any doubt that the President 'opposed … the settlement'.[19]

In London, Art O'Brien was also quick to register his disgust at the agreement. Furious at having been frozen out of the negotiations, and suffering from a bout of laryngitis, he read the terms of the Treaty in his bed at the Grosvenor Hotel. Childers had sent him a copy on 6 December, and he replied, 'not by way of complaint but for the purpose of registering a strange fact', that it was the first time the delegation had sent him 'official information in connection with the Conference'.[20] Two days later he released a public statement deriding the agreement as little more than the product of blackmail. There was 'no cause to rejoice, or offer thanksgiving' when 'under the threat of renewed and intensified warfare … five Irishmen had been compelled to sign their names to … that document'.[21] His comments were widely circulated in the British press the next day, prompting Lloyd George to denounce O'Brien as 'That swine. A little man neglected. Nothing is so pitiable', the Prime Minister told Jones, 'as a small man trying to handle big things.'[22]

The Treaty had of course put paid to the Egyptian delegation's trip to Dublin. O'Brien wrote to Makram Ebeid Pasha, the delegation's leader in London, to thank him for 'postponing his visit', acknowledging that had it gone ahead, 'it would have been very painful for all concerned'.[23] By this stage, Adly Pasha, the moderate Egyptian nationalist, had returned to Cairo and resigned the premiership, but Churchill, jubilant in the aftermath of the Treaty, predicted the Irish settlement would soon smother the long-running rebellion in the Protectorate. In a note to Curzon on 6 December, he claimed that Ireland's acceptance of 'the king & the British Empire will powerfully affect Egyptian National Sentiment', adding that the 'Egyptians seem to be taking things pretty quietly, & surely we ought to wait for the repercussions of this great event'.[24] His exuberance was misplaced. Violent protests quickly erupted again in Cairo and within months – after the radical nationalist leader, Zaghlul, had been banished to the Seychelles – the British abolished the Protectorate; with a collaborationist regime in power, they satisfied themselves with the control of Egypt's foreign policy and the free movement, within the country, of Britain's troops.

But the lapse into informal imperialism was exactly what the Conservatives in Cabinet wanted. As the historian John Darwin observes, the 'strongest emotion in this age of flux was the fear of commitments and the urge to save'.[25] The reconciliation of Tory imperialism with liberal principles of self-government – not a new phenomenon since this was how the Dominions evolved – warded off the incorrigible hostility of the separatists and kept the British Empire intact as a single geopolitical unit. Within a decade, Dominion status even became the goal of British policy in India – the linchpin of the Empire.

The Treaty fractured the United Kingdom but expanded the Commonwealth. On 7 December, when the terms of the settlement were published in the daily newspapers, the inhabitants of the twenty-six counties learned that they would soon be living in a Dominion known as the Irish Free State, which was to possess the same constitutional powers as Canada. The Treaty created, in other words, a constitutional monarchy rather than a republic. Lloyd George had seized upon the name 'Irish Free State' back in July when he first met de Valera, accompanied on that occasion by Art O'Brien. The President had handed the Prime Minister a document emblazoned with the Gaelic phrase Saorstát Éireann, and when Lloyd George asked for a translation, he was informed that the literal English meaning was 'Free State'. He then asked what the Irish word for a republic was, and according to Jones' account of the conversation, de Valera and O'Brien 'could get no further than Saorstat'.[26] As Charles Townshend speculated, this may have been a case of linguistic purism taken to absurdity, since 'Poblacht na hÉireann' or an Irish republic had been proclaimed by Pearse in 1916, but for reasons that are not clear, the term had been superseded by Saorstát Éireann by 1919. 'Poblacht', Townshend emphasises, was a neologism, 'derived from Latin rather than Gaelic', and ironically, it may have been this insistence of linguistic purity that enabled both sides to 'navigate past irreconcilable symbols' and arrive at what looked like 'a classic fudge'.[27]

Yet these same purists proved brittle and unyielding when confronted with the unholy compromises contained in the Treaty. And what galled most was the oath of allegiance to the British monarch, a meaningless form of words that had, in any case, been watered down to a pledge of fidelity, so that parliamentarians could reserve their allegiance for the future constitution of the Irish Free State. But to those wedded to the revolutionary ideal, who imagined Ireland conjured up 'in the meeting rooms of the Dáil and on the hillsides of Munster', as Roy Foster put it, these terms were nothing short of treachery.[28]

With emotions running high, Mary MacSwiney, sister of the

hunger-striker Terence MacSwiney and a member of the Dáil, suggested that the delegates should be arrested as soon as they stepped off the boat at Dún Laoghaire.

Collins and Griffith faced none of this despair and hostility during their final hours in London. On the evening of 7 December, when they and the rest of the delegation arrived at Euston station to catch the night train to Holyhead, police were struggling to hold back a huge crowd, made up mostly, according to newspaper reports, of women. And at the sight of Collins, 'with a smile on his face' and his hat at a rakish angle, a 'wild stampede' broke out; the police cordon was breached and Collins was 'heartily embraced by a young lady' who planted 'kisses upon his cheeks with wonderful rapidity'. In the ensuing melee, the 'hero of the hour' lost his hat and reached the train only 'with the utmost difficulty' and after 'twelve policemen [had] carried him along the platform'. In the midst of this chaos, Gavan Duffy and Childers slipped into the carriage unnoticed (Barton did not even warrant a mention), while Griffith escaped 'with some rather vigorous slaps on the back'. The train pulled away from the station and the 'last the enthusiastic demonstrators saw was the waving of Mr Griffith's hand and the smiling face of Mr Collins'.[29]

There was no reception party at Dún Laoghaire the next morning, just the grim news from Desmond FitzGerald that de Valera, to the surprise of both Collins and Griffith, was against the Treaty.

At a fraught and interminably long Cabinet meeting a few hours later, it was clear from the outset that the divisions were unbridgeable. Childers, whose diary provides the best source for these protracted exchanges – the meeting ran from midday until 9.30 p.m. – arrived to find de Valera with his head in his hands 'reproaching' Collins for having signed the Treaty.

Rounding on the rest of the delegates, de Valera accused them of breaking their 'instructions not to make a serious decision without consulting [the] Cabinet'. Griffith countered that de Valera 'had refused to come to London himself', an accusation that became a constant refrain among his opponents, and one that would haunt the President for the rest of his life. But confronted with it for the first time, he insisted that 'this was because he [had] trusted' the delegation to abide by their commitment.[30]

His anger was justified to a certain extent. Griffith broke his word when he signed the Treaty. At the last Cabinet meeting he had vowed not to sign the document, and the delegates were under instructions to refer the terms back to the Cabinet. But this was not so much a betrayal as a failure of leadership, for as John Regan rightly contends, the 'delegates signed because none of them individually would do what in fact they had been sent to London to do collectively: to accept responsibility for war'.[31] De Valera, too dependent on a plan that ascribed predetermined positions to the plenipotentiaries and British ministers, stuck rigidly to the one path and invested his strategy with his own sense of self-righteousness. As he confided to Joe McGarrity on 27 December, he had assumed that Barton and Childers would act as counterweights to Collins and Griffith, whose willingness to compromise 'would ... make them better bait for Lloyd George'. The break would come on Ulster, and the British would be brought to the brink, with no option other than to resume an unpopular war. He could then enter the fray and impose his own solution, an outcome that would result in a moral as well as a political triumph over his opponents.

But instead, and most unexpectedly, the plenipotentiaries buckled. De Valera blamed a lack of willpower, fulminating to McGarrity that they 'were not bold enough to dare "to make one heap of all their winnings" and stake it'. Worse, the 'win seemed almost a certainty, but they could not see it and a great occasion was missed – great not merely for Ireland but for England too, and for the world.'[32]

At the crucial hour, the delegates lost confidence in de Valera's hard-line stance. 'Coerced by both sides', as Regan put it, they 'collectively capitulated'.[33] And although Griffith's blunder ruined the delegation's Ulster plan, a mistake he compounded by unilaterally accepting the British settlement in the midst of the negotiations, his behaviour could have been disavowed by the other delegates. It was Collins who made the difference.

Like de Valera, a multiplicity of factors determined Collins' strategy, not least the recognition that the British Commonwealth was evolving, inexorably, into a league of free states, meaning that Dominion status marked the beginning of the end in terms of Ireland's ties to Britain, rather than the end of the beginning, as Childers feared. Moreover he had formed the impression that the Boundary Commission would work in the South's favour. There were also his suspicions and doubts about de Valera's motivations and judgement, which had weighed on him from the outset, but which intensified during his time in London – a state of mind not helped by Brugha's relentless attacks on his power base in the IRA. Nor could he ignore the fact that the military odds were stacked overwhelmingly in Britain's favour, rendering renewed conflict futile.

There could be no question then that he would stand by his decision at the emotional 8 December Cabinet meeting. And when de Valera speculated that the Treaty could be overturned on the grounds that it was signed under duress, he replied: 'In a contest between a great Empire & a small nation this was as far as the small nation would get. Until the British Empire was destroyed Ireland could get no more.'

In a sign of just how far de Valera's crown had slipped, Barton, too, inveighed against the President's 'vacillation', which he complained had been a problem from the beginning. After pointing out that de Valera had been asked to go to London at the 'last moment' and 'refused', he claimed, as Childers recorded in his diary, that 'the disaster was because we were not a fighting delegation'.[34]

The crunch point came when the acceptance of the Treaty was put to a vote. In a bewildering development for the anti-Treaty side, Cosgrave, who had opposed the oath to the Crown at the previous meeting, sided with Collins, Griffith and Barton, destroying in one fell swoop de Valera's carefully calibrated strategy, for he had always assumed that if a split in the Cabinet occurred, he would carry the majority. But once again, he was forced to confront a situation he had not anticipated.

Rather than publicly state that the Cabinet had recommended by a vote of 4–3 that the Dáil approve the Treaty, the President issued an explosive press statement that evening, declaring 'the terms of settlement' to be 'in violent conflict with the wishes of the majority of this nation'.[35] It was a blatant attempt to snatch back the political initiative from Collins and Griffith, and counter the deluge of favourable press coverage that the Treaty had received at home and abroad. And so the anti-Treaty campaign's official opening salvo was fired before the Dáil had even assembled. More ominously, the President had used the prestige and authority of his office to override the majority verdict of his Cabinet.

In many ways, de Valera's shock and disbelief at the Treaty mirrored the reaction of Craig and his colleagues in Belfast. At first there was 'profound astonishment', as one newspaper characterised it, but that soon turned to fury, and before long, the six counties reverberated with cries of betrayal. The *Belfast*

Telegraph proclaimed that 'Ulster stands in a position of grave peril',[36] while hard-line unionists like Sir Henry Wilson denounced the settlement as a 'complete surrender', involving a 'farcical oath of allegiance' and 'the withdrawal of our troops'. 'The British Empire', he declared, 'is doomed.'[37]

Lloyd George had always been held in low esteem by this political constituency and while he attracted a large measure of vitriol, with one newspaper labelling him a 'Judas Iscariot', it was Chamberlain and Birkenhead, the perceived Tory apostates, who came in for the heaviest opprobrium and who were branded as 'the most despicable of all'.[38]

The fear and loathing stemmed from concerns about the Boundary Commission. Ostensibly, the Treaty, as the historian Alvin Jackson emphasises, was a 'unitary settlement for the island of Ireland',[39] with the six counties automatically included in the Free State. But while the Belfast assembly could opt out of this arrangement within a month of the settlement's ratification, there was no escape from the Boundary Commission.

At about this time, Craig's 'rock-like character', as his biographer St. John Ervine put it, 'became very clear'.[40] On 9 December, he rushed over to London to demand that Lloyd George and Chamberlain clarify the implications for Ulster. True to form, the Prime Minister palmed him off with reassurances that Article 12 would result in nothing more than 'mere rectifications' of the border. But Craig put little store by Lloyd George's word and, within days, complained to Bonar Law that there was no evidence in the Treaty that the Boundary Commission 'would limit its functioning' to 'little re-adjustments'.[41]

His opposition to the Ulster clauses acquired a granite-like firmness after Lloyd George's performance in the House of Commons, where, in a lengthy speech recommending the settlement, the Prime Minister appeared to signal that large-scale territorial transfers were indeed in prospect, since 'two counties' – Tyrone and Fermanagh – 'preferred to be with their Southern neighbours'.[42] Furious, Craig fired off a letter to Chamberlain the next day, warning him that 'intense ... local feeling' would force loyalists to take up arms against the Treaty. 'Many already believe that violence is the only language understood by ... Lloyd George and his Ministers,' he raged.[43]

In response, Chamberlain sternly reminded Craig that he and his colleagues had refused to join the negotiations unless an all-Ireland parliament was ruled out, in which case, he wrote, 'there would have been no Conference for you to attend'. And he parried Craig's inflammatory rhetoric with a dose of mild incredulity: 'I know that you yourself desire peace and I cannot believe that men whose loyalty is their pride are contemplating acts of war against the King.'[44]

After two days of debate, the Treaty was adopted by both Houses of Parliament by a vote of 401 to 58 in the Commons and 166 to 47 in the Lords. The results were another triumph for Lloyd George, yet in these victories were the seeds of his defeat. For while the Irish settlement was not the cause of the Prime Minister's downfall, it weakened his grip over the Cabinet in the long term, as the confused situation in Ireland moved from sporadic outbursts of violence to full-blown civil war. The disorder galvanised the diehard movement, which could claim to have had its worst fears vindicated.

Predictably, it was this small group that provided the sole opposition to the Treaty. In the Commons, the renegade Tory MP Rupert Gwynne condemned the settlement as 'one of the most humiliating documents the British Government had ever signed'.[45] But it was Bonar Law, Lloyd George's successor, whose reaction was crucial. Although he admitted to disliking the Treaty, he accepted that it was favoured by a majority of the Conservative Party and by the 'overwhelming mass of the people'.[46] His endorsement not only limited the scale of the diehard protest, it reinforced Bonar Law's status as the Tory's leader-in-waiting. As one Conservative-leaning newspaper put it, his opinion on the Irish settlement counted for more than 'the authority of the Prime Minister or the measured ... appeals of Mr Chamberlain'.[47]

Bonar Law's cold-eyed assessment of the Treaty also reflected the uncertain mood among Tory backbenchers, who shared little of the exuberance exhibited by the Labour Party and the Asquithians. He warned there would be 'terrible difficulties ahead' and thought it 'absurd to think that we have settled the Irish question', but for all that it was 'worth going for [if] we shall be on better terms with Ireland'.[48]

Bonar Law could reluctantly accept the Treaty because, at heart, he conceived of Ireland as two separate nations; to him the Protestant-dominated north-east had little in common with the largely Catholic South. But to his old political partner, Lord Carson, the Treaty seemed a shocking defeat. All that he had fought for lay in ruins: not only was Ireland divided into two political territories, but the Union itself had fractured, and the South, his childhood home, was now to be spun off as a separate nation, free from the supremacy of Westminster.

Carson had been powerless to thwart the Treaty, which perhaps partly accounts for his extraordinary display of anger in the House of Lords, where he delivered an emotional, invective-laden speech that Nicholas Mansergh characterised as 'the authentic cry of Irish (as distinct from Ulster) Unionism at the last, with only oblivion before it'.[49] The 'old lion' as Kevin O'Higgins referred to him,[50] tore into Birkenhead, his 'galloper' from the Ulster Volunteer days, accusing him of selling out old friends in a venal scramble for power. In 'my experience,' he spat, 'these men ... are the most loathsome'. The Lord Chancellor sat expressionless and with his eyes closed throughout this diatribe. But his reply, delivered the next day to a packed chamber, and with the galleries overflowing – half the Cabinet and the Prime Minister had abandoned the debate that was simultaneously underway in the Commons to listen to Birkenhead's response – was not only devastating, it was lethal.

First, he swept away the diehards' denunciations, deriding them as the elitist views of an aristocratic cabal. 'Our difficulties,' he declared, 'lie in attempting to convince the mediaevalists among us that the world has really undergone some very considerable modification in the past few years.' Then, in a voice dripping with contempt, he dismissed Carson's speech as one that would be 'immature on the lips of an hysterical schoolgirl'.[51]

Ignoring the ferocious interjections from his former political patron, he went on to defend the Treaty as the best chance Britain had of satisfying Ireland's 'sentiment for nationhood'. To the diehards he asked, 'Is your alternative that ... we shall now resume the war, that we shall take and break this people, as we can with our military might ... ?'[52]

In the view of one historian, Birkenhead's speech provided the 'most articulate defence of the Government's policy heard in either House'.[53] And while it helped swing the peers behind the Treaty, it also sealed the political eclipse of Carson, who never recovered his standing within the Conservative Party. Yet even this fiery clash between two former political allies paled against the tortured, long-winded and frequently vindictive exchanges underway in Dáil Éireann.

History has not looked kindly on the second Dáil. The

veteran separatist P.S. O'Hegarty cruelly characterised it as 'a collection of mediocrities in the grip of a machine', which left all its thinking to a handful of leaders.[54] Although less harsh, historians tend to be equally unimpressed, dismissing it as an inadequate assembly to decide the fate of the Treaty, given that its deputies were nominated rather than elected to their seats, and were drawn, overwhelmingly, from the ranks of Sinn Féin and IRA activists. In Michael Laffan's view, the Dáil 'lacked a clear mandate from the people', while others argue that it excluded many interests, including labour and Southern Unionists.[55]

But while this was clearly something less than democracy in action, of much more significance was the fact that the revolutionary movement, and its elected leaders, had never, up until this point, collectively considered such a fundamental or divisive matter, nor one, in the words of John Regan, with 'such explosive implications'.[56] To many young republicans, the Treaty debates proved a painful awakening. The young IRA soldier Todd Andrews found it a shattering experience, for there could be no more illusions about what Mulcahy liked to describe as 'the wonderful brotherhood'. The days of collective resistance were over. Andrews recalled that 'for years I had lived on a plane of emotional idealism believing that we were being led by great men into a new Ireland. Now I had seen these "great men" in action to find that they were mostly very average in stature, some below average, some malevolent and vicious.'[57]

Held in the council chamber of University College Dublin (now the National Concert Hall) from 14 December until 7 January, the debates pitched principle against compromise, idealism against pragmatism, and reality against fantasy. But it was the choice between peace and war that circumscribed all considerations and arguments in favour of the Treaty. Seán MacEoin 'reported that he had five thousand Volunteers and ammunition enough to last only seven minutes of hard fighting' and predicted that if 'England goes to war again she will wipe all out'.[58] The movement would be finished, as the people would realise the IRA could not defend them. Mulcahy weighed in with a similar line, insisting that 'the English could not be driven into the sea, nor even expelled from their fortified centres'.[59]

Anti-Treatyites concentrated on the betrayal of the Republic, which Liam Mellows envisaged as not just an aspiration or an ideal, but a 'living and tangible thing'.[60] He dismissed concerns about further bloodshed and insisted that 'the delegates … had no power to sign away the rights of Ireland and the Irish Republic'.[61] Invocations of the dead were interspersed with accusations about the debasement of their sacrifice and no one took this rhetoric to a greater emotional pitch than Mary MacSwiney, the epitome of hard-line republicanism. She denounced the Treaty as a 'dishonour to our nation' and 'the one unforgivable crime that has ever been committed by the representatives of the people of Ireland'. In a long and exhaustive tirade, she contended that peace and war were irrelevant to the decision; what mattered was whether it was right or wrong. 'I ask you to vote in the name of the dead,' she declared, 'to vote against this Treaty and let us take the consequences'. Partway through this speech there were signs of fatigue in the Dáil, but scorning those deputies who looked at their watches, she swept on: 'I speak for the living Republic, the Republic that cannot die. That document will never kill it, never.'[62] When finally she sat down to applause, de Valera observed impatiently that 'we wish to … have the debate ended before Christmas'.[63]

From the outset it was evident the Treaty had polarised

allegiances, forcing a confrontation that many revolutionaries later looked upon as inevitable. Frank O'Connor spoke of 'two worlds, two philosophies, running in very doubtful harness'.[64] And amid the sudden realignments, personal attacks were unleashed that would have been unthinkable in the past. One deputy sneered that Collins was nothing more than a Fleet Street hero, while Brugha, as one historian put it, belittled his adversary as 'the subject of an unwarranted and self-cultivated personality cult'.[65]

Yet it was Collins who provided the most effective defence of the Treaty with a carefully calibrated speech that concentrated not on what had been lost but on the 'immense powers and liberties' gained. 'I do not recommend it for more than it is,' he declared. 'Equally, I do not recommend it for less than it is. In my opinion it gives us freedom, not the ultimate that all nations desire and develop to, but the freedom to achieve it.'[66]

Early on in the debate, in an attempt to arrest the drift towards the Treaty, de Valera unveiled his alternative proposal of External Association, rebranded as Document No. 2. It had an immediate catalytic effect, but not the one de Valera intended and, as Regan persuasively argues, the decision to introduce it to the Dáil at the beginning of the debate proved a costly mistake. 'Neither the doctrinaire republicans, pro-Treaty deputies, nor those occupying the no-man's land of the undecided were prepared to attempt to find any common ground within its provisions and Document No. 2 was ignominiously withdrawn by its author.'[67]

The near ad hoc structure of the debate, which de Valera dominated from start to finish with his superfluous interventions, left the vote on the Treaty three weeks behind schedule. During this time, the British government sank into a tense limbo as suspicions mounted about the settlement's staying power. For Lloyd George, the unexpected delay in the Treaty's ratification was a disaster and corroded the triumphant gains of a few weeks earlier. He had hoped to capitalise immediately on the settlement by calling an early general election, and the longer he held off, the more Conservative resistance grew. Confirmation of the troubles ahead came on 22 December, when the influential Tory peer, Lord Derby, notified Lloyd George that his election plans had been thrown into doubt by the protracted Dáil debates. The difficulty, he explained, was that it had 'strengthened the case of the Diehards ... and [was] making a lot of waverers incline more to their side because if what is a great gift on the part of England is not to be received in the spirit in which it is given, it does not look as if there would be any real peace in Ireland'. With a baffled air, he concluded that it 'certainly is a case of looking a gift horse in the mouth'.[68]

De Valera also felt disadvantaged by the Dáil's long-drawn-out exchanges. In his letter to Joe McGarrity he argued that the press and the Church 'were hard at work in its support' during the Christmas recess – a break that allowed deputies an opportunity to return home and gauge the opinions of their constituents.[69] On 6 January 1922, enraged at Griffith's decision to leak Document No. 2 to the press, and in a last-ditch effort to maximise his support among the extremists, de Valera submitted his resignation. Declaring that he could no longer preside over a divided government, he vowed to throw out the Treaty and pursue External Association if the Dáil re-elected him. But it was a futile and reckless tactic, for in this display of flagrant contempt for majority rule, de Valera helped set in motion the cycle of fratricidal terror to come.

'By allowing those who took up arms against the Treaty to draw on his authority, he conferred a respectability on their

cause it could never otherwise have attained.' In other words,
as his most recent biographer argued, de Valera shoulders a
large measure of the blame for 'the dimensions if not the fact
of the civil war'.[70]

The ploy to postpone the vote on the Treaty failed. Collins
and Griffith appealed to the speaker that the original standing
order took precedence over a vote on de Valera's status. The
Dáil had never been taken seriously by the Cabinet, and the
President had showed it little respect. Now, in a sign of how
quickly power was ebbing away from de Valera, the speaker
ruled that the Dáil was superior to the government. The next
evening, at 8 p.m. on Saturday 7 January, the Treaty establishing
the Irish Free State was ratified by the Dáil by a margin of
seven votes.

Todd Andrews, watching from the doorway of the council
chamber, 'saw the mixture of triumph, grief and worry with
which the deputies received the result'.[71] And while Collins leapt
to his feet to declare his affection for de Valera, the President,
overcome by emotion, buried his head in his hands and wept.

But even after the shock of the 64–57 Treaty vote, de Valera
clung to power. Spurning an invitation for political cooperation
from Collins, he offered himself for re-election as the President
of the Republic, pledging 'to carry on as before' until the people
had an opportunity to vote on the settlement.[72] This time the
tactic almost worked. Amid accusations of tyranny from the
pro-Treatyites, the margin separating the two sides narrowed
even further, and Griffith was elected as his successor by just
60 votes to 58.

In the hectic atmosphere all restraint evaporated. The next
day, with the anti-Treatyites effectively an opposition party, de
Valera led his followers out of the Dáil to a volley of abuse.
Collins roared: 'Deserters all! We will now call on the Irish

people to rally to us. Deserters all!' And to the backs of de Valera and Childers he screeched 'Foreigners – Americans – English'.[73]

Later that day, in another disquieting scene, Griffith's temper snapped. At the end of a long debate, Childers stood up to question the new President on the constitutional status of the Dáil; 'gadfly questioning', in the verdict of one historian, which 'stung [Griffith] out of his usual calm'.[74] Slamming his hand on the table, he snarled: 'I will not reply to any damned Englishman in this Assembly.'[75]

These intemperate outbursts did little to halt the rapidly widening rift within the separatist movement. In the absence of any political unity, the IRA fractured and within six months Ireland had descended into civil war. The fledgling nation's former supporters in Britain found the violence a perplexing development. As C.P. Scott commented to Margot Asquith: 'Who would have believed that having got rid of us, the Irish would start a terror of their own?'[76]

But as the historian Deirdre McMahon argued, the Treaty 'was less an object of congratulation than a festering sore at the heart of Irish political life'.[77] Lloyd George's strategic reliance on threats of coercion, a tactic that suited his short-term objectives, undermined the Treaty's legitimacy in the eyes of a substantial minority of the revolutionary movement, providing the catalyst for civil war. In Regan's view, the coercive nature of the settlement and the divisions it created corroded Ireland's parliamentary democracy in 1922, since 'militarist republicans [were released] from any obligation to the principle of majoritarianism'.[78]

And in the new terror that took hold, it was Collins, hungry for the levers of power, who became its most high-profile victim. At the time of his death, he wielded unassailable constitutional and military authority over the Free State, having prorogued the Dáil and appointed himself commander-in-chief of the National Army. To his great anger, Griffith was not consulted on any of this, but by this stage, illness had weakened the President's influence over the Provisional Government, and on 12 August, days after the dissolution of the Dáil, he died of a cerebral haemorrhage.[79]

His last weeks were spent in a state of profound misery. He believed that radical republicans had wrecked his life's work, and that the intensifying violence would, in his words, 'lay Ireland, dishonoured, prostrate again at England's feet'.[80]

Almost a fortnight later, in the encroaching darkness at Béal na mBláth in County Cork, an ambush party of six anti-Treatyites lay in wait for their former leader. They were the rump of a much larger republican group, but most had left, convinced their plan had been thwarted and that the commander-in-chief's convoy would not retrace the route travelled earlier in the day. Then, sometime between 8 p.m. and 8.30 p.m. (the precise time is disputed) on that summer evening of 22 August, Collins returned. As his convoy approached the now partially dismantled barricade, Emmet Dalton, who had stayed at Cadogan Gardens during the Treaty talks, urged the driver to drive on, but Collins countermanded the order and the vehicles stopped. Three of the ambush party, after spotting the cars on the road, had made it back to their positions by this stage, and the firing between nine 'Irregulars' and the convoy of Free Staters lasted for between thirty minutes and an hour.[81]

When the shooting stopped, there was only one casualty: Collins. He had wandered out onto the road with a rifle, and although the 'precise source of the shot' that shattered the back of his skull remains a matter of dispute, it was his own decision, as Charles Townshend argues, 'to put himself in its way'. Had he wanted to prove that he was more than a Fleet

Street hero? Or had alcohol blurred his judgement? There had been several visits to pubs and hotels earlier that day. In any case, 'there was nothing to stop the car he was travelling in from driving through to safety – nothing except perhaps his desire to demonstrate that he was truly a fighting man, not a pen pusher'.[82]

The consensus is that Collins needlessly exposed himself to danger, and died, almost accidentally, from a stray bullet. In recent years a more compelling, though controversial, narrative has been advanced, suggesting that Collins would have been lucky to survive the post-Treaty hostilities. It depicts Béal na mBláth as no haphazard ambush, but a carefully planned assassination organised by anti-Treaty elements within the IRB who believed their former leader was guilty of 'high treason' to the Irish Republic. In this telling, they lured him to Cork with the offer of peace talks that might end the Civil War, and persuaded him to pass through Béal na mBláth that fateful evening. When Collins went out onto the roadside, an unidentified sniper, armed with a Mauser sporting rifle, blew off the back of Collins' head, leaving what Dalton described as 'fearful gaping wound'.[83]

After putting his name to the Anglo-Irish Treaty in the early hours of 6 December 1921, Collins told Birkenhead that 'I have signed my own death warrant'. The Lord Chancellor retorted that he had just signed his 'political death warrant'.[84] Perhaps he had. What's certain is that of Britain's 'big four', only Churchill saw his fortunes improve after the Irish settlement. Less than two months after Collins' death, the Conservatives hounded Lloyd George from office, and although only fifty-nine, he spent the rest of his life in the political wilderness. A worse fate was in store for Birkenhead. His once brilliant career fizzled out, and as alcoholism took over, he died less than a decade later, unable, as one historian put it, 'to reconcile himself to his ultimate failure'.[85] Chamberlain, too, met an ignominious end. His relationships with leading Conservatives were scarred forever after the Treaty, and he became one of only two Tory leaders in the twentieth century to miss out on the premiership. By the time he died in March 1937, his reputation had been immortalised as the man who 'always played the game and always lost it' – a phrase variously attributed to Churchill and Birkenhead.[86]

But a century on, it is clear that the greatest casualties of the Treaty were the nationalists of Northern Ireland. The Boundary Commission, which helped persuade Collins and Griffith to sign, and which prevented the negotiations from collapsing, was nullified by its vague terms and a sinister qualifying phrase that restricted border changes to only 'so far as may be compatible with economic and geographic conditions'. The result, as Ronan Fanning has argued, 'was fifty years of persistent discriminatory repression against Northern Ireland's nationalist and Catholic minority'.[87] Southern unionists suffered some persecution in 1922–3, but there can be no comparison to the grim consequences in the North.

The Irish Free State could not have experienced a worse start. But in the end, the Treaty proved, as Collins predicted, a stepping stone to freedom, and by 1947, the year that Britain lost its imperial power over India, Churchill felt able to write, that in Ireland 'The bitter past is fading.'[88]

ENDNOTES

KEY TO ACRONYMS AND ABBREVIATIONS

AOB	Art O'Brien Papers
BMH WS	Bureau of Military History 1913–21, Military Archives, Dublin
CAC	Churchill Archives at Churchill College, Cambridge
Dáil Debates	Parliamentary Archives, Dáil Éireann
DIFP	PDF of Ronan Fanning, Michael Kennedy, Catriona Crowe, Dermot Keogh and Eunan O'Halpin (eds), Documents on Irish Foreign Policy, The Anglo-Irish Treaty: December 1920–December 1921
Hans.	Hansard, Parliamentary Archives of the United Kingdom
JMP	Joseph McGarrity Papers
LGP	Lloyd George papers, Parliamentary Archives of the United Kingdom
NAI	National Archives of Ireland
NLI	National Library of Ireland
TCD CP	Childers Papers, Trinity College Dublin Manuscripts
TNA	The National Archives of the United Kingdom
UCDA P150	De Valera Papers, University College Dublin Archives
UCDA P151	Gavan Duffy Papers, University College Dublin Archives
WB	Papers of William Bull

1. CLOSE ENCOUNTERS

1 Lloyd George formally took possession of the keys to Chequers in January 1921. The Tudor mansion was gifted to the British nation in 1917 by Sir Arthur Lee, an MP and minister during and after the First World War. He and his wife, Ruth, a wealthy American, spared no expense in modernising and furnishing

the house, and hoped the surrounding serenity and splendour would benefit the personal health of Britain's prime ministers. 'The better the health of our rulers', Lord Lee opined, 'the more sanely they will rule'. See David Stafford, *Oblivion or Glory: 1921 and the Making of Winston Churchill* (New Haven and London, 2019), pp. 78–9.

2 Frances Stevenson, in A.J.P. Taylor (ed.), *Lloyd George: A Diary by Frances Stevenson* (London, 1971), p. 210. Lloyd George eventually married Frances Stevenson on 23 October 1943, nearly three years after the death of his first wife, Dame Margaret Lloyd George, in January 1941. He died in Wales on 26 March 1945, almost eighteen months after his second marriage.

3 Lord Riddell, *Intimate Diary of the Peace Conference and After, 1918–1923* (London, 1923), p. 332.

4 Thomas Jones, in Keith Middlemas (ed.), *Whitehall Diary*, Vol. III: *Ireland 1918–1925* (London, 1971), p. 41.

5 Gerard Noonan, *The IRA in Britain, 1919-1923: 'In the Heart of Enemy Lines'* (Liverpool, 2014), pp. 277–8.

6 Ibid., p. 249.

7 Jon Lawrence, 'Forging a Peaceable Kingdom: War, Violence, and Fear of Brutalization in Post-First World War Britain' in *The Journal of Modern History*, Vol. 75, No. 3 (2003), p. 587.

8 Jones, *Whitehall Diary*, Vol. III, p. 69.

9 *Western Mail*, 22 February 1921.

10 Kenneth O. Morgan, *Consensus and Disunity: The Lloyd George Coalition Government 1918–1922* (Oxford, 1979) p. 169.

11 Ibid., p. 115.

12 Richard Toye, *Lloyd George & Churchill: Rivals for Greatness* (London, 2007), pp. 215–16; Lord Beaverbrook (Max Aitken), *The Decline and Fall of Lloyd George* (London, 1963), pp. 79–81.

13 Taylor (ed.), *Lloyd George: A Diary by Frances Stevenson*, p. 218.

14 Ibid.

15 Ibid.

16 Ibid.

17 As assistant commissioner of the Metropolitan Police, Thomson's fiefdom was variously known as special branch, the directorate of intelligence and the secret service. At the end of October 1921, he was forced to resign after General Horwood complained directly to Lloyd George about 'the independence of the Special Branch' under Thomson. His criticism followed an investigation into the Secret Services by a committee chaired by Sir Warren Fisher, permanent undersecretary at the Treasury. The Fisher report, published in July of that year, castigated Thomson for his unit's excessive spending, the duplication of work carried out by other agencies, and the production of misleading reports. But Thomson's departure caused a furore with the diehards and came at a sensitive time during the Treaty talks. See pp. 135–6 in Chapter Six. For further details on Thomson's resignation – he later claimed that he was 'kicked out by the

P.M.' – see Andrew Christopher, *The Defence of the Realm: The Authorized History of MI5* (London, 2009), pp. 114–20 and Eunan O'Halpin, 'Sir Warren Fisher and the Coalition, 1919–1922' in *The Historical Journal*, Vol. 24, No. 4 (1981) pp. 924–7.

18   Frank Thornton, BMH WS 615, p. 31.

19   Ibid.

20   *The Observer*, 12 November 1961.

21   Morgan, *Consensus and Disunity*, pp. 213–35; Peter Clarke, *Hope and Glory: Britain 1900–2000* (London, 2004), pp. 106–7; Ralph Desmarais, 'Lloyd George and the Development of the British Government's Strikebreaking Organization' in *International Review of Social History*, Vol. 20, No. 1 (1975), pp. 1–15; Laura Beers, '"Is This Man an Anarchist?" Industrial Action and the Battle for Public Opinion in Interwar Britain' in *The Journal of Modern History*, Vol. 82, No. 1 (2010), pp. 30–60.

22   J.L. Hammond, *C.P. Scott of the Manchester Guardian* (New York, 1934), p. 278; Roy Hattersley, *David Lloyd George: The Great Outsider* (London, 2010), p. 537.

23   Martin Gilbert, *Winston S. Churchill*, Vol. IV, Companion, Part 3, Documents April 1921–November 1922 (London, 1967), p. 1219.

24   Morgan, *Consensus and Disunity*, p. 130.

25   Jones, *Whitehall Diary*, Vol. III, pp. 63–70.

26   Riddell, *Intimate Diary of the Peace Conference and After*, p. 290.

27   Arthur Mitchell, *Revolutionary Government in Ireland: Dáil Éireann 1919–1922* (Dublin, 1995), pp. 281–9; David Fitzpatrick, *Politics and Irish Life 1913–1921: Provincial Experience of War and Revolution* (Cork, 1977), pp. 104–5; Michael Laffan, *The Resurrection of Ireland: The Sinn Féin Party, 1916–1923* (Cambridge, 1999), pp. 340–2; Michael Hopkinson, *The Irish War of Independence* (Dublin and Montreal, 2002), pp. 192–4; Charles Townshend, *The Republic: The Fight for Independence* (London, 2013), pp. 282–6.

28   Townshend, *The Republic*, pp. 290, 297.

29   Ibid., p. 289; *The Freeman's Journal*, 27 April 1921.

30   Paul McMahon, *British Spies and Irish Rebels: British Intelligence and Ireland 1916–1945* (Woodbridge, 2008), p. 52.

31   Jones, *Whitehall Diary*, Vol. III, p. 73. See also Anne Dolan, 'The British Culture of Paramilitary Violence in the Irish War of Independence' in Robert Gerwarth and John Horne (eds), *War and Peace: Paramilitary Violence in Europe after the Great War* (Oxford, 2012), p. 203

32   Dolan, 'The British Culture of Paramilitary Violence in the Irish War of Independence', p. 203.

33   Townshend, *The Republic*, p. 288.

34   Keiko Inoue, 'Propaganda II: Propaganda of Dáil Éireann, 1919–21' in Augusteijn (ed.), *The Irish Revolution*, pp. 87–99; Laffan, *The Resurrection of Ireland*, pp. 264–5.

35   Ibid; Charles Townshend, *Political Violence in Ireland: Government and*

Resistance since 1848 (Oxford, 1983), pp. 358–9; Sir Nevil Macready, *Annals of an Active Life*, Vol. II (London, 1924), p. 476. The newspaper, its two directors, Martin Fitzgerald and Hamilton Edwards, and the editor, Patrick Hooper were named as defendants in the case, which was brought under the Restoration of Ireland Act, legislation which provided the authorities with emergency powers. Fitzgerald, Edwards and Hooper were imprisoned in Mountjoy for about a month over Christmas 1920. According to Macready, Downing Street's intervention aroused 'disgust and contempt in the hearts of those who were risking their lives for the policy of the Government'. See also *The Freeman's Journal*, 8 January 1921.

36 Paul Adelman, *The Decline and Fall of the Liberal Party 1910–1931* (London and New York, 1995, 2nd ed.), p. 32.

37 Francis Costello, 'The Role of Propaganda in the Anglo-Irish War 1919–1921' in *The Canadian Journal of Irish Studies*, Vol. 14, No. 2 (1989) p. 12; Morgan, *Consensus and Disunity*, pp. 70–3.

38 Kenneth O. Morgan, 'Lloyd George', in A.J.P. Taylor (ed.) *British Prime Ministers* (London, 1974), p. 7.

39 Cited in Kevin Matthews, *Fatal Influence: The Impact of Ireland on British Politics 1920–1925* (Dublin, 2004), p. 16.

40 Ibid.

41 Patrick Moylett, BMH WS 767, pp. 51–80; Ronan Fanning, *Fatal Path: British Government and Irish Revolution 1910–1922* (London, 2013, ebook ed.); S.M. Lawlor, 'Ireland from Truce to Treaty: War or Peace? July to October 1921' in *Irish Historical Studies*, Vol. 22, No. 85 (1980), p. 50.

42 Jones, *Whitehall Diary*, Vol. III, p. 71.

43 Cited in Hopkinson, *The Irish War of Independence*, p. 194.

44 TNA CAB 23/26/2.

45 Jones, *Whitehall Diary*, Vol. III, p. 67.

46 Morgan, *Consensus and Disunity*, p. 259.

47 Taylor (ed.), *Lloyd George: A Diary by Frances Stevenson*, p. 223.

48 Beaverbrook, *The Decline and Fall of Lloyd George*, p. 264.

49 R.J.Q. Adams, *Bonar Law* (Stanford, 1999, ebook ed.).

50 *The Times*, 22 and 23 June 1921.

51 Jones, *Whitehall Diary*, Vol. III, p. 80.

2. IMPROVISING A NATION

1 *Irish Independent*, 29 June 1921; *The Freeman's Journal*, 29 June 1921.

2 *Daily Herald*, 29 June 1921.

3 Mark Sturgis, in Michael Hopkinson (ed.), *The Last Days of Dublin Castle: The Diaries of Mark Sturgis* (Dublin, 1999), p. 191; *Irish Independent*, 29 June 1921; *The Freeman's Journal*, 29 June 1921.

4 *The Irish Times*, 29 June 1921.

5   *Irish Independent*, 29 June 1921; *The Freeman's Journal*, 29 June 1921; *The Irish Times*, 29 June 1921.

6   *Official Correspondence relating to the Peace Negotiations, June–September 1921*, https://celt.ucc.ie/published/E900003-007/text001.html.

7   Earl of Longford (Frank Pakenham) and Thomas P. O'Neill, *Eamon de Valera* (London, 1970), pp. 124–5.

8   Maeve MacGarry, BMH WS 826, p. 22; Townshend, *The Republic*, p. 304.

9   Diarmaid Ferriter, *Judging Dev* (Dublin, 2007), p. 36.

10 James P. Walsh, 'De Valera in the United States, 1919' in *Records of the American Catholic Historical Society of Philadelphia*, Vol. 73, No. 3/4 (1962), p. 95.

11 Hopkinson (ed.), *The Last Days of Dublin Castle*, pp. 5–6.

12 Michael T. Foy, *Michael Collins's Intelligence War: The Struggle between the British and the IRA 1919–1921* (Stroud, 2006, ebook ed.); Longford and O'Neill, *Eamon de Valera*, p. 125.

13 Townshend, *The Republic*, p. 304.

14 Longford and O'Neill, *Eamon de Valera*, p. 127.

15 Fanning, *Éamon de Valera*, p. 99.

16 Hopkinson (ed.), *The Last Days of Dublin Castle*, p. 190.

17 Jones, *Whitehall Diary*, Vol. III, p. 81.

18 Hopkinson (ed.), *The Last Days of Dublin Castle*, p. 192.

19 Cited in McMahon, *British Spies and Irish Rebels*, p. 59.

20 Peter Hart, *Mick, The Real Michael Collins* (London, 2005), p. 293.

21 Hopkinson (ed.), *The Last Days of Dublin Castle*, p. 195.

22 *Official Correspondence relating to the Peace Negotiations, June–September 1921*, https://celt.ucc.ie/published/E900003-007/text001.html.

23 Zara Steiner, *The Lights That Failed: European International History 1919–1933* (Oxford, 2007), pp. 601–32.

24 Mark Mazower, *No Enchanted Palace: The End of Empire and the Ideological Origins of the United Nations* (New Jersey and Oxford, 2009), pp. 28–65; Marilyn Lake and Henry Reynolds, *Drawing the Global Colour Line: White Men's Countries and the International Challenge of Racial Equality* (Cambridge, 2008), pp. 213–14, 328.

25 Cited in Mazower, *No Enchanted Palace*, p. 50.

26 *The Daily Mail* (Brisbane, Queensland), 3 May 1921.

27 Mazower, *No Enchanted Palace*, pp. 34–8.

28 Ibid., p. 77.

29 Cited in Donal Lowry, 'The Captive Dominion: Imperial Realities Behind Irish Diplomacy, 1922–49' in *Irish Historical Studies*, Vol. 36, No. 142 (2008), p. 204.

30 Jones, *Whitehall Diary*, Vol. III, p. 75.

31 Townshend, *The Republic*, pp. 306–8; Longford and O'Neill, *Eamon de Valera*, p. 130; W.K. Hancock, *Smuts* (Cambridge, 1962), pp. 56–7; Pádraig Óg Ó Ruairc, *Truce: Murder, Myth and the Last Days of the Irish War of Independence* (Cork, 2016), pp. 58–61.

32 Rex Taylor, *Michael Collins* (London, 1963), p. 110. For the reliability of

Taylor's material, see Peter Hart, *Mick: The Real Michael Collins* (London, 2005), p. xvi.

33 NLI AOB MS 8340/23.

34 Jones, *Whitehall Diary*, Vol. III, pp. 82–3.

35 Ibid.

36 Macready, *Annals of an Active Life*, Vol. II, p. 577.

37 Townshend, *The Republic*, p. 309.

38 Macready, *Annals of an Active Life*, Vol. II, p. 578. For an explanation of the background to these killings, and for a study that challenges the historiography of the Truce, see Ó Ruairc's *Truce*.

39 D.W. Harkness, *The Restless Dominion: The Irish Free State and the British Commonwealth of Nations, 1921–1931* (London, 1969), p. 5.

40 Taylor (ed.), *Lloyd George: A Diary by Frances Stevenson*, pp. 227–8.

41 Laffan, *The Resurrection of Ireland*, pp. 245–6; J.J. Lee, *Ireland 1921–1985: Politics and Society* (Cambridge, 1989), pp. 47–8; Francis Costello, *The Irish Revolution and its Aftermath 1916–1923: Years of Revolt* (Dublin, 2003), pp. 237–9.

42 Costello, *The Irish Revolution and its Aftermath*, p. 237.

43 Mitchell, *Revolutionary Government in Ireland*, p. 296.

44 Ibid., p. 303.

45 Costello, *The Irish Revolution and its Aftermath*, p. 239.

46 Jones, *Whitehall Diary*, Vol. III, p. 91.

47 Robert C. Self (ed.), *The Austen Chamberlain Diary Letters: The Correspondence of Sir Austen Chamberlain with His Sisters Hilda and Ida, 1916–1937* (Cambridge, 1995), pp. 162–3.

48 Michael Hopkinson, *Green against Green: The Irish Civil War* (Dublin, 1988), p. 27; Townshend, *The Republic*, pp. 335–6.

49 Self (ed.), *The Austen Chamberlain Diary Letters*, p. 162.

50 Jones, *Whitehall Diary*, Vol. III, p. 96.

51 *Official Correspondence relating to the Peace Negotiations June–September 1921*, https://celt.ucc.ie/published/E900003-007/text001.html.

52 Kenneth O. Morgan (ed.), *Lloyd George Family Letters 1885–1936* (London, 1973), p. 194.

53 Jones, *Whitehall Diary*, Vol. III, p. 98.

54 *Official Correspondence relating to the Peace Negotiations, June–September 1921*, https://celt.ucc.ie/published/E900003-007/text001.html.

55 Ibid.

56 Self (ed.), *The Austen Chamberlain Diary Letters*, p. 167.

57 LGP F/7/4/27.

58 Cited in Steiner, *The Lights That Failed*, p. 376.

59 Stafford, *Oblivion or Glory*, p. 180.

60 LGP F/7/4/27.

61 *Official Correspondence relating to the Peace Negotiations, June–September 1921*, https://celt.ucc.ie/published/E900003-007/text001.html.

62 Townshend, *The Republic*, pp. 333–4.
63 Mitchell, *Revolutionary Government in Ireland*, p. 303.
64 Ibid.
65 Dáil Debates, Vol. S, 5.
66 Fanning, *Éamon de Valera*, p. 105.
67 Éamon de Valera to Joseph McGarrity, 27 December 1921, NLI JMP MS 17,440/4.
68 Dáil Debates, Vol. S, 10.
69 Batt O'Connor, *With Michael Collins in the Fight for Independence* (London, 1929), p. 178.
70 Hart, *Mick*, p. 425.
71 Ibid., p. 288.
72 Dáil Debates, Vol. S, 10.
73 Ferriter, *Judging Dev*, p. 68.
74 Hopkinson (ed.), *The Last Days of Dublin Castle*, p. 188; Tom Garvin, *Nationalist Revolutionaries in Ireland 1858–1928* (Dublin, 1987), p. 146.
75 Laffan, *The Resurrection of Ireland*, p. 242.
76 Ibid., p. 243.
77 Townshend, *The Republic*, pp. 318–21.
78 Fanning, *Éamon de Valera*, pp. 103–4.

3. LONDON

1 Frank Pakenham, *Peace by Ordeal* (London, 1935), p. 123. It should be noted that Pakenham's enduring study of the Treaty negotiations, published in 1935, was written long before the release of the British cabinet papers, or the publication of the Thomas Jones' and Frances Stevenson's diaries in the early 1970s. These invaluable sources lay bare the insecurities and anxieties that Ireland's claim for independence generated within Whitehall and Westminster, and reveal how the key decision-makers, motivated in large part by mutual distrust and self-interest, accommodated themselves to a settlement. They show the influence of top civil servants, and provide a vital insight into the attitudes and characters of the principal players who were born during the late Victorian heyday and who consequently shared values, ideas and prejudices common to that era. So, while Pakenham benefited from contemporary testimony, particularly from the Irish side, his scholarly study of the negotiations provides a limited perspective of the realities driving the British policy-makers. Nevertheless, *Peace by Ordeal*, the first serious work to appear on the Treaty talks, remains the most comprehensive treatment of the subject today.
2 TNA CAB 23/27/1.
3 Cited in David Gilmour, *Curzon* (London, 1994), p. 528.
4 TNA CAB 23/27/3.

5   David Dutton, *Austen Chamberlain: Gentleman in Politics* (Bolton, 1985, reprint; Oxon, 2019, ebook ed.), pp. 13–14.

6   Ibid.

7   Ibid., pp. 12–13.

8   David Cannadine, *The Decline and Fall of the British Aristocracy* (New Haven and London, 1990), p. 227.

9   Cited in the *Londonderry Sentinel*, 8 October 1921.

10 Michael Kinnear, *The Fall of Lloyd George: The Political Crisis of 1922* (London, 1973), pp. 79–80.

11 Pakenham, *Peace by Ordeal*, p. 123.

12 Jones, *Whitehall Diary*, Vol. III, p. 87.

13 David Cannadine, *The Pleasures of the Past* (London, 1989), pp. 296–7.

14 Pakenham, *Peace by Ordeal*, p. 125.

15 Martin Gilbert, *Winston S. Churchill*, Vol. IV: World in Torment 1916–1922 (London, 1975; reprint 2015, ebook ed.), p. 910.

16 Cited in John Campbell, *F.E. Smith, First Earl of Birkenhead* (London, 1982), p. 557.

17 Ibid.

18 Hansard, Series 5, Vol. 43, col. 1047, 19 August 1921.

19 Florence O'Donoghue, *No Other Law* (Dublin, 1954; reprint Dublin, 1986), p. 192.

20 Childers Diary, 6 and 7 October 1921, TCD CP 7814.

21 David Fitzpatrick, *Harry Boland's Irish Revolution* (Cork, 2003), pp. 236–7. See also Meda Ryan, *Michael Collins and the Women in His Life* (Cork, 1996), pp. 92–105.

22 *Irish Independent*, 10 October 1921.

23 Ibid.

24 *The Freeman's Journal*, 10 October 1921; *The Irish Times*, 10 October 1921; *Irish Independent*, 10 October 1921.

25 Hopkinson, *The Irish War of Independence*, p. 147.

26 *The Freeman's Journal*, 10 October 1921; *The Manchester Guardian*, 10 October 1921; *Northern Whig*, 10 October 1921.

27 *Aberdeen Press and Journal*, 10 October 1921.

28 *The Freeman's Journal*, 10 October 1921.

29 *Dundee Evening Telegraph*, 31 March 1921; see also Anne Dolan and William Murphy, *Michael Collins: The Man and the Revolution* (Cork, 2019, ebook ed.).

30 *Belfast Telegraph*, 10 October 1921.

31 *The Freeman's Journal*, 10 October 1921; *The Scotsman*, 10 October 1921.

32 Padraic Colum, *Arthur Griffith* (Dublin, 1959), pp. 162–3.

33 Roy Foster, *Vivid Faces: The Revolutionary Generation in Ireland 1890–1923* (London, 2014), p. 238.

34 Ibid., pp. 155, 158; Laffan, *The Resurrection of Ireland*, pp. 17–18; Patrick Maume, *The Long Gestation: Irish Nationalist Life 1891–1918* (Dublin, 1999), pp. 57, 85.

35   Laffan, *The Resurrection of Ireland*, pp. 33, 61, 180; Townshend, *The Republic*, pp. 24–5.

36   Laffan, *The Resurrection of Ireland*, p. 17.

37   Colum, *Arthur Griffith*, p. 281.

38   Ibid.

39   Louis J. Walsh, *On My Keeping and In Theirs: A Record of Experiences 'on the run', in Derry Gaol and in Ballykinlar Internment Camp* (Dublin, 1921), pp. 93–4; see also Liam Ó Duibhir, *Prisoners of War: Ballykinlar Internment Camp 1920–1921* (Cork, 2013, ebook ed.).

40   Justin D. Stover, 'Irish Political Prisoner Culture, 1916–1923', in *CrossCurrents*, Vol. 64, No. 1 (2014), p. 97.

41   *The Observer*, 9 October 1921.

42   Jones, *Whitehall Diary*, Vol. III, p. 118.

43   TNA CAB 43/4_1, p. 11. These files can be accessed from the UK's National Archives website. The page numbers refer to those displayed on the pdf document.

44   Frederick Winston Furneaux Smith, Earl of Birkenhead, *The Life of F.E. Smith, First Earl of Birkenhead* (London, 1965), pp. 374–5.

45   *Daily Express*, 11 October 1921.

46   Dolan and Murphy, *Michael Collins* (ebook ed.).

47   *Illustrated London News*, 2 April 1921; *Dundee Evening Telegraph*, 31 March 1921; *Western Morning News*, 11 October 1921.

48   *Daily Express*, 11 October 1921.

49   Jones, *Whitehall Diary*, Vol. III, p. 119.

50   Ibid.

51   Ibid., pp. 119–20.

52   TNA CAB 43/4_1, p. 11.

53   Childers Diary, 10 October 1921, TCD CP 7814.

54   NAI DE 2/531.

55   Jones, *Whitehall Diary*, Vol. III, p. 120.

56   NAI DE/2/531.

57   Pakenham, *Peace by Ordeal*, p. 147.

58   Jones, *Whitehall Diary*, Vol. III, p. 122. TNA CAB 43/4_1, p. 15.

59   Jones, *Whitehall Diary*, Vol. III, p. 123.

60   Tim Pat Coogan, *Michael Collins: A Biography* (London, 1990 ebook ed.).

61   DIFP, The Anglo-Irish Treaty, p. 83.

4. WAR OR PEACE?

1   Cited in Stafford, *Oblivion or Glory*, p. 239.

2   DIFP, The Anglo-Irish Treaty, p. 84.

3   Margery Forester, *Michael Collins: The Lost Leader* (London, 1971), pp. 218–20; Frank O'Connor, *The Big Fellow: Michael Collins and the Irish Revolution*

(London, 1937; reprint Dublin, 2018, ebook ed); Taylor, *Michael Collins*, p. 129; T. Ryle Dwyer, *Big Fellow, Long Fellow: A Joint Biography of Collins & de Valera* (Dublin, 1998), p. 193.

4 Hart, *Mick*, p. 299.

5 León Ó Broin, *In Great Haste: The Letters of Michael Collins & Kitty Kiernan* (Dublin, 1983), p. 31.

6 Hayden Talbot, *Michael Collins' Own Story* (London, 1923; reprint, The Internet Archive, ebook ed.).

7 Robert Barton, BMH WS 979, p. 33.

8 Deborah Lavin, *From Empire to International Commonwealth: A Biography of Lionel Curtis* (Oxford, 1995), p. 186; Andrew Boyle, *The Riddle of Erskine Childers* (London, 1977), p. 280.

9 Lavin, *From Empire to International Commonwealth*, p. 186.

10 Ibid., p. 187.

11 Jim Ring, *Erskine Childers* (London, 2011, ebook ed.); Lavin, *From Empire to International Commonwealth*, p. 8.

12 Thomas Pakenham, *The Boer War* (London, 1979, ebook ed.).

13 Boyle, *The Riddle of Erskine Childers*, pp. 69, 88; Ring, *Erskine Childers* (ebook ed.).

14 Cited in Bruce Nelson, *Irish Nationalists and the Making of the Irish Race* (Princeton and Oxford, 2012), p. 146.

15 Ibid., p. 152.

16 Hart, *Mick*, pp. 23–4.

17 Boyle, *The Riddle of Erskine Childers*, pp. 50–4, 121; Ring, *Erskine Childers* (ebook ed.).

18 Cited in Boyle, *The Riddle of Erskine Childers*, p. 144.

19 Cited in Nelson, *Irish Nationalists and the Making of the Irish Race*, p. 152.

20 Ibid., pp. 148–50.

21 Boyle, *The Riddle of Erskine Childers*, p. 144.

22 Frank O'Connor, *An Only Child* (New York, 1961), p. 214.

23 Lavin, *From Empire to International Commonwealth*, p. x.

24 Daniel Gorman, 'Lionel Curtis, Imperial Citizenship, and the Quest for Unity' in *The Historian*, Vol. 66, No. 1 (2004), pp. 67–96.

25 Paul Addison, 'Mount Amery' in *London Review of Books*, Vol. 2, No. 22 (20 November 1980).

26 Lake and Reynolds, *Drawing the Global Colour Line*, p. 217.

27 Lavin, *From Empire to International Commonwealth*, pp. 187–8.

28 TNA CAB 43/2_1, p. 60.

29 Gorman, 'Lionel Curtis, Imperial Citizenship, and the Quest for Unity', p. 95.

30 Robert Barton, BMH WS 979, p. 33.

31 Cited in Joseph M. Curran, *The Birth of the Irish Free State 1921–1923* (Alabama, 1980), p. 83.

32 Self (ed.), *The Austen Chamberlain Diary Letters*, p. 170.

33 Laffan, *The Resurrection of Ireland*, pp. 310–18; Townshend, *The Republic*,

pp. 337–9; Fergus Campbell, *Land and Revolution: Nationalist Politics in the West of Ireland 1891–1921* (Oxford, 2005), pp. 280–2.

34 Townshend, *The Republic*, p. 338.

35 Laffan, *The Resurrection of Ireland*, p. 316.

36 Ibid., p. 343.

37 Jones, *Whitehall Diary*, Vol. III, p. 123.

38 *The Times*, 13 October 1921.

39 TNA CAB 43/4_1, pp. 22–3.

40 Townshend, *The Republic*, pp. 176–8; Curran, *The Birth of the Irish Free State*, p. 42; Robert Lynch, *The Partition of Ireland 1918–1925* (Cambridge, 2019, ebook ed.).

41 Jones, *Whitehall Diary*, Vol. III, p. 126.

42 Simon Heffer (ed.), *Henry 'Chips' Channon, the Diaries 1918–38* (London, 1967; reprint, London, 2021), p. 396; Jones, *Whitehall Diary*, Vol. III, pp. 126–7.

43 DIFP, The Anglo-Irish Treaty, p. 85.

44 NAI DE/2/304/1/3; for Collins' reaction, see Lawlor, 'Ireland from Truce to Treaty', p. 55.

45 NAI DE/2/304/6/1.

46 NAI DE/2/304/1/3.

47 DIFP, The Anglo-Irish Treaty, p. 85.

48 Fanning, *Fatal Path* (ebook ed.).

49 NAI DE/2/304/8/1.

50 Ibid.

51 Jones, *Whitehall Diary*, Vol. III, p. 132.

52 Riddell, *Intimate Diary of the Peace Conference and After*, pp. 328–9.

53 Hopkinson (ed.), *The Last Days of Dublin Castle*, pp. 219–20.

54 *Belfast News-Letter*, 15 October 1921.

55 Dolan and Murphy, *Michael Collins* (ebook ed.).

56 Cited in Richard Ullman, *The Anglo–Soviet Accord*, Vol. III: Anglo–Soviet Relations: 1917–1921 (London, 1972), p. 96.

57 *Londonderry Sentinel*, 18 October 1921.

58 Dolan and Murphy, *Michael Collins* (ebook ed.).

59 NAI DE/ 2/304/6/2.

60 Coogan, *Michael Collins* (ebook ed.).

61 Talbot, *Michael Collins' Own Story* (ebook ed.).

62 NAI DE/2/304/2/2.

63 Lawlor, 'Ireland from Truce to Treaty', pp. 54–6.

64 Fanning, *Éamon de Valera*, p. 111.

65 Hopkinson (ed.), *The Last Days of Dublin Castle*, p. 202.

66 NAI DE/2/304/8/1; TNA CAB 43/4_1, pp. 34–5. See also Curran, *The Birth of the Irish Free State*, p. 85.

67 Jones, *Whitehall Diary*, Vol. III, p. 137.

68 DIFP, The Anglo-Irish Treaty, p. 93.

69 *The Times*, 22 October 1921.

70   Donald S. Birn, 'Open Diplomacy at the Washington Conference of 1921-2: The British and French Experience' in *Comparative Studies in Society and History*, Vol. 12, No. 3 (1970), p. 310.

71   Noonan, *The IRA in Britain*, p. 268.

72   Hansard (Commons), Vol. 128 cc. 1337–79 (28 April 1920).

73   Dolan and Murphy, *Michael Collins* (ebook ed.).

74   McMahon, *British Spies and Irish Rebels*, p. 101; Noonan, *The IRA in Britain*, p. 199.

75   NAI DE/2/304/1/31.

76   Pakenham, *Peace by Ordeal*, pp. 168–9.

77   NAI DE/2/304/1/31.

78   Ibid.

79   TNA CAB 43/4_1, p. 43.

80   NAI DE/2/304/1/31; TNA CAB 43/4_1, pp. 42–3.

81   McMahon, *British Spies and Irish Rebels*, p. 63.

5. OPPOSITION AND DIVISION

1   *Pall Mall Gazette*, 21 October 1921.

2   *Newcastle Daily Chronicle*, 22 October 1921.

3   *The Freeman's Journal*, 22 October 1921.

4   NAI DE/2/304/8/1.

5   Una Stack, BMH WS 418, p. 47.

6   DIFP, The Anglo-Irish Treaty, p. 102.

7   Lee, *Ireland 1912–1985*, p. 48.

8   DIFP, The Anglo-Irish Treaty, p. 102.

9   Townshend, *The Republic*, p. 87.

10 Ibid; Fergus O'Farrell, *Cathal Brugha* (Dublin, 2018), p. 57.

11 Ibid., pp. 66–7.

12 Townshend, *The Republic*, pp. 87, 327–8.

13 Dwyer, *Big Fellow, Long Fellow*, p. 200.

14 NAI DE/2/531.

15 Maryann Gialanella Valiulis, *Portrait of a Revolutionary: Richard Mulcahy and the Founding of the Irish Free State* (Dublin, 1992), p. 104.

16 TNA HO 317/46; McMahon, *British Spies and Irish Rebels*, pp. 56–60.

17 NLI AOB MS 8430/31.

18 Ó Broin, *In Great Haste*, p. 46.

19 Ibid., p. 48.

20 Ibid.

21 Childers Diary, 24 October 1921, TCD CP 7814.

22 TNA CAB 43/4_1, p. 46.

23 *Pall Mall Gazette*, 25 October 1921; *The Manchester Guardian*, 25 October 1921; *Dundee Courier*, 25 October 1921.

24   DIFP, The Anglo-Irish Treaty, p. 99.

25   TNA CAB 43/4_1, p. 45.

26   DIFP, The Anglo-Irish Treaty, p. 99.

27   NAI DE/2/304/1/27.

28   D.G. Boyce, *Englishmen and Irish Troubles: British Public Opinion and the Making of Irish Policy, 1918–22* (London, 1972), p. 184.

29   Bill Kissane, *The Politics of the Irish Civil War* (Oxford, 2005, ebook ed.).

30   NAI DE/2/304/1/27.

31   Jones, *Whitehall Diary*, Vol. III, p. 144.

32   TNA CAB 43/4_1, pp. 45–6.

33   See, for example, the editorial comments in Jones' *Whitehall Diary*, Vol. III, p. 141, as well as Dwyer, *Big Fellow, Long Fellow*, p. 201.

34   Fanning, *Éamon de Valera*, p. 114.

35   Curran, *The Birth of the Irish Free State*, p. 89; Costello, *The Irish Revolution*, p. 257.

36   Geoffrey Shakespeare, *Let Candles Be Brought In* (London, 1949), p. 82.

37   Jones, *Whitehall Diary*, Vol. III, pp. 144–5.

38   Eunan O'Halpin, 'British Intelligence in Ireland, 1914–1921', in Christopher Andrew and David Dilks (eds), *The Missing Dimension: Governments and Intelligence Communities in the Twentieth Century* (London, 1984) pp. 59–61. See also McMahon, *British Spies and Irish Rebels*, pp. 20–1.

39   Kinnear, *The Fall of Lloyd George*, p. 80.

40   NAI DE 2/304/1.

41   Trevor Wilson (ed.), *The Political Diaries of C.P. Scott* (London, 1970), p. 404.

42   NAI DE 2/531.

43   Ibid.

44   Ibid.

45   Pakenham, *Peace By Ordeal*, p. 182.

46   NAI DE 2/531.

47   Ibid.

48   Éamon de Valera to Joseph McGarrity, 27 December 1921, NLI JMP MS 17,440/4.

49   NLI AOB MS 8430/20.

50   *The Manchester Guardian*, 27 October 1921; *Daily Mirror*, 27 October 1921.

51   *The Manchester Guardian*, 28 October 1921; *The Times*, 28 October 1921.

52   Cited in John D. Fair, 'The Anglo-Irish Treaty of 1921: Unionist Aspects of the Peace' in *Journal of British Studies*, Vol. 12, No. 1 (1972), p. 140.

53   Jones, *Whitehall Diary*, Vol. III, p. 146.

54   Ibid., pp. 146–7.

55   Taylor (ed.), *Lloyd George, a Diary by Frances Stevenson*, p. 234.

56   Ibid.

57   Beaverbrook, *The Decline and Fall of Lloyd George*, p. 106.

58   Ibid.

59   Wilson (ed.), *The Political Diaries of C.P. Scott*, p. 404.

60   NAI DE/2/304/8/1.

61 Ibid.
62 Childers Diary, 27 October 1921, TCD CP 7814.
63 Childers Diary, 28 October 1921, TCD CP 7814.
64 Wilson (ed.), *The Political Diaries of C.P. Scott*, p. 404.
65 Longford and O'Neill, *Eamon de Valera*, p. 148.
66 Wilson (ed.), *The Political Diaries of C.P. Scott*, p. 402.
67 Ibid., p. 405.
68 Jones, *Whitehall Diary*, Vol. III, p. 149.
69 NAI DE/2/304/8/1.
70 Wilson (ed.), *The Political Diaries of C.P. Scott*, p. 406.
71 Jones, *Whitehall Diary*, Vol. III, p. 150.
72 Ibid., p. 151.
73 Riddell, *Intimate Diary of the Peace Conference and After*, p. 330.
74 NAI DE/2/304/8/1.
75 Jones, *Whitehall Diary*, Vol. III, p. 151.

6. CASTING AND GATHERING

1   NAI DE/2/304/8/1.
2   Ibid.
3   Ibid.
4   DIFP, The Anglo-Irish Treaty, p. 42; Fanning, *Fatal Path* (ebook ed.).
5   Cited in Matthews, *Fatal Influence*, p. 44.
6   Maurice Cowling, *The Impact of Labour 1920–1924: The Beginning of Modern British Politics* (Cambridge, 1971), pp. 122–4.
7   Cited in Matthews, *Fatal Influence*, p. 44.
8   NAI DE/2/304/8/1.
9   Forester, *Michael Collins*, p. 231.
10 Sir John Lavery, *The Life of a Painter* (London, 1940), p. 215.
11 Taylor, *Michael Collins*, p. 122.
12 Ibid; O'Connor, *The Big Fellow* (ebook ed.).
13 Forester, *Michael Collins*, p. 231.
14 Pakenham, *Peace by Ordeal*, p. 125.
15 Richard Davenport-Hines, *Enemies Within: The Communists, the Cambridge Spies and the Making of Modern Britain* (London, 2018), pp. 64, 66.
16 Ibid., p. 63.
17 Cited in Campbell, *F.E. Smith*, p. 713.
18 Cited in Taylor, *Michael Collins*, p. 122.
19 NAI DE/2/304/8/1.
20 *The Scotsman*, 31 October 1921; *Shields Daily News*, 1 November 1921.
21 *The Manchester Guardian*, 1 November 1921; *The Scotsman*, 1 November 1921.
22 *Daily Express*, 1 November 1921.

23 *The Manchester Guardian*, 1 November 1921; *The Times*, 1 November 1921.

24 *The Scotsman*, 1 November 1921.

25 Ibid.

26 Cited in *Belfast News-Letter*, 1 November 1921.

27 *Daily Express*, 1 November 1921.

28 Bayford, Lord (Robert Sanders), *Real Old Tory Politics: The Political Diaries of Sir Robert Sanders, Lord Bayford, 1910–1935* (London, 1984), p. 163.

29 Jones, *Whitehall Diary*, Vol. III, p. 152.

30 Ibid.

31 NAI DE/2/531.

32 Ibid.

33 Ibid.

34 Childers Diary, 1 November 1921, TCD CP 7814.

35 NAI DE/2/531.

36 Eunan O'Halpin, *Defending Ireland: The Irish State and its Enemies Since 1922* (Oxford, 1999), pp. 81–3, 91.

37 Hart, *Mick*, p. 293.

38 Childers Diary, 3 November 1921, TCD CP 7814.

39 NAI DE/2/531.

40 O'Halpin, *Defending Ireland*, p. 32.

41 Terence de Vere White, *Kevin O'Higgins* (London, 1948), pp. 240–2. Kevin O'Higgins' derogatory view of the republicans was no doubt strengthened by the death of his father four and a half years previously. On 11 February 1923, Dr. Thomas Higgins was shot and killed by the IRA at the family home in Stradbally, County Laois. See ibid., pp. 148–50.

42 See, for example, John M. Regan, *The Irish Counter-Revolution 1921–1936* (Dublin, 1999), pp. 78–9, 89, 270; Anne Dolan, *Commemorating the Irish Civil War: History and Memory, 1923–2000* (Cambridge, 2006). For a reappraisal of the actions of Kevin O'Higgins and W.T. Cosgrave at the time of the Treaty, see Jason Knirck, 'Apostates or Imperialists? W. T. Cosgrave, Kevin O'Higgins, and Republicanism' in *New Hibernia Review*, Vol. 14, No. 4 (2010), pp. 51–73.

43 Townshend, *The Republic*, p. 424. Eunan O'Halpin's recent study on the doomed teenage revolutionary Kevin Barry, highlights that leaders on the military side of the anti-Treaty forces also tended to come from elitist or middle-class, Jesuit-educated backgrounds; an analysis that complements Roy Foster's investigation of the 1916 revolutionary generation. See Eunan O'Halpin, *Kevin Barry: An Irish Rebel in Life and Death* (Kildare, 2020), and Foster, *Vivid Faces*, pp. 38–42.

44 De Vere White, *Kevin O'Higgins*, pp. 60–1.

45 Childers Diary, 3 November 1921, TCD CP 7814.

46 *The Manchester Guardian*, 4 November 1921; *The Times*, 4 November 1921.

47 Eunan O'Halpin, 'Sir Warren Fisher and the Coalition, 1919–1922' in *The Historical Journal*, Vol. 24, No. 4 (1981), pp. 917–19.

48 Ibid., pp. 907–27.

49 *Dublin Evening Telegraph*, 5 November 1921. See also St. John Ervine, *Craigavon: Ulsterman* (London, 1949), p. 444.

50 *The Scotsman*, 30 November 1921.

51 Boyce, D.G., in David Cannadine (ed.), *Oxford Dictionary of National Biography*, https://doi.org/10.1093/ref:odnb/32609.

52 Beaverbrook, *The Decline and Fall of Lloyd George*, p. 84.

53 *The Scotsman*, 30 November 1921.

54 Taylor (ed.), *Lloyd George, a Diary by Frances Stevenson*, p. 235.

55 Robert Blake, *Unrepentant Tory: The Life and Times of Andrew Bonar Law, 1858–1923, Prime Minister of the United Kingdom* (New York, 1956), p. 432.

56 Keith Jeffrey, *Field Marshal Sir Henry Wilson* (Oxford, 2006), p. 274.

57 Diarmaid Ferriter, *A Nation and Not a Rabble: The Irish Revolution 1913–23* (London, 2015, ebook ed.); David Fitzpatrick, *The Two Irelands: 1912–1939* (Oxford, 1998), pp. 118–19.

58 In Hopkinson (ed.), *The Last Days of Dublin Castle*, p. 33. See also Michael Hopkinson, 'Negotiation: The Anglo-Irish War and the Revolution' in Joost Augusteijn (ed.), *The Irish Revolution, 1913–1923* (Hampshire, 2002) pp. 129–30.

59 Fanning, *Fatal Path* (ebook ed.); Jones, *Whitehall Diary*, Vol. III, p. 154.

60 R.J.Q. Adams, *Bonar Law* (Stanford, 1999, ebook ed.).

61 Jones, *Whitehall Diary*, Vol. III, p. 154.

62 Ibid.

63 Cited in Matthews, *Fatal Influence*, p. 45.

64 Jones, *Whitehall Diary*, Vol. III, p. 155.

65 Ibid., p. 156.

66 Ibid., p. 155.

67 Ibid., p. 156.

68 DIFP, The Anglo-Irish Treaty, p. 118.

69 Ó Broin, *In Great Haste*, pp. 52–3.

70 Childers Diary, 8 November 1921, TCD CP 7814.

71 Right Rev. Monsignor M. Curran, BMH WS 687 (section 1), pp. 559–60.

72 Regan, *The Irish Counter-Revolution*, p. 12.

73 DIFP, The Anglo-Irish Treaty, p. 120.

74 NAI DE/2/531.

75 Gilbert, *Winston S. Churchill*, Vol. IV, Companion, Part 3, pp. 1666–7.

76 John McColgan, *British Policy and the Irish Administration, 1920–1922* (London, 1983), p. 69.

7. POWER AND INTENT

1 Taylor (ed.), *Lloyd George: A Diary by Frances Stevenson*, p. 236.

2 Jones, *Whitehall Diary*, Vol. III, pp. 157–8.

3 H.H. Asquith, *Memories and Reflections, 1852–1927* (Boston, 1928), p. 238.

4 Morgan, *Consensus and Disunity*, p. 17, pp. 112–14; Gilmour, *Curzon*, pp. 549–52; Peter Hennessy, *Whitehall* (New York, 1989), pp. 68–75.

5 Robert Blake, *The Conservative Party from Peel to Major* (London, 1970; reprint, London, 2010, ebook ed.)

6 Ibid.

7 John Maynard Keynes, *Essays in Biography* (New York, 1963), p. 36.

8 Margaret MacMillan, *Peacemakers: The Paris Peace Conference of 1919 and its Attempt to End War* (London, 2001), p. 46.

9 Hattersley, *David Lloyd George*, pp. 5–10.

10 Ibid., pp. 7–8.

11 TNA CAB 43/2_2, p. 119.

12 Jones, *Whitehall Diary*, Vol. III, p. 159.

13 Ibid., pp. 159–60.

14 Ibid., p. 160.

15 Ibid.

16 Ibid.

17 Gilmour, *Curzon*, p. 383.

18 Jones, *Whitehall Diary*, Vol. III, p. 161.

19 Ibid., p. 162.

20 TNA CAB 43/2_2, p. 124.

21 Alvin Jackson, *Home Rule: An Irish History 1800–2000* (London, 2004), p. 242.

22 Jones, *Whitehall Diary*, Vol. III, p. 161.

23 Lavin, *From Empire to International Commonwealth*, p. 191.

24 Jones, *Whitehall Diary*, Vol. III, p. 163.

25 Stafford, *Oblivion or Glory*, pp. 236–7.

26 Cannadine, *The Decline and Fall of the British Aristocracy*, pp. 313–18.

27 Cited in ibid., p. 314.

28 Ibid., pp. 313–39; Hattersley, *David Lloyd George*, pp. 567–8; Morgan, *Consensus and Disunity*, pp. 339–40.

29 Jones, *Whitehall Diary*, Vol. III, p. 164.

30 Ibid.

31 NAI DE/2/531.

32 Jones, *Whitehall Diary*, Vol. III, p. 163.

33 Ibid.

34 Maye, *Arthur Griffith*, p. 11.

35 Pakenham, *Peace by Ordeal*, p. 213.

36 Curran, *The Birth of the Irish Free State*, p. 107.

37 Morgan, *Lloyd George* in Taylor (ed.), *British Prime Ministers*, p. 8.

38 Earl of Birkenhead, Frederick Edwin Smith, *Contemporary Personalities* (London, 1924), p. 35.

39 Hattersley, *David Lloyd George*, p. 193.

40 NAI DE/ 2/304/8/2.

41   Ibid.

42   Childers Diary 12 November 1921, TCD CP 7814.

43   Curran, *The Birth of the Irish Free State*, 106–7; Matthews, *Fatal Influence*, p. 52.

44   Pakenham, *Peace by Ordeal*, p. 218.

45   Taylor (ed.), *Lloyd George: A Diary by Frances Stevenson*, p. 237; Matthews, *Fatal Influence*, p. 52.

46   Taylor (ed.), *Lloyd George: A Diary by Frances Stevenson*, p. 237.

47   Ibid; Pakenham, *Peace by Ordeal*, pp. 219–20.

48   Taylor (ed.), *Lloyd George: A Diary by Frances Stevenson*, p. 237.

49   Fair, 'The Anglo-Irish Treaty of 1921', pp. 144–5.

50   Cited in Kinnear, *The Fall of Lloyd George*, p. 81.

51   Self (ed.), *The Austen Chamberlain Diary Letters*, pp. 170–1.

52   Blake, *Unrepentant Tory*, p. 433.

53   Ibid., p. 432.

54   During Bonar Law's short premiership – he died from throat cancer in 1923 – the terms of the Treaty were mostly adhered to, and his administration propped up the Cosgrave government with much-needed military and financial aid. See Paul Canning, *British Policy Towards Ireland 1921–1941* (Oxford, 1985), p. 69.

55   Matthews, *Fatal Influence*, p. 49.

56   Bonar Law wrote to Lord Rothermere on 16 November 1921. See Beaverbrook, *The Decline and Fall of Lloyd George*, p. 286.

57   Morgan, *Consensus and Disunity*, p. 247.

58   Ibid., pp. 247–9; Kinnear, *The Fall of Lloyd George*, pp. 98–9; Campbell, *F.E. Smith*, pp. 577–9.

59   *The Scotsman*, 18 November 1921.

60   Jones, *Whitehall Diary*, Vol. III, p. 168.

61   Cited in Kinnear, *The Fall of Lloyd George*, p. 99.

62   Pakenham, *Peace by Ordeal*, p. 225.

63   Childers Diary, 14 November 1921, TCD CP 7814; Nelson, *Irish Nationalists and the Making of the Irish Race*, p. 147.

64   Childers Diary, 15 November 1921, TCD CP 7814.

65   Ibid.

66   Ibid., 16 November 1921.

67   TNA CAB 43/4_1, pp. 75–7; NAI DE/2/531.

68   Matthews, *Fatal Influence*, p. 53; Paul Murray, *The Irish Boundary Commission and its Origins 1886–1925* (Dublin, 2011, ebook ed.).

69   Childers Diary, 16 November 1921, TCD CP 7814.

70   Ó Broin, *In Great Haste*, p. 58.

71   Ibid., footnote 1; Lavery, *The Life of a Painter*, pp. 214–5.

72   Hart, *Mick*, pp. 342–3, 351–2; Coogan, *Michael Collins: A Biography* (ebook ed.).

73   Ó Duibhir, *Prisoners of War* (ebook ed.).

74 Childers Diary, 15 November 1921, TCD CP 7814; NAI DE/2/304/6/3.
75 Ó Broin, *In Great Haste*, p. 58.
76 Childers Diary, 17 November 1921, TCD CP 7814.
77 NAI DE/2/304/8/2.
78 Taylor, *Michael Collins*, p. 130.
79 Lowry, 'The Captive Dominion: Imperial Realities Behind Irish Diplomacy', p. 205.
80 Ibid., pp.133, 136.
81 Lavin, *From Empire to International Commonwealth*, p. 192.
82 NAI DE/2/531.
83 Childers Diary, 21 November 1921, TCD CP 7814.
84 Ibid., 22 November 1921.
85 Jones, *Whitehall Diary*, Vol. III, p. 170.
86 Taylor (ed.), *Lloyd George: A Diary by Frances Stevenson*, p. 238.

8. CROSSINGS

1 Jones, *Whitehall Diary*, Vol. III, p. 171.
2 Rodney Lowe, 'Jones, Thomas' in (David Cannadine ed.), *Oxford Dictionary of National Biography*, https://doi.org/10.1093/ref:odnb/34238.
3 Kenneth O. Morgan, 'Lloyd George's Premiership: A Study in "Prime Ministerial Government"' in *The Historical Journal*, Vol. 13, No. 1 (1970), pp. 134–6; Hennessy, *Whitehall*, p. 56.
4 Jones' perceived integrity also enabled him to survive Lloyd George's downfall, and for much of the inter-war period he remained a trusted adviser to a succession of Prime Ministers. See, Lowe, Rodney in (David Cannadine ed.), *Oxford Dictionary of National Biography*, https://doi.org/10.1093/ref:odnb/34238.
5 Lavin, *From Empire to International Commonwealth*, p. 187.
6 Jones, *Whitehall Diary*, Vol. III, pp. 171–2.
7 Ibid., p. 172.
8 TNA CAB 23/27/15; *The Guardian*, 15 June 2020.
9 Jones, *Whitehall Diary*, Vol. III, p. 172.
10 Ibid.
11 Childers Diary, 22 November 1921, TCD CP 7814.
12 Ibid.
13 NAI DE/2/304/1/64.
14 Childers Diary, 22 November 1921, TCD CP 7814.
15 Jones, *Whitehall Diary*, Vol. III, p. 173.
16 NAI DE/2/304/8/2.
17 Ibid.
18 Jones, *Whitehall Diary*, Vol. III, p. 173.
19 Ibid.

20   Childers Diary, 23 November 1921, TCD CP 7814.

21   Childers Diary, 24 November 1921, TCD CP 7814.

22   Ibid.

23   Ibid.

24   DE/2/304/2/5.

25   Ibid.

26   Ibid.

27   Childers Diary, 24 November 1921, TCD CP 7814.

28   Jones, *Whitehall Diary*, Vol. III, p. 175.

29   Eunan O'Halpin, 'Long Fellow, Long Story: MI5 and de Valera', in *Irish Studies in International Affairs*, Vol. 14 (2003), p. 188.

30   CAC WB 5/2, Sir William Bull's notes on the Anglo-Soviet trade negotiations, 5 and 6 August 1920; Ullman, Anglo-Soviet Accord, p. 428. Cf. Christopher Andrew, *The Defence of the Realm: The Authorized History of MI5* (London, 2009), p. 145.

31   Private correspondence in the possession of the author.

32   TNA HO 317/46.

33   Taylor, *Lloyd George: A Diary by Frances Stevenson*, p. 238; Morgan, *Lloyd George Family Letters*, pp. 194–5.

34   Jones, *Whitehall Diary*, Vol. III, p. 175.

35   Regan, *The Irish Counter-Revolution*, p. 9.

36   Valiulis, *Portrait of a Revolutionary*, pp. 104–6.

37   Ibid.; Townshend, *The Republic*, p. 329.

38   Ibid.

39   Valiulis, *Portrait of a Revolutionary*, pp. 107–8.

40   Tom Garvin, *1922: The Birth of Irish Democracy* (Dublin 1996), p. 59.

41   Kissane, *The Politics of the Irish Civil War* (ebook ed.).

42   Valiulis, *Portrait of a Revolutionary*, pp. 108–9.

43   Regan, *The Irish Counter-Revolution*, pp. 12–13.

44   Ibid., pp. 27–30.

45   Dáil Cabinet Minutes, 25 November 1921, NAI DE/1/3.

46   Townshend, *The Republic*, pp. 330–1.

47   Childers Diary, 26 November 1921, TCD CP 7814.

48   *The Manchester Guardian*, 28 November 1921.

49   Pakenham, *Peace by Ordeal*, p. 246.

50   NAI DE/2/531.

51   NAI DE/2/304/2/5.

52   Thomas Jones to Maurice Hankey, 25 November 1921, TNA CAB/63/34.

53   Cited in Maye, *Arthur Griffith*, p. 37.

54   Ibid., p. 35.

55   Ibid., p. 42.

56   Dolan, *Commemorating the Irish Civil War*, p. 102.

57   Ibid., pp. 100–1.

58   Ibid., pp. 1–13, 30.

59   Maume, *The Long Gestation*, p. 217.

60   Jones, *Whitehall Diary*, Vol. III, p. 176.

61   Cited in Curran, *The Birth of the Irish Free State*, p. 114.

62   Childers Diary, 28 November 1921, TCD CP 7814.

63   Jones, *Whitehall Diary*, Vol. III, p. 176.

64   Ibid.; Childers Diary, 28 November 1921, TCD CP 7814.

65   NAI DE/2/304/2/5.

66   TNA CAB 43/4_1, pp. 101–5.

67   NAI DE/2/304/2/5.

68   *Belfast Telegraph*, 30 November 1921; TNA CAB 43/4_1, p. 106.

69   Cited in *Belfast Telegraph*, 30 November 1921.

70   Childers Diary, 29 November 1921, TCD CP 7814.

71   Ó Broin, *In Great Haste*, p. 63; Childers Diary, 30 November 1921, TCD CP 7814.

72   Ibid.

73   Dáil Debates, vol. T, No. 15.

74   Peter Hart, *The I.R.A. and its Enemies: Violence and Community in Cork, 1916–1923* (Oxford, 1998), p. 269.

75   DIFP, The Anglo-Irish Treaty, p. 136.

76   Taylor, *Michael Collins*, p. 140.

9. LAST DAYS

1   Childers Diary, 1 December 1921, TCD CP 7814.

2   Ibid.

3   Ibid.

4   John Darwin, *Unfinished Empire, The Global Expansion of Britain* (London, 2013), p. 314.

5   David Gilmour, *The Long Recessional: The Imperial Life of Rudyard Kipling* (London, 2003), pp. 310–11.

6   Gilmour, *Curzon*, p. 525.

7   NLI AOB MS 8430/32.

8   Ibid; Childers Diary, 24 November 1921, TCD CP 7814.

9   Cited in McMahon, 'Ireland, the Empire, and the Commonwealth' in Kevin Kenny (ed.), *Ireland and the British Empire* (Oxford, 2004), p. 210.

10 TNA CAB 43/4_1, pp. 108–10.

11 Jones, *Whitehall Diary*, Vol. III, p. 178.

12 Childers Diary, 1 December 1921, TCD CP 7814.

13 Dolan, *Commemorating the Irish Civil War*, p. 114.

14 Colum, *Arthur Griffith*, p. 296.

15 Wilson (ed.), *The Political Diaries of C.P. Scott*, p. 408.

16 Ibid., pp. 406–7.

17 Ibid.

18   Lawlor, 'Ireland from Truce to Treaty', p. 60.
19   Longford and O'Neill, *Eamon de Valera*, p. 160.
20   Lawlor, 'Ireland from Truce to Treaty', p. 64.
21   *Dublin Evening Telegraph*, 3 December 1921; *Sunday Post*, 4 December 1921; *The Irish Times*, 5 December 1921.
22   NAI DE/2/304/1/80.
23   Childers Diary, 3 December 1921, TCD CP 7814.
24   NAI DE/2/304/1/80.
25   Austin Stack, BMH WS 418, p. 54.
26   NAI DE/2/304/1/80.
27   Ibid.
28   Austin Stack, BMH WS 418, p. 53; NAI DE/2/304/1/80.
29   Pakenham, *Peace by Ordeal*, pp. 256–7.
30   NAI DE/2/304/1/80.
31   Regan, *The Irish Counter-Revolution*, p. 15.
32   NAI DE/2/304/1/80.
33   Stack, BMH WS 418, p. 54.
34   Regan, *The Irish Counter-Revolution*, p. 30.
35   Ibid., pp. 29–30.
36   Cited in ibid., p. 30.
37   Ibid.
38   Garvin, *1922: The Birth of Irish Democracy*, p. 60.
39   McMahon, *British Spies and Irish Rebels*, p. 61.
40   Ibid., p. 63.
41   TNA CAB 43/4_1, pp. 115.
42   NAI DE/2/531 (111).
43   Childers Diary, 4 December 1921, TCD CP 7814.
44   Hart, *Mick*, p. 313.
45   O'Connor, *The Big Fellow* (ebook edition); Coogan, *Michael Collins: A Biography*, p. 326.
46   Childers Diary, 4 December 1921, TCD CP 7814.
47   Jones, *Whitehall Diary*, Vol. III, p. 180.
48   NAI DE/2/531 (122–123).
49   TNA CAB 43/4_2, p. 116.
50   Ibid; NAI DE/2/531 (122–123).
51   Childers Diary, 4 December 1921, TCD CP 7814.
52   Ibid.
53   Pakenham, *Peace by Ordeal*, p. 270.
54   Childers Diary, 4 December 1921, TCD CP 7814.
55   NAI DE/2/531 (123).
56   Maye, *Arthur Griffith*, p. 75.
57   Taylor, *Michael Collins*, pp. 135–6.
58   Jones, *Whitehall Diary*, Vol. III, p. 180.
59   Ibid.

60 Ibid., p. 181.
61 Cited in Jackson, *Home Rule*, p. 243.
62 Costello, *The Irish Revolution and its Aftermath*, p. 268.
63 NAI DE/2/304/2/7 (008–010).
64 Wilson (ed.), *The Political Diaries of C.P. Scott*, pp. 410–11.
65 Ibid.
66 TNA CAB 43/4_2 , p. 118.
67 Ibid., pp. 119–20.
68 *The Daily Express*, 5 December 1921; *The Manchester Guardian*, 5 December 1921.
69 *The Freeman's Journal*, 5 December 1921; *Aberdeen Press and Journal*, 5 December 1921.
70 *Irish Independent*, 6 December 1921.
71 *The New York Times*, 6 December 1921.
72 Churchill, *The World Crisis: The Aftermath* (London, 1929), p. 305.
73 NAI DE/2/531 (133–138); TNA CAB 43/4_2, pp. 122–8.
74 Churchill, *The World Crisis*, p. 306.
75 *The Freeman's Journal*, 6 December 1921.
76 Cited in Hart, *Mick*, p. 317.
77 Childers Diary, 5 December 1921, TCD CP 7814.
78 Pakenham, *Peace by Ordeal*, p. 305.
79 Robert Barton, BMH WS 979, p. 41.
80 Cited in Regan, *The Counter-Revolution*, p. 25.
81 Ibid.
82 Churchill, *The World Crisis*, p. 306.
83 Austen Chamberlain, *Down the Years* (London, 1935), p. 150.
84 Churchill, *The World Crisis*, p. 306.
85 Childers Diary, 5 December 1921, TCD CP 7814.
86 NAI DE/2/531 (133–138); TNA CAB 43/4_2, pp. 122–9.
87 *Pall Mall Gazette*, 6 December 1921; *The New York Times*, 6 December 1921.
88 *Pall Mall Gazette*, 6 December 1921; *Hull Daily Mail*, 6 December 1921.

10. AFTERMATH

1 Childers Diary, 6 December 1921, TCD CP 7814.
2 *The New York Times*, 7 December 1921.
3 *The Times*, 7 December 1921.
4 TNA CAB 23/27/17.
5 Jackson, *Home Rule*, p. 380.
6 H.A.L. Fisher: Diary, 6 December 1921, quoted in Gilbert, *Churchill Companion*, Vol. IV, p. 1685.
7 Fanning, *Fatal Path* (ebook ed.).
8 *The Age*, 7 December 1921.

9   McMahon, *British Spies and Irish Rebels*, p. 64.
10 *The Manchester Guardian*, 7 December 1921.
11 Matthews, *Fatal Influence*, p. 61.
12 Maurice Hankey to Lloyd George, 9 December 1921, TNA CAB 63/34.
13 *The Scotsman*, 7 December 1921.
14 *Pall Mall Gazette*, 6 December 1921.
15 Valiulis, *Portrait of a Revolutionary*, p. 109.
16 BMH WS 418, pp. 55–8; Longford and O'Neill, *Eamon de Valera*, pp. 166–7.
17 Ibid.
18 Hopkinson, *Green against Green*, p. 35.
19 Fanning, *Eamon de Valera*, p. 125.
20 Art O'Brien to Erskine Childers, 6 December 1921, NLI AOB MS 8430/31.
21 *Daily Record*, 9 December 1921.
22 Jones, *Whitehall Diary*, p. 186.
23 NLI AOB MS 8430/32.
24 Winston Churchill to Lord Curzon, 6 December 1921, Gilbert, *Churchill Companion*, Vol. IV, pp. 1685–6.
25 Darwin, *The Empire Project*, p. 415.
26 Jones, *Whitehall Diary*, pp. 88–9.
27 Townshend, *The Republic*, p. 344.
28 Foster, *Vivid Faces*, p. 278.
29 *The Scotsman*, 8 December 1921; *Lancashire Evening Post*, 8 December 1921.
30 Childers Diary, 8 December 1921, TCD CP 7814.
31 Regan, *The Irish Counter-Revolution*, p. 24.
32 Éamon de Valera to Joseph McGarrity, 27 December 1921, NLI JMP MS 17,440/4.
33 Regan, *The Irish Counter-Revolution*, p. 34.
34 Childers Diary, 8 December 1921, TCD CP 7814.
35 Longford and O'Neill, *Eamon de Valera*, p. 169.
36 Quoted in the *Aberdeen Press and Journal*, 9 December 1921.
37 Charles Edward Caldwell, *Field Marshal Sir Henry Wilson: His Life and Diaries*, Vol. 2 (London, 1927), p. 315.
38 Matthews, *Fatal Influence*, p. 58.
39 Jackson, *Home Rule*, p. 243.
40 Ervine, *Craigavon*, p. 470.
41 Matthews, *Fatal Influence*, p. 59.
42 *The Manchester Guardian*, 15 December 1921.
43 Jones, *Whitehall Diary*, pp. 189–90.
44 Ibid., p. 191.
45 *The Scotsman*, 16 December 1921.
46 Ibid.
47 *Aberdeen Press and Journal*, 16 December 1921.
48 Ibid.
49 Cited in Murray, *The Irish Boundary Commission and its Origins* (ebook ed.).

50   Regan, *The Irish Counter-Revolution,* p. 266.
51   Campbell, *F.E. Smith,* pp. 577–9.
52   Ibid., p. 580.
53   Canning, *British Policy Towards Ireland: 1921–1941,* p. 9.
54   Cited in Townshend, *The Republic,* p. 362.
55   Laffan, *The Resurrection of Ireland,* p. 359; Hopkinson, *Green against Green,* p. 36; R.F. Foster, *Modern Ireland 1600–1972* (London, 1988), p. 509.
56   Regan, *The Irish Counter-Revolution,* p. 40.
57   Foster, *Vivid Faces,* p. 280.
58   Townshend, *The Republic,* p. 351.
59   Ibid., p. 352.
60   Dáil Debates, vol. T, No. 11.
61   Ibid.
62   Dáil Debates, vol. T, No. 8.
63   Ibid.
64   Cited in Townshend, *The Republic,* p. 353.
65   Maye, *Arthur Griffith,* p. 246.
66   Dáil Debates, vol. T, No. 6.
67   Regan, *The Irish Counter-Revolution,* p. 42.
68   Beaverbrook, *The Decline and Fall of Lloyd George,* p. 287.
69   Éamon de Valera to Joseph McGarrity, 27 December 1921, NLI JMP MS 17,440/4.
70   Fanning, *Éamon de Valera,* pp. 265–6.
71   Townshend, *The Republic,* p. 360.
72   Dáil Debates, vol. T, No. 16.
73   Dáil Debates, vol. T, No. 17.
74   Cited in Maye, *Arthur Griffith,* p. 232.
75   Dáil Debates, vol. T, No. 17.
76   Hopkinson, *Green against Green,* p. 276.
77   Deirdre McMahon, '"Transient Apparition": British Policy towards the de Valera Government, 1932–5' in *Irish Historical Studies,* Vol. 22, No. 88 (1981), p. 332.
78   Regan, *The Irish Counter-Revolution,* p. 49.
79   John M. Regan, *Myth and the Irish State: Historical Problems and Other Essays* (Kildare, 2013); Hopkinson, *Green against Green,* p. 140.
80   Cited in Townshend, *The Republic,* p. 426; See also Laffan, *The Resurrection of Ireland,* p. 417; Ferriter, *A Nation and Not A Rabble* (ebook ed.).
81   Hart, *Mick,* pp. 410–12; Hopkinson, *Green against Green,* pp. 177–9; Townshend, *The Republic,* pp. 432–3.
82   Ibid.
83   Gerard Murphy, *The Great Cover-Up: The Truth about the Death of Michael Collins* (Cork, 2018), p. 127.
84   Forester, *Michael Collins,* p. 256.
85   Cannadine, *The Pleasures of the Past,* p. 302.

86 Self (ed.), *The Austen Chamberlain Diary Letters,* p. 14.

87 Fanning, *Fatal Path* (ebook ed.).

88 Winston Churchill, 'The Dream', https://winstonchurchill.hillsdale.edu; see also Andrew Roberts, *Churchill* (London, 2018), pp. 904–6.

BIBLIOGRAPHY

PUBLISHED DIARIES AND MEMOIRS

Amery, Leo, *The Leo Amery Diaries, Vol. I: 1896–1929* (London, 1980).

Asquith H.H., *Memories and Reflections, 1852–1927* (Boston, 1928).

Bayford, Lord (Robert Sanders), *Real Old Tory Politics: The Political Diaries of Sir Robert Sanders, Lord Bayford, 1910–1935* (London, 1984).

Beaverbrook, Lord (Max Aitken), *The Decline and Fall of Lloyd George* (London, 1963).

Birkenhead, Earl of, Frederick Edwin Smith, *Contemporary Personalities* (London, 1924).

Chamberlain, Austen, *Down the Years* (London, 1935).

Childers, Erskine, *In the Ranks of the C.I.V.: a Narrative and Diary of Personal Experiences with the C.I.V.* (London, 1901).

Churchill, Winston, *The World Crisis: The Aftermath* (London, 1929).

Ewart, Wilfrid, *A Journey in Ireland, 1921* (London and New York, 1922; reprint, Dublin, 2008).

George, William, *My Brother and I* (London, 1958).

Heffer, Simon (ed.), *Henry 'Chips' Channon, the Diaries 1918–38* (London, 1967; reprint, London, 2021).

Hinkson, Pamela, *Seventy Years Young: Memories of Elizabeth Countess of Fingall* (Dublin, 1991, ebook ed.).

Jones, Thomas, in Keith Middlemas (ed.), *Whitehall Diary, Vol. III: Ireland 1918–1925* (London, 1971).

Keynes, John Maynard, *Essays in Biography* (New York, 1963).

Lavery, Sir John, *The Life of a Painter* (London, 1940).

Macready, Sir Nevil, *Annals of an Active Life, Vol. II* (London, 1924).

Midleton, Earl of, *Records & Reactions 1856–1939* (London, 1939).

Naughton, Lindie (ed.), *Markievicz: Prison Letters & Rebel Writings* (Kildare, 2018).

O'Connor, Batt, *With Michael Collins in the Fight for Independence* (London, 1929).

O'Malley, Cormac K. H. and Anne Dolan (eds), *'No Surrender Here!' The Civil War Papers of Ernie O'Malley 1922–1924* (Dublin, 2007, ebook ed.).

Pottle, Mark (ed.), *Champion Redoubtable: The Diaries and Letters of Violet Bonham Carter 1914–1945* (London, 1998).

Riddell, Lord, *Intimate Diary of the Peace Conference and After, 1918–1923* (London, 1923).

Scott, C.P., in Trevor Wilson (ed.), *The Political Diaries of C.P. Scott 1911–1928* (London, 1970).

Shakespeare, Geoffrey, *Let Candles Be Brought In* (London, 1949).

Stevenson, Frances, in A.J.P. Taylor (ed.), *Lloyd George: A Diary by Frances Stevenson* (London, 1971).

Sturgis, Mark, in Michael Hopkinson (ed.), *The Last Days of Dublin Castle: The Diaries of Mark Sturgis* (Dublin, 1999).

Walsh, Louis J., *On My Keeping and In Theirs: A Record of Experiences 'on the run', in Derry Gaol and in Ballykinlar Internment Camp* (Dublin, 1921).

Wilson, Henry, in Calwell, Charles Edward, *Field Marshal Sir Henry Wilson: His Life and Diaries*, Vol. II (London, 1927).

BOOKS AND ARTICLES

Adams, R.J.Q., *Bonar Law* (Stanford, 1999, ebook ed.).

Addison, Paul, 'Mount Amery' in *London Review of Books*, Vol. 2, No. 22 (20 November 1980).

— *Churchill: The Unexpected Hero* (Oxford, 2005).

Adelman, Paul, *The Decline and Fall of the Liberal Party 1910–1931* (London and New York, 1995, 2nd ed.).

Akenson, D.H., 'Was De Valera a Republican?' in *The Review of Politics*, Vol. 33, No. 2 (1971), pp. 233–53.

Andrew, Christopher, *The Defence of the Realm: The Authorized History of MI5* (London, 2009).

Augusteijn, Joost (ed.), *The Irish Revolution, 1913–1923* (Hampshire, 2002).

Beers, Laura, '"Is This Man an Anarchist?" Industrial Action and the Battle for Public Opinion in Interwar Britain' in *The Journal of Modern History*, Vol. 82, No. 1 (2010), pp. 30–60.

Bew, Paul, 'Moderate Nationalism and the Irish Revolution, 1916–1923' in *The Historical Journal* 42.3 (1999), pp. 729–49.

— *Ireland: The Politics of Enmity, 1789–2006* (Oxford and New York, 2007).

— *Churchill and Ireland* (Oxford, 2016).

Birkenhead, Earl of, Frederick Winston Furneaux Smith, *The Life of F.E. Smith, First Earl of Birkenhead* (London, 1965).

Birn, Donald S., 'Open Diplomacy at the Washington Conference of 1921–2: The

British and French Experience' in *Comparative Studies in Society and History*, Vol. 12, No. 3 (1970), pp. 297–319.

Blake, Robert, *Unrepentant Tory: The Life and Times of Andrew Bonar Law, 1858–1923, Prime Minister of the United Kingdom* (New York, 1956).

— *The Conservative Party from Peel to Major* (London, 1970; reprint, London, 2010, ebook ed.)

Bourke, Richard and Ian McBride (eds), *The Princeton History of Modern Ireland* (New Jersey, 2016, ebook ed.).

Bowman, John, *De Valera and the Ulster Question 1917–1973* (New York, 1982).

Boyce, D.G., 'British Conservative Opinion, the Ulster Question, and the Partition of Ireland, 1912–21' in *Irish Historical Studies*, Vol. 17, No. 65 (1970), pp. 89–112.

— *Englishmen and Irish Troubles: British Public Opinion and the Making of Irish Policy, 1918–22* (London, 1972).

— 'From War to Neutrality: Anglo-Irish Relations, 1921–1950' in *British Journal of International Studies*, Vol. 5, No. 1 (1979), pp. 15–36.

— 'Craig, James, first Viscount Craigavon' in David Cannadine (ed.), *Oxford Dictionary of National Biography* (2004), https://doi.org/10.1093/ref:odnb/32609.

Boyle, Andrew, *The Riddle of Erskine Childers* (London, 1977).

Campbell, Fergus, *Land and Revolution: Nationalist Politics in the West of Ireland 1891–1921* (Oxford, 2005).

Campbell, John, *F.E. Smith: First Earl of Birkenhead* (London, 1982).

Cannadine, David, *The Pleasures of the Past* (London, 1989).

— *The Decline and Fall of the British Aristocracy* (New Haven and London, 1990).

— *Aspects of Aristocracy* (New Haven and London, 1994).

— *Ornamentalism: How the British Saw Their Empire* (London, 2001).

— *George V: The Unexpected King* (London, 2014, ebook ed.).

— *Victorious Century: 1800–1906* (London, 2017)

Canning, Paul, *British Policy Towards Ireland 1921–1941* (Oxford, 1985).

Carlton, David, *Churchill and The Soviet Union* (Manchester, 2000).

Christopher, Andrew, *The Defence of the Realm: The Authorized History of MI5* (London, 2009).

Clarke, Peter, *Hope and Glory: Britain 1900–2000* (London, 2004).

Collins, Damian, *Charmed Life: The Phenomenal World of Philip Sassoon* (London, 2016, ebook ed.).

Colum, Padraic, *Arthur Griffith* (Dublin, 1959).

Coogan, Tim Pat, *Michael Collins, A Biography* (London, 1990, ebook ed.).

— *De Valera: Long Fellow, Long Shadow* (London, 1993, ebook ed.).

Costello, Francis, 'Lloyd George and Ireland, 1919–1921: An Uncertain Policy' in *The Canadian Journal of Irish Studies*, No. 14, Vol. 1 (1988), pp. 5–16.

— 'The Role of Propaganda in the Anglo-Irish War 1919–1921' in *The Canadian Journal of Irish Studies*, Vol. 14, No. 2 (1989) pp. 5–24.

— *The Irish Revolution and its Aftermath 1916–1923: Years of Revolt* (Dublin, 2003).

Cowling, Maurice, *The Impact of Labour 1920–1924: The Beginning of Modern British Politics* (Cambridge, 1971).

Curran, Joseph M., *The Birth of the Irish Free State 1921–1923* (Alabama, 1980).

Darwin, John, *The Empire Project: The Rise and Fall of the British World-System, 1830–1970* (Cambridge, 2009).

— *Unfinished Empire: The Global Expansion of Britain* (London, 2013).

Davenport-Hines, Richard, *Enemies Within: The Communists, the Cambridge Spies and the Making of Modern Britain* (London, 2018).

Davies, Norman, *The Isles: A History* (London, 1999).

— *Vanished Kingdoms: The History of Half-Forgotten Europe* (London, 2011).

Desmarais, Ralph, 'Lloyd George and the Development of the British Government's Strikebreaking Organization' in *International Review of Social History*, Vol. 20, No. 1 (1975), pp. 1–15.

Dolan, Anne, 'Killing and Bloody Sunday, November 1920' in *The Historical Journal*, Vol. 49, No. 3 (2006), pp. 789–810.

— *Commemorating the Irish Civil War: History and Memory, 1923–2000* (Cambridge, 2006).

— 'The British Culture of Paramilitary Violence in the Irish War of Independence' in Robert Gerwarth and John Horne (eds), *War in Peace: Paramilitary Violence in Europe after the Great War* (Oxford, 2012).

Dolan, Anne and William Murphy, *Michael Collins, The Man and The Revolution* (Cork, 2019, ebook ed.).

Dooley, Terence A.M., 'From the Belfast Boycott to the Boundary Commission: Fears and Hopes in County Monaghan, 1920–26' in *Clogher Record*, Vol. 15, No. 1 (1994), pp. 90–106.

— 'The Organisation of Unionist Opposition to Home Rule in Counties Monaghan, Cavan and Donegal, 1885–1914' in *Clogher Record*, Vol. 16, No. 1 (1997), pp. 46–70.

Dutton, David, *His Majesty's Loyal Opposition: The Unionist Party in Opposition 1905–1915* (Liverpool, 1992).

— *Austen Chamberlain: Gentleman in Politics* (Bolton, 1985, reprint; Oxon, 2019, ebook ed.).

Dwyer, T. Ryle, *Big Fellow, Long Fellow: A Joint Biography of Collins & de Valera* (Dublin, 1998).

— *The Squad and the Intelligence Operations of Michael Collins* (Cork, 2005).

Ervine, St. John, *Craigavon: Ulsterman* (London, 1949).

Fair, John D., 'The Anglo-Irish Treaty of 1921: Unionist Aspects of the Peace' in *Journal of British Studies*, Vol. 12, No. 1 (1972), pp. 132–49.

Fanning, Ronan, *The Irish Department of Finance: 1922–58* (Dublin, 1978).

— 'The British Dimension' in *The Crane Bag*, Vol. 8.1, Ireland: Dependence & Independence (1984), pp. 41–52.

— *Fatal Path: British Government and Irish Revolution 1910–1922* (London, 2013, ebook ed.).

— *Éamon de Valera: A Will to Power* (London, 2015).

Ferriter, Diarmaid, *Judging Dev* (Dublin, 2007).

— *A Nation and Not A Rabble: The Irish Revolution 1913–23* (London, 2015, ebook ed.).

Fitzpatrick, David, *Politics and Irish Life 1913–1921: Provincial Experience of War and Revolution* (Cork, 1977).

— *The Two Irelands 1912–1939* (Oxford, 1998).

— *Harry Boland's Irish Revolution* (Cork, 2003).

Forester, Margery, *Michael Collins: The Lost Leader* (London, 1971).

Foster, R.F., *Modern Ireland 1600–1972* (London, 1988).

— *Vivid Faces: The Revolutionary Generation in Ireland 1890–1923* (London, 2014).

Foy, Michael T., *Michael Collins's Intelligence War: The Struggle between the British and the IRA 1919–1921* (Stroud, 2006, ebook ed.).

Garvin, Tom, *Nationalist Revolutionaries in Ireland 1858–1928* (Dublin, 1987).

— *1922: The Birth of Irish Democracy* (Dublin, 1996).

Gilbert, Martin, *Winston S. Churchill*, Vol. IV, Companion, Part 3, Documents April 1921–November 1922 (London, 1967).

— *Winston S. Churchill*, Vol. IV: World in Torment 1916–1922 (London, 1975; reprint, 2015, ebook ed.).

Gillis, Liz, *The Hales Brothers and the Irish Revolution* (Cork, 2016, ebook ed).

Gilmour, David, *Curzon* (London, 1994).

— *The Long Recessional: The Imperial Life of Rudyard Kipling* (London, 2003).

Glandon, Virginia E., 'Arthur Griffith and the Ideal Irish State' in *An Irish Quarterly Review*, Vol. 73, No. 289 (1984), pp. 26–36.

Gorman, Daniel, 'Lionel Curtis, Imperial Citizenship, and the Quest for Unity' in *The Historian*, Vol. 66, No. 1 (2004), pp. 67–96.

— *The Emergence of International Society in the 1920s* (Cambridge, 2012).

Hammond, J.L., *C.P. Scott of the Manchester Guardian* (New York, 1934).

Hancock, W.K., *Smuts* (Cambridge, 1962).

Harkness, D.W., *The Restless Dominion: The Irish Free State and the British Commonwealth of Nations, 1921–1931* (London, 1969).

Harrington Jr., Joseph F., 'The League of Nations and the Upper Silesian Boundary Dispute, 1921–1922' in *The Polish Review*, Vol. 23, No. 3 (1978), pp. 86–101.

Hart, Peter, *Mick, The Real Michael Collins* (London, 2005).

— *The I.R.A. and Its Enemies: Violence and Community in Cork 1916–1923* (Oxford, 1998).

— 'The Social Structure of the Irish Republican Army, 1916–1923' in *The Historical Journal*, Vol. 42, No. 1 (1999), pp. 207–31.

Hattersley, Roy, *David Lloyd George: The Great Outsider* (London, 2010).

Hennessy, Peter, *Whitehall* (New York, 1989).

Hopkinson, Michael, *Green against Green: The Irish Civil War* (Dublin, 1988).

— 'Biography of the Revolutionary Period: Michael Collins and Kevin Barry' in *Irish Historical Studies*, Vol. 28, No. 11 (1993), pp. 310–16.

— *The Irish War of Independence* (Dublin and Montreal, 2002).

— 'From Treaty to Civil War, 1921–2' in J.R. Hill (ed.), *A New History of Ireland*, Vol. VII: Ireland, 1921–1984 (Oxford, 2003).

Howe, Stephen, *Ireland and Empire: Colonial Legacies in Irish History and Culture* (Oxford, 2000; reprint 2002, ebook ed.).

Jackson, Alvin, *Home Rule: An Irish History 1800–2000* (London, 2004).

— *The Ulster Party: Irish Unionists in the House of Commons, 1884–1911* (Oxford, 1989).

Jalland, Patricia, *The Liberals and Ireland: The Ulster Question in British Politics to 1914* (Brighton, 1980).

Jeffrey, Keith, *Field Marshal Sir Henry Wilson* (Oxford, 2006).

— 'Field Marshal Sir Henry Wilson: Myths and the Man' in *Journal of the Society for Army Historical Research*, Vol. 86, No. 345 (2008), pp. 57–82.

— *MI6: The History of the Secret Intelligence Services 1909–1949* (London, 2010).

Kenny, Colum, *The Enigma of Arthur Griffith: 'Father of Us All'* (Dublin 2020).

Kenny, Kevin (ed.), *Ireland and the British Empire* (Oxford, 2004).

Kinnear, Michael, *The Fall of Lloyd George: The Political Crisis of 1922* (London, 1973).

Kissane, Bill, *The Politics of the Irish Civil War* (Oxford, 2005, ebook ed.).

Knirck, Jason, 'Apostates or Imperialists? W.T. Cosgrave, Kevin O'Higgins, and Republicanism' in *New Hibernia Review*, Vol. 14, No. 4 (2010), pp. 51–73.

Koss, Stephen E., *Asquith* (London, 1976).

Laffan, Michael, *The Resurrection of Ireland: The Sinn Féin Party, 1916–1923* (Cambridge, 1999).

Lake, Marilyn and Henry Reynolds, *Drawing the Global Colour Line: White Men's Countries and the International Challenge of Racial Equality* (Cambridge, 2008).

Lavin, Deborah, *From Empire to International Commonwealth: A Biography of Lionel Curtis* (Oxford, 1995).

Lawlor, S.M., 'Ireland from Truce to Treaty: War or Peace? July to October 1921' in *Irish Historical Studies*, Vol. 22, No. 85 (1980), pp. 49–64.

Lawrence, Jon, 'Forging a Peaceable Kingdom: War, Violence, and Fear of Brutalization in Post-First World War Britain' in *The Journal of Modern History*, Vol. 75, No. 3 (2003), pp. 557–89.

Lee, J.J., *Ireland 1912–1985: Politics and Society* (Cambridge, 1989).

Lentin, Antony, *Lloyd George and the Lost Peace: From Versailles to Hitler, 1919–1940* (London, 2001, ebook ed.).

Lewis, Geoffrey, *Carson: The Man Who Divided Ireland* (London and New York, 2005, ebook ed.).

Longford, Earl of (Frank Pakenham) and Thomas P. O'Neill, *Eamon de Valera* (London, 1970).

Lowe, Rodney, 'Jones, Thomas' in David Cannadine (ed.), *Oxford Dictionary of National Biography* (2004), https://doi.org/10.1093/ref:odnb/34238.

Lowry, Donal, 'The Captive Dominion: Imperial Realities Behind Irish Diplomacy, 1922–49' in *Irish Historical Studies*, Vol. 36, No. 142 (2008), pp. 202–26.

Lynch, Robert, *The Partition of Ireland 1918–1925* (Cambridge, 2019, ebook ed.).

Macardle, Dorothy, *The Irish Republic* (New York, 1937; reprint, New York, 1965).

MacMillan, Margaret, *Peacemakers: The Paris Peace Conference of 1919 and its Attempts to End War* (London, 2001).

Mansergh, Martin, 'Sovereign Independence, but "A Family of Nations" to Belong to' in *Irish Studies in International Affairs*, Vol. 30 (2019), pp. 21–39.

Mansergh, Nicholas, *The Unresolved Question: The Anglo-Irish Settlement and Its Undoing, 1912–1972* (New Haven, 1991).

Matthews, Ann, *Renegades: Irish Republican Women 1900–1922* (Cork, 2010, ebook ed.).

Matthews, Kevin, *Fatal Influence: The Impact of Ireland on British Politics 1920–1925* (Dublin, 2004).

Maume, Patrick, *The Long Gestation: Irish Nationalist Life 1891–1918* (Dublin, 1999).

Maye, Brian, *Arthur Griffith* (Dublin, 1997).

Mazower, Mark, *Dark Continent: Europe's Twentieth Century* (London, 1998).

— *No Enchanted Palace: The End of Empire and the Ideological Origins of the United Nations* (New Jersey and Oxford, 2009).

McColgan, John, 'Implementing the 1921 Treaty: Lionel Curtis and Constitutional Procedure' in *Irish Historical Studies*, Vol. 20, No. 79 (1977), pp. 312–33.

— *British Policy and the Irish Administration, 1920–1922* (London, 1983).

McMahon, Deirdre, '"Transient Apparition": British Policy towards the de Valera Government, 1932–5' in *Irish Historical Studies*, Vol. 22, No. 88 (1981), pp. 331–61.

McMahon, Paul, 'British Intelligence and the Anglo-Irish Truce, July to December 1921' in *Irish Historical Studies* Vol. 35, No. 140 (2007), pp. 519–40.

— *British Spies and Irish Rebels: British Intelligence and Ireland 1916–1945* (Woodbridge, 2008).

Mitchell, Arthur, *Revolutionary Government in Ireland: Dáil Éireann 1919–1922* (Dublin, 1995).

Morgan, Kenneth O., 'Lloyd George's Premiership: A Study in "Prime Ministerial Government"' in *The Historical Journal*, Vol. 13, No. 1 (1970), pp. 130–57.

— 'Welsh Nationalism: The Historical Background' in *Journal of Contemporary History*, Vol. 6, No. 1, Nationalism and Separatism (1971), pp. 153–59 and 161–72.

— *Lloyd George Family Letters 1885–1936* (London, 1973).

— 'Lloyd George', in A.J.P. Taylor (ed.), *British Prime Ministers* (London, 1974).

— *Consensus and Disunity: The Lloyd George Coalition Government 1918–1922* (Oxford, 1979).

Murphy, Gerard, *The Great Cover-Up: The Truth about the Death of Michael Collins* (Cork, 2018).

Murray, Patrick, 'Obsessive Historian: Éamon de Valera and the Policing of his Reputation', *Proceedings of the Royal Irish Academy: Archaeology, Culture, History, Literature*, Vol. 101C, No. 2 (2001), pp. 37–65.

Murray, Paul, *The Irish Boundary Commission and its Origins 1886–1925* (Dublin, 2011, ebook ed.).

Nelson, Bruce, *Irish Nationalists and the Making of the Irish Race* (Princeton and Oxford, 2012).

Nicholson, Harold, *King George the Fifth: His Life and Reign* (London, 1952).

Noonan, Gerard, *The IRA in Britain, 1919–1923: 'In the Heart of Enemy Lines'* (Liverpool, 2014).

Ó Broin, León, *In Great Haste: The Letters of Michael Collins & Kitty Kiernan* (Dublin, 1983).

O'Connor, Frank, *The Big Fellow: Michael Collins and the Irish Revolution* (London, 1937; reprint Dublin, 2018, ebook ed).

— *An Only Child* (New York, 1961).

O'Donoghue, Florence, *No Other Law* (Dublin, 1954; reprint: Dublin, 1986).

Ó Duibhir, Liam, *Prisoners of War: Ballykinlar Internment Camp 1920–1921* (Cork, 2013, ebook ed.).

O'Farrell, Fergus, *Cathal Brugha* (Dublin, 2018).

O'Halpin, Eunan, 'Sir Warren Fisher and the Coalition, 1919–1922' in *The Historical Journal*, Vol. 24, No. 4 (1981), pp. 907–27.

— 'British Intelligence in Ireland, 1914–1921', in Christopher Andrew and David Dilks (eds), *The Missing Dimension: Governments and Intelligence Communities in the Twentieth Century* (London, 1984).

— *Defending Ireland: The Irish State and its Enemies Since 1922* (Oxford, 1999).

— 'Historical Revisit: Dorothy Macardle, "The Irish Republic" (1937)', *Irish Historical Studies*, Vol. 31, No. 123 (1999), pp. 389–94.

— 'Long Fellow, Long Story: MI5 and de Valera', in *Irish Studies in International Affairs*, Vol. 14 (2003), pp. 185–203.

— *Kevin Barry: An Irish Rebel in Life and Death* (Kildare, 2020).

O'Mahony, Patrick and Gerard Delanty, *Rethinking Irish History: Nationalism, Identity and Ideology* (London, 1998, ebook ed.).

Ó Ruairc, Pádraig Óg, *Truce: Murder, Myth and the Last Days of the Irish War of Independence* (Cork, 2016).

Packer, Ian, *Lloyd George* (London, 1998).

Pakenham, Frank, *Peace by Ordeal* (London, 1935).

Pakenham, Thomas, *The Boer War* (London, 1979 ebook ed.).

Pašeta, Senia, *Irish Nationalist Women, 1900–1918* (Cambridge, 2013, ebook ed.).

Regan, John M., *The Irish Counter-Revolution 1921–1936* (Dublin, 1999).

— 'Michael Collins, General Commanding-in-Chief, as a Historiographical Problem' in *History*, Vol. 92, No. 3 (2007), pp. 318–46.

— *Myth and the Irish State: Historical Problems and Other Essays* (Kildare, 2013).

Reid, Colin, 'Stephen Gwynn and the Failure of Constitutional Nationalism in Ireland, 1919–1921' in *The Historical Journal* , Vol. 53, No. 3 (2010), pp. 723–45.

Ring, Jim, *Erskine Childers* (London, 2011, ebook ed.).

Roberts, Andrew, *Churchill* (London, 2018).

Ryan, Meda, *Michael Collins and the Women in His Life* (Cork, 1996).

Self, Robert C. (ed.), *The Austen Chamberlain Diary Letters: The Correspondence of*

Sir Austen Chamberlain with His Sisters Hilda and Ida, 1916–1937 (Cambridge, 1995).

Sheehan, William, *British Voices from the Irish War of Independence 1918–1921: The Words of British Servicemen Who Were There* (Cork, 2005).

Sloan, G., 'Hide seek and negotiate: Alfred Cope and counter intelligence in Ireland 1919–1921' in *Intelligence and National Security*, Vol. 33, No. 2 (2018), pp. 176–95.

Smith, Jeremy, 'Federalism, Devolution and Partition: Sir Edward Carson and the Search for a Compromise on the Third Home Rule Bill, 1913–14' in *Irish Historical Studies*, Vol. 35, No. 140 (2007), pp. 496–518.

Stafford, David, *Oblivion or Glory: 1921 and the Making of Winston Churchill* (New Haven and London, 2019).

Steiner, Zara, *The Lights That Failed: European International History 1919–1933* (Oxford, 2007).

Stevenson, John, *British Society 1914–45* (London, 1984).

Stover, Justin D., 'Irish Political Prisoner Culture, 1916–1923' in *CrossCurrents*, Vol. 64, No. 1 (2014), pp. 90–106.

Talbot, Hayden, *Michael Collins' Own Story* (London, 1923; reprint, The Internet Archive, ebook ed.)

Taylor, Rex, *Michael Collins* (London, 1958; reprint: London, 1963).

Townshend, Charles, 'The Irish Republican Army and the Development of Guerrilla Warfare, 1916–1921' in *The English Historical Review*, Vol. 94, No. 371 (1979), pp. 318–45.

— *Political Violence in Ireland: Government and Resistance since 1848* (Oxford, 1983).

— *The Republic: The Fight for Independence* (London, 2013).

Toye, Richard, *Lloyd George & Churchill: Rivals for Greatness* (London, 2007).

Ullman, Richard, *The Anglo–Soviet Accord*, Vol. III: *Anglo–Soviet Relations: 1917–1921* (London, 1972).

Valiulis, Maryann Gialanella, *Portrait of a Revolutionary: Richard Mulcahy and the Founding of the Irish Free State* (Dublin, 1992).

Walsh, James P., 'De Valera in the United States, 1919' in *Records of the American Catholic Historical Society of Philadelphia*, Vol. 73, No. 3/4 (1962), pp. 92–107.

Walsh, Maurice, *Bitter Freedom: Ireland in a Revolutionary World 1918–1923* (London, 2015).

Ward, Margaret, *Fearless Woman: Hanna Sheehy Skeffington, Feminism and the Irish Revolution* (Dublin, 2019).

White, Terence de Vere, *Kevin O'Higgins* (London, 1948).

ACKNOWLEDGEMENTS

I owe a great debt of gratitude to Jonathan Williams, my literary agent, whose help and encouragement spurred me on to the finishing line. He picked up this project at a very difficult time, and without his support I doubt this book would have been published. I am also extremely grateful to Professor Eunan O'Halpin, who was a source of inspiration and advice from the outset. He was kind enough to read the manuscript and saved me from several egregious errors, although I alone bear the blame for any remaining mistakes or omissions.

While this book is a product of the Covid era, I am very grateful for the help I received from the archivists at the National Library of Ireland, University College Dublin and Trinity College Dublin. I also want to thank Wendy Logue at Merrion Press, who brought everything to fruition with remarkable patience, efficiency and skill. Thanks are due, too, to my publisher Conor Graham.

Throughout the trials and tribulations of the last year and a half, Lorraine Morris has proved a pillar of strength and encouragement, and I could not have survived the troughs without the help of Paul and Barry Gaster. Finally, I want to thank my family, Fintan, Fionn and Rory, whose love and support made everything possible.

INDEX